Short-Term Couples Therapy

The Imago Model in Action

Wade Luquet, A.C.S.W.

With Foreword by Harville Hendrix, Ph.D.

BRUNNER/MAZEL, *Publishers* • New York

Based upon the concepts of Imago Relationship Therapy©
and the couples workshops developed by Harville Hendrix, Ph.D., author of the
best-selling works *Getting the Love You Want* and *Keeping the Love You Find.*

To Marianne,
  my friend for life

To Cory, Alex, and Aubree,
  may you always look at the world with awe

Library of Congress Cataloging-in-Publication Data

Luquet, Wade.
    Short-term couples therapy : the imago model in action /
by Wade Luquet, with a foreword by Harville Hendrix.
        p.   cm.
    "Based on the best-selling book Getting the love you want : a
guide for couples by Harville Hendrix."
    Includes bibliographical references
    ISBN 0-87630-802-7 (paper)
    1. Marital psychotherapy.   2. Brief psychotherapy.
3. Communication in marriage.   I. Title.
RC488.5.L826   1996
616.89′156—dc20   96-1961
                                                          CIP

Copyright © 1996 by Wade Luquet

Published by
BRUNNER/MAZEL, INC.
19 Union Square West
New York, New York 10003

Manufactured in the United States of America

10 9 8 7 6 5 4 3 2

Contents

  A week-by-week plan for couples to continue the process learned in therapy.

List of Homework/Handout Sheets for the Couple

Foreword

For decades proponents of long-term therapy and short-term therapy have been engaged in a debate about the definition of therapy, its structure, goals, duration, and comparative effectiveness.

Long-term therapy advocates define therapy as a healing process that consists of the treatment of emotional, developmental and characterological disorders that have their roots in childhood and are activated by precipitating life situations or events. The therapeutic structure for treating these disorders generally includes an intense, emotionally complicated and nonjudgmental therapist/patient relationship, usually a therapeutic dyad or a group context. The goal of this structure is to allow the patient to regress into his childhood memories and achieve such a powerful emotional insight into his early cognitions, experiences, affects, and defensive behaviors that his repressions are undone. The role of the therapist as expert is generally passive, sometimes empathic, listening that is interrupted only to provide timely and catalytic interpretations intended to provoke emotional sights. Some contemporary long term therapists may be more active and employ specific techniques such as breathing procedures or body exercises to evoke buried emotions or provoke insights. Successful outcome includes characterological reorganization and restoration to his or her presumably normal state of emotional and behavioral freedom. Essentially, childhood is relived in a benign context which facilitates repair. The duration of this process is usually deemed to be three to five years to achieve permanent results. Outcome studies of long-term therapy tend to verify its effectiveness, although this evaluation is sometimes mitigated by the thesis that life itself changes over time as a result of sustained reflection.

Advocates of short-term therapy are more "result" than healing oriented. They tend to define therapy as treatment of specific dysfunctional emotional reactions (such as phobias or depression), irrational cognitions (such as rigid and erroneous beliefs) or inappropriate behaviors (such as addictions or kleptomania), all of which, for the long term therapist, would be considered symptoms of deeper historical, emotional and characterological disorders. For the short-term therapist, the symptoms may be rooted in childhood or may be consequences of stresses in the patient's current life situation, but the etiology of the symptom is unimportant or secondary to its function for the patient in his current life. The structure for short-term therapy is similar to long-term therapy, that is, a therapy dyad in which the therapist is an expert or treatment of the patient's symptom in a group context. In contrast to the long-term therapist who tends to be passive except for the offering of catalytic interpretations or special exercises, the short-term therapist actively intervenes in the patient's symptoms with interpretations, confrontations, behavioral prescriptions, information, and verbal and emotional support. The method is both therapeutic and educational and the goal is a specific result. Rather than healing the whole person, the short-term therapist's aim is the excision of the symptom, by therapeutic and educational means, from an otherwise intact system and its replacement by a functional feeling, thought or behavior, thus restoring the patient to normal functioning by removing the symptomatic impediment. The time frame for such treatment is usually short, ranging from one session to about a year. Outcome studies usually give short therapy high grades in the short haul but indicate that without long-term follow up, the symptom usually returns, thus collapsing somewhat the distinction of long- and short-term therapies.

Currently, the debate about the desirability, necessity, and effectiveness of short-term versus long-term therapy is being profoundly impacted by a non-therapeutic other, the managed care mental health provider. While the traditional insurance provider has influenced the frequency and duration of therapy by policy limits, that in most cases have been generous, the managed care mental health insurance provider has made the debate practically moot by prescribed and generally non-negotiable short term sessions and financial limits. Most mental health analysts see this as the almost certain future for mental health care. If this is the case, then providers of mental health care are challenged to develop a therapy modality and delivery system for short term requirements that combines the best features of the long term and short therapies.

From my perspective, there is no such thing as short-term therapy. Therapy is a healing process that requires a long time, but not necessarily a long time in formal therapy sessions. But, we need to envision a mental health delivery system that is responsive to the contemporary situation created by managed care and capable of reconciling the issues between long- and short-term therapy models. As I see it, such a system cannot be created out of traditional views of the human condition and its restitution because of a theoretical defect in the assumptions of both long-term and short-term therapy systems. Both are based on an outdated medical model which sees mental health problems, both symptomatic and characterological, as pathologies of the individual that need treatment whether viewed as cure or healing. To stay within these two modalities is to be left with an either–or situation and the winner, given the current climate in the mental health market, will be the short-term model with its questionable long-term results. For me, the debate about the effectiveness of these methods is moot, not because of the current challenge of managed care, but because of the limited value of the systems themselves.

What is needed is a new theoretical orientation at the level of a paradigm shift from the individual as the locus of being and individual pathology as the human problem to an ontology of relationality as constitutive of being and its rupture as the source of the human condition. Such a shift has been in the making for decades with the appearance of conjoint therapy for couples, family systems theory and group therapist of all sorts. These innovations registered our awareness of the restriction of the individual paradigm and the need for a more inclusive vision of the human situation, but they are half way points on the journey to a new paradigm because they tend to use the dynamics of the individual as the model for the dyad, family, and group. In addition, some of these therapies focused on the individual in context (conjoint therapy and group psychotherapy) while others lost the individual in the context (family systems therapies and group therapy). The needed new theoretical orientation must understand relationality or inherent connectedness as the structure of being and preserve the individual as points of connection. Such a theory will see the reciprocal effect of context on individual psychodynamics and intra-psychic functioning and the influence of the latter on the former. In other words, all things, including persons, are in relationship and they are what they are because of their relationship to each other and their relationship to each other is function of who they are individually. Relationship is seen as the essence of being at the personal and cosmic level.

Imago Relationship Therapy, on which this book is based, is an exhibit of such a paradigm. The challenge and inspiration which led to its development was to create a couples therapy that was effective in helping partners understand and maintain their relationship. Reflecting the course of my education, its original theses reflected the individual model operating in the context of conjoint therapy. Later it was modified by systems theory and group therapies. Its meta-theoretical assumptions were inspired by quantum physics and religious mysticism which evolved finally into a view of the human situation as essentially relational. Couples therapy became the door through which a vision of cosmos emerged.

The basic thesis of Imago Relationship Therapy is that each person is a creation and function of relationship and in turn is a creator of the relationship in which they function. Each person begins life essentially connected to all aspects of himself and to his physical, social and cosmic context. He is whole and experiences a oneness with everything. The human problem results from a rupture of this essential connection, a rupture caused by unconscious parenting which does not support the maintenance of original connection. This results in separation from self-parts and alienation from others which creates the problematic character of the social context in which we live—flawed mental health, interpersonal tension, and social ills. The fundamental human yearning is to restore this original connection. Marriage, having evolved historically since the eighteenth century from a utilitarian social structure to a personal relationship serving personal needs, is a contemporary means by which persons unconsciously attempt to restore the lost connection. Romantic love functions as a selection process which unconsciously creates a relationship with a person similar to one's original caretaker with whom they anticipate the healing of their emotional wounds and the recovery of their wholeness. The attempt at reconnection inevitably fails however, because the similarity of the selected partner to the original parents results in the recreation of the original, wounding childhood situation, resulting in the power struggle.

It is at this point that most couples visit a therapist. In Imago Relationship Therapy, the goal of therapy is to help couples co-create a conscious marriage. The role of the Imago therapist, in contrast to both traditional long term and short term therapists who function as experts and the source of healing, is to facilitate a therapeutic process that empowers the partners in the relationship to heal each other and grow towards wholeness. To help them become therapists for each other, he functions as a coach rather than as expert or source of healing.

Essentially, the therapist helps partners in a committed partnership make contact with each other and eventually achieve empathic connection through a process called dialogue. The conscious and consistent use of the three phases of dialogue—mirroring, validation and empathy—ultimately restores connection between partners, and this connection leads to healing of emotional wounds, resumption of developmental growth and spiritual evolution. The ultimate outcome of a dialogical relationship is the creation of a conscious relationship within which both partners experience the restoration of the original condition of connection to all parts of oneself, to one's physical and social context and to the cosmos—the experience of oneness which was lost in childhood.

In Imago Relationship therapy the issues of long-term versus short-term therapy do not arise. There is no distinction between characterological issues and symptoms, for the focus is not upon the intrapsychic functioning of the individuals but upon their relationship. If the work is with an individual not in relationship, the focus is the same—his or her functioning in relationship. Since the dialogical process can be learned quickly, the need for the therapist becomes optional after a few sessions and can be maintained for as long as the couple chooses. Childhood issues and the transference are catalyzed by the relationship, and contained and resolved in the relationship. The process of complete healing may take years, but the internalization of the process can be achieved in a few weeks. Consequently, the requirements of a managed care program to produce results as well as the desire by some persons for a longer term relationship can be met.

What Wade Luquet has done in this book is provide a condensed version of Imago Relationship Therapy that can serve as a framework for relational healing for therapists and clients that are presented with short term situations. The model he has developed is creatively responsive to the issues of the short term requirements of managed care. With his added insights, illustrations, examples and guidelines, any therapist can effectively utilize this model in any therapeutic context that presents itself. He is to be congratulated for his courageous and brilliant work.

Harville Hendrix, Ph.D.
Abiquiu, N.M.
January, 1996

Preface

If you think relationship problems can be "fixed" through negotiation or compromise, this book may change your mind. Or if you are one who contends that there really is a short-term cure for the frustrations experienced in every relationship, this book may surprise you. Based on the premise that relationships are vehicles for growth, this book is a support system and a solution for those therapists who are presented with short-term situations. It has been designed to help you not only to teach couples about relationships, but also to give them the tools and the encouragement they need to continue the relationship and grow.

Today's managed care, managed competition, and governmental health policies are changing the face of psychotherapy. Although psychotherapy will continue to be covered, companies are placing limits on both the number of sessions and the amounts they pay for these services. They are relying heavily on their Employee Assistance Programs (EAPs) or on their preferred providers to provide quality service at a lower cost. Moreover, therapists in private practice also feel the pinch by being asked to do more in a shorter period of time.

If short-term couples therapy provided by these professionals is to be successful, it needs to be specific and powerful, and it must teach skills. It also needs to be organized in such a way that the information provided for the counselor is clearly presented. Therapists need to know exactly what it is that they want a couple to learn about relationships, and they need to be able to give the couple an experience of healthy communication. This book has been designed to fulfill those needs.

DEVELOPING A DIFFERENT APPROACH

When I first started my practice, I disliked working with couples. Sessions never seemed to go anywhere, and sometimes couples would leave far angrier than when they had first come in. They rarely seemed willing to negotiate or compromise; in those instances when they did, the agreement would usually last only a few weeks. In my frustration I would think, "Why don't they just have fun?" or "Why do they keep arguing about the same things all the time? Why don't they just let it go?" The truth is that I was being a little self-righteous. In hindsight, I can now see that I didn't really know what I was doing. And this may be true for many of today's professionals, if only because many graduate programs are weak in the area of couples therapy. Most of those programs teach us to apply individual or family skills to marriages—*and that just doesn't work!*

Several years ago, my wife Marianne and I began to experience some glitches in our own "perfect" relationship. Our problems were common enough: we weren't meeting each other's expectations. We'd exchange little remarks such as "you weren't this way when I married you," and "you've changed." We went from always wanting to be together to trying to find ways to be apart.

One day during our summer vacation at the New Jersey shore, an otherwise ordinary afternoon was to mark the beginning of a major change for us. Marianne was sitting on the beach reading an article on relationships by Harville Hendrix, Ph.D., in *Family Circle*. Dr. Hendrix had written the book *Getting the Love You Want: A Guide for Couples* (1988) and was a contributing editor to the magazine. As Marianne read on, she commented on how wonderful the article was—how Dr. Hendrix really seemed to know what he was talking about. I listened and smiled and changed the subject, figuring he couldn't know anymore than I already knew. I didn't realize how serious Marianne was until she announced, "One day, I'm going to study with that man!"

Less than a year later—in spite of my resistance—I found myself with my wife and our struggling relationship in New York attending a two-day couples workshop led by Dr. Hendrix himself. That experience changed the way I look at relationships—forever! Through Dr. Hendrix's program, I learned that all relationships go through a power-struggle stage: couples may split up, they may fight, or they may live in the same house and never talk, but all relationships struggle—and most of them remain at this stage. Only a small percentage of couples use their relationships for their intended purpose: growth and healing.

Marianne and I began applying the skills we learned in the workshop to our marriage, and we saw immediate results. Sometimes we were more volatile than usual, and sometimes we experienced a shorter frustration time, but we were never the same again. We then began to use these skills in our practice, and I actually found that I enjoyed working with couples! Moreover, Marianne's prediction came true: we both went on to study with Dr. Hendrix. In the process, we became Certified Imago Relationship Therapists. The most amazing development is that I, the Great Skeptic, went on to become a workshop presenter for Imago Relationship Therapy and now conduct the same two-day workshops that I was so reluctant to attend at first. The consistently positive results of Imago Therapy have made me a firm believer in this work.

With the increasing number of limitations being placed upon therapists by managed care and new government regulations, our ability to be of real help to our clients is being greatly hampered. In graduate school, many of us were trained in long-term models; yet, we are now witnessing the gradual transformation of our profession into an "industry," wherein regulations are mandating that we see clients in fewer sessions. To further compound this situation, we have been offered little in the way of rethinking our long-term models. It's like trying to squeeze Texas into Rhode Island: it doesn't fit and we are frustrated.

Unfortunately, there is very little we will be able to do about insurance policies that shorten our time with clients. However, we do have to realize that our old long-term models will not fit into this scenario. We cannot spend a month taking a history and getting to know the client. Establishing and using a transference are things of the past if couples only have 10 to 20 sessions in which to work with you. This is a dilemma that will be shared by practitioners of all long-term models: how do we take what we have been doing, take out its essence, and package it so that therapists on the "front line" can use it in their daily work with clients? These new models will have to educate and empower clients. They will have to be fast, structured, and easy for clients to do on their own—after the therapy is over.

This book aims to give therapists the essence of Imago Therapy. It was developed out of a need, following my many discussions with employee assistance professionals and managed-care therapists. This short-term intervention has been tested in an EAP setting, with clients reporting better-than-expected results. If presented as described, it will work for the couple who are ready to take in the information and use the techniques daily. For the therapist, it is simple and structured.

Short-term Imago Therapy is a model for the future. It takes the best of a proven model and gives it to the therapist in a usable package that educates, empowers, and gives couples skills they can use for the duration of their relationship. In doing so, it makes couples less dependent on the therapist and more aware of their available support systems: that is, themselves. Furthermore, upon the conclusion of this type of couples therapy, the therapist can feel a sense of accomplishment and need no longer lament, "If only I had more time."

How to Use This Book

In preparing this information, I have assumed that you—the therapist—are limited to between three and 12 sessions to work with couples, and I have included six detailed sessions for you to use with them. If you have more than six sessions available, spread the work out over the extra sessions, or include a session specifically for the practice of skills. In the first three sessions, you will be providing information to the couples, as well as teaching them an effective communications skill. In Sessions Three through Six, you will be teaching the couple how to reromanticize their relationship, change behaviors, and deal with anger. I strongly recommend a minimum of six sessions in order to give couples an ample opportunity to practice while you are present. If this is not possible, and you feel that they need more work, see the suggested referral resources provided in the back of the book.

One of the things you will have to get used to is the pace of this work—it's *fast!* You will be squeezing 12 weeks of work into six to 10 sessions. To pull this off, you should take full advantage of the session format, that is, have the couple perform and monitor some of the work at home. Also, take advantage of the couple's eagerness. Typically, the couple coming to therapy are ready to do the work. So put them to task on the skills in this book. In addition, rather than spending an entire session gathering information from them, get your history from the work they are doing. From their childhood work and what they do in the sessions, you should be able to gather enough information to prepare an adequate history and report for your files.

OVERVIEW

This book is set up with an introductory chapter on Imago Theory and Therapy followed by six chapters that correspond to the six-session course of treatment for couples. Each session is comprised of similar sections: starting the session, suggested lecture, exercises, and homework.

If you were to read this book straight through, it may begin to seem repetitive to you. As you read on from session to session, you will probably begin to feel that you've heard much of the material before—and you'll be partially correct. The introductory chapter is repeated to some degree in each session, depending upon the material's applicability. The book has been deliberately constructed this way for two reasons: to help you quickly familiarize yourself with Imago Therapy through the reinforcement of its principles, and to avoid the need to continually refer back to earlier material or sessions as you progress with the couples from week to week. Following Session One, each subsequent session will, therefore, start out with a review of the preceding week to help you keep your presentations on track. Session One itself will briefly recount the Basic Imago Theory to get you on your way. The more couples you are treating at any given time period, the more this built-in convenience may come in handy.

You will also notice that the lectures—what you are to say to the couple—are set off from the regular text. However, it is not recommended that you read these lectures to the couple; rather, familiarize yourself with the material so that you can present it to them.

A Note About Time

At the beginning of each session, you will see a page with a suggested time frame and goals for the session. This is the average amount of time it takes a therapist to present this portion of the material. At first, you may not be able to complete the work within this time frame, but as you become familiar with it, your speed will improve. I suggest that you go into the session knowing what your goals are and what you want to accomplish within the hour, and the rest will follow. Remember, short-term therapy is not the client telling you his or her problems with you wrapping your theory around them. Rather, it is the client wrapping his or her problems around your theory and techniques.

Also, you may find that couples therapy takes longer than the traditional 50- to 60-minute therapy hour. To find more time, you may want to be creative with your session hour. In my own practice, I see couples for an hour and a half, but I see them every other week. This amounts to 3 hours a month rather than 4 and allows the couple 2 weeks to practice the skills learned. They are free to call me during the 2-week interval between sessions with any questions that may arise about the material.

For those working with managed care, it is possible to negotiate with case managers around the time issues—ask approval for six one-and-a-half hour biweekly sessions rather than 10 one-hour sessions. This gives the couple 12 weeks of contact and practice with the therapist rather than 10 weeks of rushed contact. Although this can sometimes create a scheduling nightmare for the therapist, there is no evidence that weekly sessions are more beneficial than biweekly. It seems that weekly hour-long sessions were created for therapist convenience during the era when dependence and transference were thought to be important to the therapeutic process. With Imago Relationship Therapy's emphasis on the couple's relationship as the primary healing relationship, biweekly sessions may be preferred, with the therapist more of a teacher and consultant to the process. Nonetheless, because therapy is traditionally about an hour, the six sessions are presented here in a one-hour time frame.

Having said that, I also want to say that the therapist must use good judgment if the clients are obviously in too much distress to continue with the sessions as written. We have found that the best way to handle couples in distress is to keep them in the dialogue process you will teach them in the first session. If all you do is dialogue for the entire length of treatment, you will still be of great help to the couple. Also be aware that you cannot help every marriage and your best intervention may be to help them end the relationship successfully. In addition, be aware of problems that may be of an organic nature that may require medical attention (see Asaad, 1995).

About the Homework

At the end of each chapter that is devoted to a session are handouts to give to the couple for that session. You have permission to photocopy the handouts to give to the couple to complete their homework. For ease of photocopying, all handouts are also reproduced in the back of the book. Each set of handouts includes instructions regarding their purpose and when to give the couple the handouts in the session. You may want to consider copying all of the handouts together to produce a packet, making multiple copies for future couples.

The book is organized as follows:

Introduction to Imago Relationship Theory and Therapy

Imago Relationship Therapy was developed by Harville Hendrix, Ph.D., and is explained in his books *Getting the Love You Want: A Guide for Couples* and *Keeping the Love You Find: A Guide for Singles*. Dr. Hendrix has refined this work through his 25 years of couples work by applying the theory and skills in the hundreds of two-day couples workshops he has conducted. He has taught these skills to over 1000 therapists nationwide who have since become Certified Imago Relationship Therapists. (A listing of therapists in your area is available from the Institute for Imago Relationship Therapy (IIRT), and you may contact them with your questions and referrals. See Resources at the end of this book.) You should find that the Imago Therapy sessions presented in this book will be applicable to most of the couples who come to you for therapy—regardless of age, race, religious beliefs, or sexual preference.

Couples Dialogue: The Essential Skill

This chapter will be a detailed description of the basic skill of this work, the Couples Dialogue. Following a description of the dialogue, we will look at the importance of couples learning this skill to connect, differentiate, heal developmental wounds, and create gender understanding.

Session One: The Cosmic Journey, the Brain, and Couples Dialogue

In this session, you will briefly introduce the couple to Imago Therapy, and you will present a lecture: "The Cosmic Journey and the Brain." You will also introduce the basic communications skill—Couples Dialogue.

Session Two: Development, Childhood Wounds, and Mate Selection

This session deals with how couples meet and fall in love. After monitoring the couple in an actual practice of the Couples Dialogue, you will present a lecture on "Development and Childhood Wounds." You will end the session by doing a guided imagery, and you will give the couple homework that has been designed to illustrate why they picked each other as partners.

Session Three: Developing Empathy and Reimaging the Partner

You will help the couple to develop empathy for each other by giving them work that will ask them to "reimage" each other. They will begin to see each other as wounded allies rather than as enemies; furthermore, they will begin to see each other as a source of healing, rather than as a source of pain. This session is very experiential and involves two powerful exercises.

Session Four: Reromanticizing the Relationship

Couples use their new-found empathy and begin the process of "reromanticizing" their relationship, as well as reinstating "caring behaviors." There will also be a time for high-energy fun and belly laughs. In an important homework assignment, the couple will create a vision for their relationship.

Session Five: Restructuring Frustrations

Couples usually present their frustrations in a way that infuriates their partners—and nothing gets done! In this chapter, you will teach couples how to state their frustrations so that they can be **heard**, and the receiving partners will learn that their resistance usually lies in an area in which they most need to grow in order to become whole. This session will also introduce the couple to Behavior Change Requests and to an important principle in Imago Therapy called "stretching."

Session Six: Resolving Rage

In this session, you will teach the couple a seven-step process known as the Container, which—if done correctly—will help them to express their rage and do so in a safe atmosphere. Because the Container Process is not always needed for every couple, you will be given the option to continue in problem solving using the Behavior Change Request. The Container is very powerful, and prior to conducting this exercise on your own for the first time, you may want to consider getting some additional training or to see an actual Container process. However, because the Container is structured, it is safer and more productive than what couples have probably been using at home. Although this is a tough way to end a therapy relationship, for many couples it is the answer that they have been looking for in their marriage—one that clearly illustrates how the therapy works.

The remaining chapters are devoted to posttherapy work for the couples—optional sessions and ways to be creative with this book, case studies, and an unusual epilogue titled "To What End—Couples Therapy." I have also included a section called "What If the Therapy Does Not Work" (we have to be a realists). Last, you will find an appendix containing resources for the therapist and couple; another appendix that reports the preliminary findings on a study devoted to the efficacy of short-term Imago Therapy; a bibliography; an index; and a section with all the homework assignments for easy photocopying.

1

INTRODUCTION TO IMAGO RELATIONSHIP THEORY AND THERAPY

Quite frequently, therapists ask me, "What is Imago Theory based on?" Imago Relationship Therapy was developed by Harville Hendrix, Ph.D., and is explained in his books *Getting the Love You Want: A Guide for Couples* (1988) and *Keeping the Love You Find: A Guide for Singles* (1992). Those who are familiar with Imago work often say that it seems analytical or Jungian, and that the exercises seem Gestalt-like or resemble psychodrama. Actually, Imago Theory is based on a combination of established theories, some recent biological discoveries and some very old philosophical and mythological ideas. Also, it is continually being refined by Imago Relationship Therapists who are putting the theory to the test in their own practices. The theory presented herein is as it stands in its current stage of development.

CUPID AND PSYCHE

The ancient Greeks learned early on that one of the most effective ways to get a message across to their people was to transform that message into a story. From their mythology, we have evidence that they understood the true meaning of love relationships, and their tale of Cupid and Psyche sums this up rather well.

Once there lived a beautiful mortal named Psyche, whose name is the Greek word meaning soul or mind. So lovely was Psyche that she attracted the attention of Venus, the Goddess of Beauty. Despite her status as a Greek deity, Venus was prone to great jealousy, and she felt threatened by Psyche's very existence. And so she decided to cast a spell on Psyche via her son Cupid (aka Eros), the God of Love.

Cupid was an archer whose arrows would cause anyone struck by them to fall instantly in love. Venus thought it would be funny to have Cupid's arrow strike Psyche who, in turn, would fall desperately in love with the first thing she came upon—such as a frog or an ogre. Venus's vengeful plan backfired. Upon Cupid's first glimpse of Psyche, he was so taken by her beauty that he accidentally cut himself on his own arrow. Indeed, he fell so madly in love with her that he took the lovely mortal as his wife. There was a catch, however: he did not want her to know that he was a god, so he would never let her actually see him. During the day he would appear to her as a voice; he would only come to her in the dark of night. Although she was well taken care of by Cupid, Psyche longed to actually see her husband. When she would tell him of her longing, he would explain that she might be afraid of his true form. He would then ask her to love him, and to trust and believe in him.

In the meantime, Psyche's sisters were growing suspicious and convinced her to try to get a look at him in case he might, in reality, be a monster. Finally, at their urging, Psyche approached Cupid in the night, holding a light over him while he slept. Upon seeing that he was hardly a monster but a god, she was so startled that she spilled a drop of oil from her lamp on him, and he awoke. Naturally, Cupid was angry that Psyche had tried to see his true identity, and so he stripped her of all the luxuries that he had given her, condemning her to roam the land alone.

The remorseful Psyche longed for her husband and finally came up with the idea that the way to get him back might be to ask his mother, Venus, to intervene on her behalf. Venus, still quite jealous of Psyche, was now furious with the mortal woman for hurting Cupid. In a wave of vindictiveness, Venus agreed that Psyche could have Cupid back—but only after the successful completion of some humanly impossible tasks! Little did Venus realize that her son, who—

despite his disappointment in his wife—still longed for her, would be by Psyche's side, helping her undertake each task.

As a final measure, Venus decided to give Psyche the hardest task of all: to go to Hades (the underworld) and bring back some beauty from the goddess Proserpine. This Venus knew to be an impossible venture for poor Psyche, since no mortal could travel to the underworld and hope to return alive. Psyche was so convinced that she would not be able to complete the task that she decided to kill herself.

As Psyche was about to jump to her death, Cupid came to her as a soothing voice and whispered assurances in her ear that he would keep her safe throughout the treacherous journey. And, with his help, the tired and tattered Psyche was able to make the dreaded journey. As her husband had promised, she returned safely. Finally, Cupid, who could no longer bear to be without her, implored the other gods to make Psyche a god as well. The gods were so touched by the trials of Cupid and his mortal wife that they hosted a great feast at which they gave Psyche ambrosia and nectar. Thus, Psyche herself became immortal and was able to remain with Cupid forever.

This Greek myth provides a good outline for Imago Theory, as well as an illustration for how Imago Therapy works.

ROMANTIC LOVE

Like Cupid and Psyche, we are usually taken in by *Romantic Love*. We feel lightheaded and lost and would sacrifice anything to be with the object of our romance. Romantic Love gives us hope. But just what is it?

Physiologically, romantic love is a chemical reaction. Scientists are now telling us that when we fall in love, a chemical called phenylethylamine, or PEA, is released in the brain, causing feelings of elation, exhilaration, and euphoria (Fisher, 1992). PEA is a natural amphetamine and works to rev up the brain. This amphetamine pools in the emotional center of the brain and causes a natural high. Another curious fact is that it is only present in the presence of the object of love. Also, the brain seems to be able to tolerate PEA for a maximum of two years. You see, romantic love is supposed to happen, and it is supposed to end.

Imago Theory sees Romantic Love as a way that nature has devised to get two people together who, during their individual development, have been emotionally wounded in the same place. It is Nature's way of helping us recreate that scene of our childhood in which the wounding occurred so that we can at long last get what we really needed back then. Dr. Hendrix likes to call Romantic Love "Nature's Anesthesia," because nature somehow numbs us to the faults of the person with whom we establish a love relationship. And Nature does this in order to fulfill its purpose: to heal the wounds of our childhood and provide us with what we need to finish our development—so we can grow!

Humans are very complex creatures, having the longest childhood of any animal. As babies, we are unable to survive away from the watchful eye and caretaking of an adult; moreover, we have extensive developmental needs that must be met before we can consider ourselves as "whole." Other mammals only need to learn to hunt, survive, and live in groups. In contrast, humans have a need to form an identity, develop competence and skills, as well as develop friendships and intimacy. It is when we do not get what we need developmentally that the Imago begins.

THE IMAGO AND THE BRAIN

The word *Imago* is the Latin word for *image* and refers to the idea that, inside our minds, we hold an image of both the positive and negative aspects of our early childhood caretakers. This image is held in the "unconscious" or, as I like to think of it, that part of the brain that can hold memories but has no speech. The unconscious is actually a very old part of the brain and is found in all mammals. For our purposes, the unconscious will be referred to as the "old brain."

Starting with the brain stem, the old brain extends into the center of the brain and is comprised of two segments: the "reptilian" brain and the "mammalian" brain (Maclean, 1964). The reptilian brain is where control of our bodily functions are located—the things we don't think about, such as heartbeat, digestion, and breathing. It is also where our survival mechanisms are located, which explains why—when danger strikes—we fight, flee, freeze or "play dead," hide, or submit. The reptilian brain is also concerned with safety; therefore, if something or someone is safe, animals play, nurture, and mate. In addition to these activities, humans work or are creative.

The mammalian part of the old brain is where we store our feelings, our need for relationships, and our tendency for living in groups. This part of the brain evolved with the mammals and influenced the practice of animals living in groups, feeding their young, and experiencing feelings. Animals and humans have these same two parts of the old brain and they are similar in function. Because our brain evolved out of the reptile and mammal brain, we too are always concerned about safety, we live in groups, take care of our young, and experience feelings. What separates us from other animals is the third layer of brain matter.

This third layer of brain matter is the cerebral cortex, sometimes known as the grey matter or "logical" brain. The cerebral cortex is five times larger than the old brain and completely surrounds it. Among the animal kingdom, only humans have evolved this part of the brain that contains speech, writing, reading, and all logical processes. (The exceptions to this are dolphins who have a larger cerebral cortex and the apes, who have a smaller one.) It is the cerebral cortex that is mainly responsible for the technological advances (and, some might argue, the ecological destruction) of humans. It is what may be described as "consciousness."

However, consciousness may not be the best word for this brain function; for the most part, it has not been totally aware of itself. Remember that speech is located in this logical brain part and, because of this, the old brain has an almost impossible time sending direct messages to it. For example, when we see a vicious dog, we don't hear the word "run"—we just instinctively take off. This is an old brain function. It is unconscious and, as mentioned earlier, comes from that part of the brain that has instinct and memory but no speech.

This unconscious aspect is of significance to a couple. When a couple meet and fall in love, they are experiencing a sense of safety. Young lovers, for instance, can be observed playing with and nurturing each other. Some report intense sexual activity; others report a renewed interest in work and in being creative. These are all aspects of what the old brain does when it is feeling "safe." When the romantic love fades—and it always does—and things feel dangerous, couples will either fight or flee (try to leave the situation). Some will stare through their partner (play dead) as a response to that partner's complaints. Some will submit and yell, "Okay . . . whatever you want to do! Just leave me alone!" Others will try to hide from their partners by coming home late or by isolating themselves. You see, when it is dangerous, the old brain is just doing what it has been designed to do.

Another aspect of the old brain (where the Imago is formed and comes into play) is that although it has no speech, it appears to be the place where traumas, deprivations, frustrations, and childhood memories are stored. Also, because it has no sense of time (that's in the logical brain), the old brain often cannot distinguish between being frustrated in the *present* or being frustrated by someone from the *past*. This is where the intense reactions in relationships get their energy!

Bob and Barbara had been married for ten years. Bob often felt trapped by Barbara's desire to have the family together all the time. He felt that this regularly kept him from doing things with "the guys." One day, Bob came home 20 minutes late without calling, and Barbara was furious. She called him every name in the book and told him that she wanted to be called if he expected to be late. This caused an equally intense reaction in Bob, who felt trapped.

When they brought this up in their therapy, Bob and Barbara were able to access how this incident stirred up their early childhood wounds. By using Couples Dialogue (an Imago Therapy tool), Barbara was able to determine that her intense reaction was from a sense of abandonment she experienced as a child. When she was 2 years old, her brother was born, and her mother suffered a serious postpartum depression. Through Couples Dialogue, it dawned on Barbara—who was often told about the "terrible" year her mother experienced—that her intense desire to keep her own family together, as well as her reactions when things do not necessarily go her way, were most likely the result of her being "abandoned" while her mother healed.

Bob, on the other hand, had parents who ruled with an "iron thumb." When he was born, his family lived with his grandmother, and they expected him to "be good" all the time. He has since felt under their thumb and, consequently, has always wanted some "space."

Although some may balk at the idea that things that happen to us in our childhood affect our choices in relationships, couples who undergo even a short amount of Imago Therapy begin to see this very clearly. When they see how they touch their partner's wounds and how their partner touches theirs, couples develop an empathy for each other and begin to work together for their marriage and for their growth. And, as in any growth, there are growing pains that require partners to really hear each other in order to develop empathy and to reimage their partner as "wounded." When partners do this, they are able to see their partner's pain and—at the same time—come in touch with their own.

As the therapist, you will be concerned with two issues in this therapy: *safety* and *growth*. When couples come in for therapy, they are not feeling safe with each other and will demonstrate this by fighting, fleeing, playing dead or freezing, hiding, or submitting. They will come in and point fingers as to who is the most "messed up," but they are both equally "messed up." What they really need is for you to make it safe so they can work with each other, and one of the ways to do that is to begin to normalize their frustrations.

THE POWER STRUGGLE

The power struggle is that stage of the relationship with which most couples are too familiar. Our society has a cliché that begins, "you know the honeymoon is over when . . . ," and the list can be a mile long: he stays out too late; she spends too much money; he works too much; she doesn't understand his feelings; he doesn't understand how hard it is to raise a family; she's too involved with activities; he plays too much softball. Couples go from always wanting to be together to finding ways to be apart. They use coercive methods to get what they need from the other, such as screaming for their partner to spend an extra hour with them. As one seeks more closeness, the other tries to get more distance. And, regardless of the tactics used, frustrations set in.

I envision the frustrations in relationships as mile markers. Most highways have markers at every mile along the road to let you know where you are in case you need help. Some roads even have phones every mile so that you can call and have a tow truck sent to the specific mile marker, to get you on your way again. Frustrations in relationships are very similar. They tell couples the exact spot where they are broken down and need to grow; then they can get the help they need to move on a little further together (that is, of course, until they break down again).

But what is it that they need to repair? According to Imago Theory, frustrations alert us to three main areas in need of repair:

I. Defending Against the Loss of Romantic Love

When couples first begin to fall out of the romantic-love stage, they themselves go through stages. These stages are not unlike other stages that people go through when they experience loss. They will experience **shock** as to why their partner is acting "that way." They might then use **denial** in regard to what their partner is doing, chalking it up as an isolated incident. They may then go through an intense **anger** because their partner is behaving in a certain way or not giving them what they need. Partners often use coercive means to get their partners either to change back to how they were or to give them what they need. When that doesn't work, couples go into a period of **sadness** or despair that their relationship is not giving them what they wanted or hoped for. It is at this point that couples might split up, begin to live parallel lives, or fight constantly.

Joe and Kathy met in school and for three years did everything together. They were so in love that they gave up some of their friends to spend time only with each other. They would give each other gifts and surprises and were always affectionate. By the time they graduated, they were ready to get married and settle down. About a year into the marriage, both were working for large corporations and moving up the ladder. However, to do this, they had to work long hours and sometimes take work home.

Things began to change. They did less and less for each other, yet still expected their partner to do the same as before for them. Kathy began to notice that Joe stopped bringing her flowers. As an explanation, he said, "Flowers die." At first she couldn't believe this, because he used to bring them to her often. Then she thought that it was a phase, but things did not change back. Then, for a period of time, she got angry at the way he was treating her. He, in turn, accused her of nagging. Her anger often temporarily got her what she wanted, but Joe would soon revert to his earlier behavior. After about a year of trying, Kathy regretfully gave up and assumed that she would have to have her needs met through work, friends, or—as a last resort—an affair.

II. Healing the Wounds Created in the Developmental Process

Developmental theories vary in length of time that is deemed necessary to complete the process. Margaret Mahler's separation-individuation developmental theory (Mahler, Pine, & Bergman, 1975) takes place over a 4-year period and results in what she calls the psychological birth of the infant. Erik Erikson's developmental theory (Erikson, 1959) takes place over a lifetime and involves the completion of social tasks, including the development of trust, autonomy, and initiative. Erikson considers each stage a "crisis," because a change is taking place at each stage. Imago borrows from both of these theories and sees development as a 7- to 10-year process that repeats itself several times over the life span. A basic—but important—difference, however, is that Mahler and Erikson see their stages as necessitating separation and difference, whereas Imago sees developmental stages as occurring in connection with the caretaker. In other words, the child needs to be mirrored and validated by a primary caretaker to accomplish each stage without experiencing wounding. Imago identifies five distinct stages:

1. **Attachment** (birth–2 years). Children need to attach to a caretaker; parents need to be available and warm.

2. **Exploration** (2–3 years). Children need to be able to explore (usually just as far as the next room or four steps ahead at the mall) and need to be able to come back to tell their parents about their explorations and adventures. The parents need to allow exploration, and they need to be there to mirror the child's excitement about exploring when he returns to them.

3. **Identity** (3–4 years). Children are beginning to explore different parts of their personality. For example, they will pretend to be dogs, cats, or cartoon characters. Boys and girls will try on their mother's makeup or their father's shoes or shirt. Parents need to mirror ("you're a puppy dog!") so the child gets a sense that others see them as they are pretending to be.

4. **Power and Competence** (4–6 years). Children at this age are beginning to do things outside of the home, such as in school, and have an intense need (and usually a frustrating lack of skill) to be helpful around the house. They are developing a sense of competence. Parents need to give praise, affirmation, and mirroring.

5. **Concern** (6–9 years). Children are now outside of the house and with friends. Their developmental needs are to make friends, find a best friend, and learn the intricacies and jealousies of having and maintaining friends. Parents need to promote friendships and serve as good role models in terms of their own friendships.

Imago Therapy's developmental model is a cyclical process that starts up all over again in adolescence. First, the adolescent will attach to a peer group. When this takes place, adolescents will then explore with their peers, and the peer group will form an identity. Adolescents develop a sense of power in their peer groups, and they develop competency skills. Eventually, they will form an intimate relationship with one of the members of the peer group.

This process repeats itself yet again in young adult relationships wherein partners will attach to each other. They then begin to explore each other, and, if all goes well, they will form an identity as a couple and as competent individuals. Once they do this, they are able to develop their power and competence, both in their lives and in their work. And once they are able to accomplish that, they are able to become intimate friends and give freely to each other, developing a supportive friend network.

At this point, if you are wondering what planet I am from, I want to assure you that it is Earth. As we most assuredly find out, life rarely gets to play itself out in such a tidy scenario, either in adolescence or adulthood, and the reason for this is that many of us did not get our needs met in childhood—*and we cannot seem to get past it!* As hard as many of our parents tried, they could not give us everything that we needed, and our old brain—which has no sense of time—still wants and needs what it did not get! Therefore, we try to get these needs met during the second part of the cycle with our peers, and, when that doesn't work, we try on the third part of the cycle with our partners. But what are we trying to accomplish? That depends on what we missed—in what ways do we feel unfulfilled?

In the attachment phase, if the child was not held enough, or if the parent was not available, the child will develop a personality "type." In this stage, that type would be either a **Clinger** ("I didn't get held so, when I find someone, I'm going to hold on and never let go!") or an **Avoider** ("I didn't get held, so now I don't want anyone to hold me!"). In relationships, these people seek availability and warmth (even though the avoiders say they don't want it). Diagnostically, these individuals are often seen as schizoid personality types. The Clinger often seeks therapy for human contact. The Avoider most often stays by himself or herself.

In the exploration stage, if a child cannot explore ("You must not leave this room and must always stay next to me"), or is shamed upon his or her return, or there is no one to return to (parent leaves the room or is not enthusiastic about what the child finds), the child again develops a personality type. He or she will either become a **Fuser** ("No one got excited about me or what I liked, so I'm going to find someone and make them like what I like—or I'll scream!") or an **Isolator** ("I couldn't do anything when I was a kid, so now I'll do anything I want—and no one is going to stop me!") Diagnostically, these people might be termed as having borderline or narcissistic personality disorders, respectively.

In the identity stage, if the child received no mirroring (was ignored) or poor mirroring ("You're not a puppy, you're a girl!" or "Boys don't wear makeup; only girls wear makeup!"), the personality will either be **Diffuse** ("I don't know what I want to do; I think I want to be either a doctor, a lawyer, or a hairdresser") or they become **Rigid** ("*I* make the rules around here, and we do things *my* way" or "There is only one right way to do things"). Diagnostically for this stage as well as for the remaining stages, clinicians might be more apt to see neurotic disorders, such as anxiety or mild depression.

In the power and competence stage, if the child received partial mirroring ("You colored that okay, but you are all out of the lines, and flowers are not green, they are purple and red") or shaming ("You can't do anything right!"), he or she will develop a personality that is **Competitive** (*"I'm* the best! Can't you see that?") or **Passive/Manipulator** ("I can't do that, so why even try? I've never been able to do anything right! You have to do this for me. I feel so dumb.").

In the concern stage, if the child is unable to make friends or has received poor modeling in regard to making friends, he or she will become either a **loner** and keep to himself or herself, or become a **caretaker** ("I'll take care of these people so they will like me").

According to Imago Theory a funny thing happens to these various personality types when they become adults: *"opposites" fall in love with each other!* The Clinger always falls in love with the Avoidant person. The Isolator always falls for the Fuser. The Rigid personality always falls for the Diffuse, and the Competitive person always falls for the Passive/Manipulator. Last, the Loner always finds the Caretaker (often, the alcoholic/codependent couple). Nature, as Imago Theory defines it, determines that two people *injured at the same place developmentally* find each other and fall in love!

Sample Couplings According to Personality Type

Clinger/Avoider. The Avoider might be a scientist who prefers computers to people; his lab to his home. The Clinger is always screaming at him that she wants closeness, that everything she does is for him and to make him feel special, and that he never notices. He responds to her screaming by not noticing. When they finally decide to separate, it usually means that he sleeps on the couch. Because of the early nature of their wounding, these couples are severely impaired, and typically they are socially isolated.

Fuser/Isolater. The Fuser might be a flamboyant type, always calling attention to himself or herself through dress, demands, or loud outbursts. The Isolator might be a successful "self-made" person, whom others might admire but soon realize they cannot get close to. In this pairing, although Fusers may appear self-centered (since these types try to attract attention to themselves), Isolators are actually the more self-centered ones, because they cannot see past their own actions. Isolators can be very successful in business, since their work is the center of their concentration and their means of not feeling trapped. Fusers respond by screaming and by causing very emotional scenes in an attempt to get Isolators to notice their accomplishments or discoveries.

Rigid/Diffuse. The Rigid partner in this couple is firm and stubborn in what he or she believes: there is only one right way, and it is his or her way. The Diffuse partner has difficulty in making decisions and has few opinions other than the ones dictated by the Rigid partner. This couple might best be described as Archie and Edith types from the TV show "All in the Family."

Competitive/Passive Manipulator. This pairing might be the dual career couple, where one partner is doing fabulously well and moving up the career ladder, while the other is having a hard time getting his or her feet off the ground on the job. In this couple, the Competitive partner typically chooses a life's work in which he/she can be seen and praised. This partner is the one who tries to find ways of making more money and commonly participates in sports or other activities with high visibility. The Passive-Manipulator partner is one who does not want to be seen for fear of failure or humiliation. The Passive partner has difficulty with giving praise to the Competitive partner, which adds to the frustration of both. At the same time the Competitive partner doles out advice to the Passive-Manipulator partner which also adds to their struggle.

Caretaker/Loner. In general, this couple might be quiet and keep to themselves. They work hard and life is neither happy nor sad to them. This description can also fit some alcoholic/codependent couples. The Caretaker learns that the best way to get someone to like him/her is to take care of that person. The Caretaker is attracted to the Loner because of the latter's high-care needs; however, no matter how hard they try, Caretakers cannot get Loners to love them in the way they want to be loved. Loners keep to themselves.

III. Restoring Functions of the Self That Were Lost in the Socialization Process

Astronomers and physicists are now contending that the universe had its beginning in a Big Bang that occurred 15 billion years ago. Moreover, according to those scientists, we are an actual part of that explosion. So it goes that if we are a part of the explosion, then we are energy. And we express this energy in four ways: through our thinking, feeling, acting, and sensing.

If we were "whole," we would have full access to these four areas of energy expression. All of us would think clearly, and we would be able to act on our thoughts to accomplish things. We would all know how we feel every moment, and we'd have ready access to how we felt in the past. We would also have an awareness of our bodies and trust our intuitive natures. What happens in the process of our socialization, however, is that we are usually cut off from two ways of expressing our energy.

On the coast of California, the trees on the cliffs above the beach have adapted in an interesting way. All of their lives, they've been exposed to an almost constant wind off the ocean. Because of this continual pressure during their growth, many trees have branches on one side but not on the side where the wind hits them. Since they do not have branches on both sides, they are not whole. Humans are similar to these trees in that we also adapt to our environment.

According to Imago Theory, when we come into this world we are "whole." Our environment brings about our adaptation, and in the process we lose two means of energy expression. Many of us lived in families in which we were told "don't feel!" We heard, "Boys don't cry!" "Keep your feelings to yourself!" or "You don't feel that way!" When this happened, we adapted by losing the *"feeling"* part of our energy expression or our "selves." Some people live in families in which they are told "don't do!" They hear, "You can't do anything right!" "Don't do that!" "Everything you do, you mess up!" "Girls don't work!" or even, "I'll do that!" And they hear this all too often. The adaptation to this environment is that the person feels that he or she can't do anything right, and so this person loses his or her ability to "act" as a means of energy expression. When this person does something, he or she has the feeling that somehow it is wrong.

In contrast, others were told "don't think!" They heard, "You're so stupid!" "That's the dumbest idea I've ever heard!" "I'll do the thinking around here!" or "Girls don't think as well as boys!" The adaptation to this environment is to cut off "thinking" as an expression. These people are generally unsure of their thoughts; many even have learning difficulties. Finally, others were told "don't trust your body!" They heard, "That doesn't hurt!" "Don't trust your instincts!" "Use your head, it doesn't matter how you feel!" or "You're not sick!" Again, these people cut off their "senses" as an energy expression. They tend to know themselves from the neck up and are stiff and unaware of the body's messages, except when the body expresses symptoms such as in physical illness.

In our society, there seems to be a gender difference in that men lose their feeling and sensing expressions, whereas women lose their thinking and acting expressions. This, however, is most likely the result of our environment and not at all related to ability, and any differences may be rooted in the development and proliferation of our patriarchal society (See Chapter 12, Epilogue: To What End—Couples Therapy?).

Yet wholeness seems to be our number one quest, and our biggest clue to this is the person with whom we fall in love: we fall in love with those who possess our "lost self." That is, thinker/doers fall in love with feeler/sensers; thinker/feelers fall in love with doer/sensers; and thinker/sensers fall in love with feeler/doers. Moreover, when we find them, we tell everyone that we have found the greatest person in the world: "He's so smart!" "She's so sensual!" "She's such a go-getter!" "I've never known a man who feels so deeply." And, for a period of time, we feel whole. We've found the part of ourselves that socialization had told us to turn off.

Eventually, however, something odd begins to happen. We begin to resent or become frustrated by those parts of our partners that first attracted us. "He's so smart!" becomes "He thinks too much and never pays attention to my feelings!" "I've never known a man who feels so deeply!" becomes "He's always so depressed and never does anything about it!" "She's such a go-getter!" becomes "She's always on the run and never has time for the family." This is not because we now hate those parts; rather, it's because the part of our partner that he or she uses as the main way of expression begins to "tickle" those parts that socialization told us to turn off.

For example, when our partner is *feeling*, our own feelings are stimulated, and our socialization message "don't feel!" becomes activated—*and we have to turn it off!* We may begin to scream "quit feeling!" in an effort to turn off this stimulation. Or we may leave the highly emotional situation. According to Imago Theory, the old brain becomes stimulated by those parts our partners have that socialization taught us to turn off. This stimulation is interpreted by the old brain as danger because we are involved in something our caretakers told us to avoid. Just remember what our old brains do when they sense something is unsafe: fight, flight, play dead/freeze, hide, or submit!

Those parts of ourselves that we do not primarily use—whether thinking, feeling, acting, or sensing—are still there. They may have been turned off by our socialization, but they've been stimulated by our partners—and rightly so! We *need* those other parts of ourselves to become whole. Otherwise, we are like the trees on the California coast: surviving and adapting, but not really whole.

Romantic love is supposed to happen, *and* it is supposed to end. Couples are also expected to go through power struggles, but this, too, is supposed to end. Too often, couples get stuck in their power struggles or end the relationship before the struggles can bring about growth. Actually, most couples have no idea what power struggles and frustrations are, let alone that they serve a purpose. With this in mind, if you can teach the couple about these struggles, their relationship will seem more normal to them; in turn, the whole process of struggling will not seem so unsafe. Although their relationship may still be conflictual, at least they can take comfort in realizing that their frustrations do serve a purpose.

COMMITMENT, SAFETY, COUPLES DIALOGUE, AND THE STRETCHING PRINCIPLE

According to Imago Theory, the bottom line is this: Nature has put together two totally incompatible people—injured at the *same* place developmentally and missing opposite parts of themselves—in an effort to get their developmental needs met and to regain lost parts of themselves. Not surprisingly, most of us don't know this secret and—rather than cooperating with Nature—we reinjure our partners in our effort to defend ourselves. For us to heal in our relationships, we must grasp the concept that Nature is using relationships to help us regain our wholeness. The trick is for us to cooperate with Nature!

Commitment

The first step towards accomplishing wholeness is *commitment*. Certainly, a couple must be committed to the relationship in order to do this type of therapy, and we have found that most couples who present to us are indeed committed to each other. Couples who come to your office would certainly like to see the relationship work—otherwise they'd be seeing a lawyer. Be sure to use their commitment to your advantage—even on those days when they're considering ending the relationship. Unless there is a history of abuse or the couple absolutely do not like each other, I believe the relationship is worth saving. One exception to this: if there is an active alcoholic or drug abuser in the relationship, that problem must be addressed first before the therapy can work.

Couples also need to make a commitment to their own growth and to the process of the therapy. Imago Therapy is more than a "couples therapy." It is cooperating with nature to restore individual wholeness. To do this, the couple needs to understand their woundedness and must be committed to restoring both their own wholeness and their partner's wholeness. Be aware that the process of becoming whole is often painful. Dr. Hendrix likes to say, "Nature is not concerned with your comfort. It is only concerned with your growth." Because the path to wholeness is sometimes paved with pain, there must be a commitment to the process of therapy.

Imago Therapy employs three principles in restoring wholeness: *safety*, *couples dialogue*, and *stretching*. Imago Therapy strongly contends that nothing changes if it is not safe. This is because when a situation is dangerous our old brain goes into its defense mode. It's how we are wired. Our old brain kept us from being eaten by tigers in the wild, and it keeps us from being eaten by our partners now. Confrontational therapies may manage to coerce people into changing their behavior, but many times this is only temporary. You see, we cannot change our brain, but we can learn to work with it. And, to do so, we first have to make it safe.

Safety

We can create safety in two ways. One way is within ourselves, by means of evoking mental images that we are safe. Our old brains are very trigger happy, which is probably a leftover from our having lived in the wild. People who live in the wild have to be on the constant lookout for wild animals preying upon them. At the slightest inclination of danger, the tribesman has to be ready to fight or run. In a similar vein, if you ever come face to face with a bear, some say it is better to play dead and—in some cases—even better to submit or to hide. The problem in our modern-day society, where we are seldom confronted with this kind of danger, is that nature forgot to turn the mechanism off. Still, we can learn to use our logical brain to create images of safety.

Typically, early on in the therapy, we tell couples to find a place in their minds—real or imagined—where they can go to feel safe. I will usually tell them that mine is my Italian grandmother's kitchen where there were always a lot of people, and children were especially treasured. Now, when my wife and I are doing this work, and I am feeling danger, I will mentally transport myself to my grandmother's kitchen; yet, at the same time, I am fully with my wife and listening to what she has to say. We also tell couples that "frustrations in relationships are a little bit about now and a lot about the house you grew up in." This does not ignore the fact that partners frustrate each other and have to make changes, but it lets them know that the intensity of the frustration may have its roots in an earlier time in their lives. These two simple techniques, imaging a safe place and realizing that frustrations have roots in earlier times, begin to soothe the old brain. As a result, we've seen fewer impulsive and more thought-out responses to frustrations.

A big part of establishing safety will lie with you, the therapist, as you create safety and guide couples through the process. You should be prepared for couples to slip back into old-brain responses many times; after all, old habits die hard. This is why you will need to acknowledge to yourself—or validate—the fact that changing their responses is a difficult undertaking for you or for any therapist. In other words, to help a couple learn to stay out of their old-brain responses, we must be careful to stay out of their and our own old-brain responses.

If you find this to be a challenge, you are not alone! We are certainly not immune to feeling danger, especially if we feel we have lost control of the session. If a dog senses you are afraid of him, it is quite common for that dog to become frightened and bite you. We are very much that way ourselves; therefore, to create a safe environment for you, the therapist, I suggest the following: find a safe place within yourself from which you can work, especially if conflict upsets you. Also, remember that the conflict and frustration in the session have very little to do with you but more to do with what has been going on for some time in the couple's relationship.

Another way to create safety within yourself is to always remember to "stay with the process." In this book, you will be introduced to and become familiar with "mirroring," "validating," and "empathizing" as the main communication processes you will be teaching couples. Make it a point to learn these tools for yourself and use them to help yourself maintain control of the sessions and to create safety with the couples, thus avoiding danger. For instance, if a couple should confront you, *mirror*, *validate*, and *empathize* with their concern. When you use the tools you have given them, they will grasp the idea behind the process all the more quickly.

Couples Dialogue

In Imago therapy, dialogue is primordial. If a couple leaves your office learning nothing else, they should learn the process of Couples Dialogue. Humans have a basic need to know that they were heard and understood. We need to know that we make sense, are acknowledged as having feelings—that we exist. Couples Dialogue helps to fulfill this desire.

To many, Couples Dialogue will sound like other communication tools they have learned—active listening or parroting. In part, that is correct. The difference is the paradigm that the therapist will package it in. Couples Dialogue is more than fully listening. It also adds the dimension of fully understanding that the other has a valid point or feeling: that the other person's reality is very real to him/her and does not have to be blended with the listeners or compromised. In other words, dialogue teaches couples that their thoughts and beliefs do not have to be symbiotic. There can be two realities and points of view.

Most couples live in a symbiotic state. The *American Heritage Electronic Dictionary* (1992) defines symbiosis as "A close, prolonged association between two or more organisms of different species that may, but does not necessarily benefit the other." I used to joke about some couples: "together, they make one good person." That stopped being funny to me when I realized that this outlook was the underlying source for problems in marriages. We have lived under the theory that the two shall become one. However, the belief that promotes growth is that the two shall remain two and get together often to talk in dialogue in order to create closeness, understanding, and passion in a way that benefits the other. Couples Dialogue is the key to understanding, healing, and creating interdependent relationships.

The Stretching Principle

Once you have created safety and taught couples dialogue, couples can do the work they have come to do. The work not only improves the relationship, it cooperates with Nature, helping each partner complete childhood development and, at long last, become whole. And this is possible through a principle called *stretching*.

Stretching is one of the most difficult aspects of Imago Therapy. It is, in a sense, becoming what you are not. Better yet, it is becoming what you think you are not, because what you are "stretching" into are the lost parts of yourself or those parts that were turned off in your childhood. Stretching goes against the messages you received way back then. If you say "I don't feel," that's not a true statement at all, because you have a whole part of your brain—the mammalian brain—that is dedicated to feelings. You may not be connected to these feelings because of the way you were socialized ("boys don't cry!"), but the capacity is there, and the way to reclaim this part is through stretching.

Here is a common question that may arise: if the part is "lost," how do you know where to find it—or even *know* what you are looking for? The answer is found in the most unlikely and, many would say, the most dreaded of places: our partners! Our partners have been screaming at us from the place in which we need to grow. As we say in this work, "Your partner has the blueprint for your growth."

The problem is twofold: we haven't been listening, and they've been saying it in a way that we cannot hear because it's too dangerous for us. They've been stating it as a frustration: "Don't you have any feelings?" "Are you stupid or something?" "You can't do anything right!" These are but a few of the statements our partners may scream at us. Although they are reinjuring us in a very hurtful way, these statements tell us precisely where we need to grow. To create safety, however, couples need a better way to state their frustrations so their partners can hear their needs and, at the same time, know the area in which they have to grow in order to become whole. Imago Therapy uses Behavior Change Requests to accomplish this.

Behavior Change Requests

A Behavior Change Request is one partner's (the "sender's") detailed request for a change in the other's (the "receiver's") behavior. It is based on the sender's frustrations in the relationship, yet it is phrased in a manner that the receiving partner can hear and respond to. Grouped together, Behavior Change Requests become what is called a "blueprint for growth." This blueprint is the way for one partner to tell the other exactly how to reclaim those parts of himself or herself that were turned off either in childhood or because of societal expectations.

In a Behavior Change Request, a frustration ("Don't you have any feelings?") becomes a desire ("I need your feelings"), which then becomes a very specific Behavior Change Request: for example, "When I am talking about things that are important to me, such as how the kids have been driving me crazy, I need you to listen and to validate that I have had a hard day and to take a guess at how I might be feeling." The Behavior Change Request tells one partner what it is that the other partner needs in order to feel fully heard and understood; however, what the sending partner is in need of is always the thing that is most difficult for the other to give: that need is requesting something of the receiving partner's "lost" part. Using the example above, a typical scene would be the following:

> Bill came home after a long day at work to find Linda overwhelmed by the children. Linda told Bill about all the fights, spills, and arguments of the day. Bill immediately responded to her by saying, "Why don't you just put them in their room and make them clean up their own mess?" Linda, who did not want to hear that, yelled, "What do you think I am—stupid? You stay with these kids all day and see what it's like!" Bill then retorted, "I was just offering you some advice." And from this point on, their "shouting match" accelerated.

Bill was an action person. His lost part was his feeling, and that's just what Linda needed—his feeling. In the therapy, she made that known to him in her Behavior Change Request:

When you come home from the office, I would like you to come to me and say, "I am here to listen to you." I would like you to mirror what I say, to validate that I am having the feelings I tell you I am, and to take a guess at what I may be feeling. I would like you to do this for 15 minutes, and then I want you to say to me, "I can see that you have been having a very difficult day." I would like you to do this three times a week.

Although Bill was able to hear this, he stated how difficult it was going to be for him. He considers himself a "take-charge" kind of guy, and he has a hard time with feelings. He would rather take action. Nevertheless, since he is committed to the process of Imago Therapy and understands that it is necessary to his partner's needs as well as to reclaim his own lost parts, he decides to make the "stretch."

Linda mapped out the stretch for Bill in the Behavior Change Request. The combination of listening, validating, and empathizing was the start Bill needed to begin the process of reclaiming his feelings. It was difficult for Bill, but Linda had given him *the* way. Remember, "the partner has the blueprint for growth."

REIMAGING YOUR PARTNER

How can someone possibly follow this blueprint for change when one is so angry at one's partner? Imago offers two ways of dealing with this dilemma, the first of which is *reimaging*. Again, we go back to the Greeks for the basics of reimaging.

The great Greek thinkers wanted to find a way to end wars. They were tired of fighting and wanted to find a way to permanent peace. What they came up with gave birth to one of their words for love: *agape*. They found that in order for people to be able to slaughter other people, they had to learn to visualize those people as nonhumans. We've seen this in our lifetime with the rampant use of derogatory terms. When we indiscriminately group a race or nation under a derogatory term we dehumanize them, and it becomes easier for us to kill them. The Greeks decided to change this way of thinking. Instead of killing those who entered their land, they would befriend them. Thus, the word agape was coined, meaning: "When you are in my territory, I will make you safe."

Couples are quite often guilty of "slaughtering" each other. They first dehumanize each other with pronouns: "*You* always . . ." "*He* never . . ." "*She* is . . . ." By dehumanizing each other, the "kill" becomes easier. In order to change this battle, they have to be like the Greeks and reimage each other. They need to begin to see each other as allies in growth rather than as enemies in a relationship. They need to see that Nature has brought them together for a purpose, rather than to view their relationship as a mistake or wish they'd never met. This does not mean they won't feel tension—after all, the Greeks certainly must have tensed up when others entered their territory. But it does mean that they will be safe, and no one will get killed as they explore what the tension is all about.

Imago Therapy employs two very specific tools to help partners reimage each other: the Holding Exercise and the Parent/Child Dialogue. These are explained at length later in this book, but their basic purpose is to help couples see what we stated earlier: that frustrations in marriage are a little bit about now and a lot about the house they grew up in. These tools also enable partners to view the hurt that underlies each other's behavior and allow them to develop empathy for each other. When a couple really sees the partner's pain, they can never view each other in the same way again. After all, if you saw a car injure somebody, you wouldn't go and kick him or her; you would provide help and "feel" the hurt.

THE CONTAINER PROCESS

The second way to deal with anger is with the Container Process. In relationships, intense anger is usually either expressed loudly or not expressed at all. Quite commonly, those who do not express anger have a partner who expresses frustration about that very lack of expression—that the partner does not tell what he or she feels. The expression of anger usually calls up the reptilian-brain response, and those who do express anger tend to have a partner who responds by freezing, hiding, or submitting. Whether the anger goes unexpressed or is expressed through yelling, partners do not hear each other, and this pent-up anger turns to rage. Rage may best be described as stored or unheard anger.

Anger, on the other hand, is a survival mechanism or a fight response from the reptilian brain. It is also a feeling from the mammalian brain. Anger is not something that we can lose or take away from people; it has kept us alive when we needed it. Again, the best way to deal with anger and rage is to learn to cooperate with Nature. Imago Therapy makes anger and rage *safe* so that the angry partner can be heard, validated, and understood, and it does so through the Container Process.

The Container, which is described in detail in Chapter 8 (Session Six), is basically a structured way to express anger and rage in a relationship. In fact, it is so structured that partners must ask for an appointment from each other in order to use the Container and thus express rage. Ask for an appointment? Shouldn't feelings be spontaneous? The answer is a flat "NO!" Spontaneous expressions of anger or criticism elicit an immediate response of defensiveness from the old brain.

Have you ever been startled by a scream? One day, as I was walking down a street in New York, I came upon a homeless woman. Now I'd walked those streets often enough to know that homeless people are much more concerned with their own survival than they are with hurting pedestrians. Generally, they will politely ask for money, are gracious if you give them some, and won't pester you if you decide not to give them a handout. This particular woman appeared to be approaching me similar to the way others had in the past, giving me little reason to be alarmed. Then, suddenly, she screamed at the top of her lungs, "Pleeeeeease!" This startled me to such a degree that I ran to get away from her. Her spontaneous scream brought out my flight response.

As farfetched as this may sound, had that woman come to me and said, "I need to scream. Could you possibly give me a moment to scream?", I would have thought her weird, but I may have been able to calm myself enough to know that I was safe and actually have agreed to listen to her. And this is precisely what we ask of couples when they wish to express anger: to give adequate warning to enable their partners to first find their safe place. As a result, they allow their partners to fully hear the anger that they wish and need to express. When partners are able to do this for each other, they can usually get through the anger and reach the hurt underneath. When couples are able to get to the frustration's underlying hurt, they seem to be able to cover more ground, and the interactions become more productive. The Container Process gives couples a structured seven-step process to create safety, feel heard, express rage, and push through the hurt. In many cases, this creates passion between them.

CUPID AND PSYCHE REVISITED

We started this chapter on Basic Imago Theory and Therapy with the Greek mythology story of Cupid and Psyche, referring to it as a basic outline for Imago Theory. As was the case with our mythical couple, Romantic Love always begins a relationship; however, we do not know whom our real lover is, because we have not really seen him or her. When we finally do, our magic kingdom seems to suddenly disappear, and we are left looking for the love we once had.

When we cannot get Romantic Love back, a sense of despair sets in, and we either give up or fight constantly. One hope is to go with Nature and take on the task of becoming whole through our partner. Like Psyche's trying journey, the journey to wholeness (looking at our wounds and stretching into our lost selves) is difficult and painful. Psyche was able to do it with the help of her partner Cupid who was working alongside her to help make her journey safe. When we are able to make the journey into our "underworld" and do so with our lover's help, we emerge stronger and closer to wholeness. Imago Therapy gives couples the tools they need to help each other make that journey and return safely.

But what about love? If we are saying that Romantic Love is a no-growth kind of love that is supposed to end, what kind of love can we hope for? Our English language has limited us to only one word for it. The Greeks have at least three: *eros*, the initial romantic love; *agape*, a transformative love, making an enemy an ally; and, the highest form of love, *philia* or brotherly love. We now know from couples who have made the journey through to the end that this third type of love, philia, is better and even more intense than Romantic Love. They report a sense of desireless valuing, empathetic communication, nondefensive relating, joy, and they feel fully alive. Philia is the payoff for toughing out the treacherous journey—and it's well worth the trip!

The Greeks knew this, too. Following their demanding journey to be together at last, Psyche and Cupid gave birth to a daughter. They named her Pleasure.

2

COUPLES DIALOGUE

The Essential Skill

One thing I have come to look upon as almost universal is that when a person realizes he has been deeply heard, there is a moistness in his eyes. I think in some real sense he is weeping for joy. It is as though he were saying, "Thank God, somebody heard me. Somebody knows what it is like to be me." In such a moment I have had the fantasy of a prisoner in a dungeon tapping out day after day a Morse code message, "Does anybody hear me? Is there somebody there? Can anyone hear me?" And finally one day he hears some faint tapping that spells out "Yes." By that simple response he is released from his loneliness, he has become a human being again. There are many, many people living in private dungeons today, people who give no evidence of it whatever on the outside, where you have to listen very sharply to hear the faint message from the dungeon.

Carl Rogers
Freedom to Learn (1969 p. 224)

Carl Rogers' words still ring true today; being heard and understood truly sets us free from our own world. It puts us in relationship with another, and lets us know that the thoughts and feelings we are having on the inside can be validated by someone on the outside. This is something we, as therapists, have always known. Research conducted on the therapeutic process by Lambert (1992) indicates that the therapeutic relationship contributes 30% to the outcome in psychotherapy. Outcome depends very little on what technique or model a therapist uses but relies heavily on the warmth, trustworthiness, nonjudgmental attitude, and empathy of the therapist. Paradoxically, while being validated by someone puts us in connection with that person, at the same time it sets us apart; it differentiates us.

What you will be doing over the course of this therapy is teaching couples what therapists have known all along and what makes the therapeutic relationship so important: If you truly hear a person, he or she feels both connected and differentiated. Like the therapeutic relationship, couples who take the time to understand one another can help each other step out of his or her box. These partners will be more inclined to take chances, pursue goals, change behaviors, and develop a sense of self. Most importantly, they can do this within the relationship—but this time, in a different type of relationship. Not a relationship with someone they found in a phone book or who was referred by a friend or who was assigned to them by a case manager. These steps will be taken with the person whom Nature chose to make the journey with them: their partner. Together, they begin a process of collaborative self-development.

COUPLES DIALOGUE

To make this journey, the couple first needs a dialogue process. In Imago Therapy, we call this process the Couples Dialogue or Intentional Dialogue. The second moniker is more descriptive of what we ask couples to do, because they will intentionally and consciously listen to their partners. However, this is far different from what commonly occurs in couples who usually communicate in what is called a diatribe. A diatribe occurs when a couple trying to communicate are observed to be thinking of what they will say back to their partners to defend themselves or their stance. Such action immediately invalidates what their partners said just before their response and creates unsafe communication. A typical diatribe might go like this:

Lisa: What a day! I'm so tired. I had a school meeting this morning, and Lila is not doing so well in her reading. I then had to drive over to that client and drop off the proposal and I got held up there for two hours, so I missed my lunch with my mom. I hate hectic days like this.

Alan: Yeah. Did you see that bill for the lawn service?

Lisa: Did you hear what I said?

Alan: Yes, did you hear what I said?

Lisa: You never listen to me. I'm really tired, and you don't care!

Alan: I'm tired, too. I can't stop what I'm doing to talk about that. I've got a lot to do.

Lisa: And I've done a lot. I'm near exhaustion, and all you're concerned about is the bill for the lawn service.

Alan: I do a lot around here, too.

Lisa and Alan are not listening to each other, and this sets up a power struggle. Couples in a power struggle look for ways to defend their position and typically feel frustrated and distant afterwards. They may become discouraged and begin to keep their feelings to themselves, or they may do things without asking for help because they fear the response. This may look like differentiation because they are handling things on their own, but it is really distance.

Couples Dialogue allows the sender of a statement to feel fully heard and understood. When a person feels understood, he or she can redirect the energy used to hold onto his or her position to move towards the more useful purpose of developing a sense of self. At the same time, Couples Dialogue allows the receivers of the statement to hear it without feeling as if he or she has to agree or become symbiotic with the other. It allows for two realities of a situation rather than the one that the diatribe strives for. When couples are able to understand that there are two realities through the dialogue process, they are able to facilitate each other's growth. This occurs through a complete, albeit difficult, understanding by one partner of the needs of the other. In order to tread into these uncharted territories, couples need the safety of the Couples Dialogue process.

Couples Dialogue is a three-part process consisting of mirroring, validating, and empathizing. When the couple first learns it, it is very structured and may seem rote. Some may even complain that it seems fake when they do it. But this will pass, and the dialogue will become more natural and fluid. Watch a one-year-old walk, and you'll find that it's really more of a controlled fall. Only after a period of awkward practice does walking become integrated. Likewise, the payoff for the awkward period of Dialogue is a couple who understand and appreciate each other.

Mirroring

The first step of the Dialogue process—mirroring—has the receiving partner repeating back to the sending partner what was said—not what he or she thought was said or what he or she wanted to be said, but what the sender actually said. This part of the process establishes contact and lets the sending partner know that he or she was heard. It also prevents the receiver from responding with a defensive answer so quickly, because he or she has to concentrate and listen intentionally to fully hear the partner. Mirroring becomes an important part of establishing contact between sender and receiver, so it is important that it be done accurately. It is perfectly appropriate for the receiver to ask the sender to repeat the statement; the idea is to get the message across.

Validating

Once the receiver has accurately mirrored the partner, he or she then validates what the partner said. Validation is not agreeing, although agreement may occur. Validation is a way of saying, "If I could look at things through your eyes, which I cannot, but if I could, I could see how you would see it that way." In other words, validation means, "Your ideas make sense from your point of view." This is a very important part of the dialogue process and what sets it apart from "active listening." It asks the receiver to momentarily place him or herself into the thoughts of the other and understand the sense of the partner's point of view.

Validation can be momentary. Some may describe it as a small "aha!" experience. It is listening long enough, without defending oneself, to understand that the other has a valid point. At the same time, it is not losing one's "self" to the other. Validation creates two points of view, neither of which is wrong. It is what sets the other apart in the relationship and creates personhood. At the same time, it sets the receiver apart in that he or she has to learn to integrate the anxiety they both are feeling because the sending partner does not feel, think, or believe like he or she does. In other words, validation breaks the symbiotic thought and creates a healthy differentiation through relationship.

Empathizing

Therefore, if the receiver can validate the partner, he or she can usually understand that the partner will have feelings about what was said. This brings us to the third part of the Dialogue process: empathizing. For the receiving partner to empathize, he or she merely needs to guess what the sending partner may be feeling. Quite often a person is able to have two, three, or more feelings at the same time. Even contradictory feelings are noticed. The receiving partner may say something like, "I can imagine that might make you feel sad, lonely, and scared." The receiving partner may have guessed incorrectly, but this was, after all, a guess and an attempt at connection through empathy. If the receiver is able to stay in the process, there are no wrong moves. If the receiver missed the feelings of the partner, he or she can start over by mirroring the correction the partner gives and attempt to understand these feelings through the Dialogue process.

Dialogue occurs in blocks. Rather than teaching the partners to take turns, saying what each has to say by sentence or paragraph, you will show

how the receiving partner intentionally mirrors, validates, and empathizes with the sending partner until the sending partner feels fully heard. Of course things will crop up during this process that the receiver will want to defend, but he or she is asked to hold his or her thoughts and anxieties until the sending partner feels fully heard and understood. Then it will be the receiving partner's turn to be the sender in the dialogue process. If partners can endure their anxieties, over time they will reach a new level of understanding of and empathy for the significant other. The receivers will also find that the anxiety of the process becomes tolerable, which will allow them to listen to their partner for longer periods of time in the future.

Dialogue is an evolving process for the couple; if practiced regularly, it becomes easier, more fluid, and again produces less anxiety. Staying in the process is everything in this work. If a couple falls out of the dialogue process when they are discussing difficult issues, they will revert to old, hurtful ways of communicating. To consciously and intentionally participate in the dialogue process is to strive for understanding the other, and this promotes growth. Frustrations are growth trying to happen; Couples Dialogue promotes this growth.

CASE STUDY: MIKE AND LINDA

Throughout this book, you will be introduced, through case studies, to couples who are just learning the process of Couples Dialogue. To give you an idea of the end result, I would like to start with a couple who have been using the process for several years. Mike and Linda have been married for twelve years and have two sons, ages 8 and 6, and a 3-year-old daughter. They entered therapy four years ago and spent ten sessions learning the dialogue process as well as the other processes that will be described herein.

Prior to the therapy, Mike and Linda were frustrated with the way their marriage was going. They found they had little time for each other as they took care of their young sons and built their business. There were constant misunderstandings and hurt feelings, which caused them to seek ways to avoid each other. They were tired most days and had little time for affection. They decided to enter therapy out of concern for what this atmosphere was doing to their children. They made a commitment to learn the processes and practice as often as they could—despite their busy lives.

Initially, the work was difficult for them due to time pressures and Mike's skepticism of the processes—especially how his childhood played into his present marriage. However, he became more involved as he saw their communication improve and how the processes helped him become more responsive to Linda. In the four years since their therapy sessions, they've often reverted to talking in diatribes. Invariably they come back to Couples Dialogue when they realize that diatribe and unsafe communication get them nowhere, whereas Couples Dialogue moves them along. Now, their dialogues sound like this:

Mike: I need to talk to you. Can you get safe?

Linda: Yeah, give me one minute. . . . Okay, I can hear you now.

Mike: It's 11:30 and I thought you were going to be back at 11:00. I was feeling really angry, anxious, and worried that something happened.

Linda: (*mirroring*) If I got that right, you thought that I was going to be back at 11:00 and it is now 11:30. You were feeling angry, worried, and anxious that something happened. Did I get that?

Mike: Yes.

Linda: Is there more?

Mike: I found myself pacing and being really angry at you for the past 30 minutes. I felt really mad that you didn't call me to let me know that you'd be late. It felt disrespectful to me.

Linda: (*mirroring*) So if I'm getting this, you said that you've been pacing and feeling angry for the past 30 minutes. You were mad that I didn't call you and you said that feels disrespectful. Did I get that?

Mike: Yes.

Linda: (*validating and empathizing*) Well, that makes sense to me, because I was late and you were wondering what happened. I can understand how you would wonder why I didn't call you and that felt disrespectful. I can imagine that you would feel angry, worried, anxious, and scared.

Mike: Yeah, really anxious and scared, because it reminded me of when I was a kid and my parents would go out and leave me in charge of my sisters. They'd always come back late and never call me, and I'd get worried that something had happened to them and that I would be in charge forever. It was really scary, and that's why this is so scary to me. I need to know that you are alright.

Linda: (*mirroring*) So if I'm getting this, it really scares you when I'm late and don't call, because it reminds you of when you were a kid and your parents would put you in charge and they'd be late and not call. You felt like something may have happened to them and that would put you permanently in charge and that scared you. You needed to know that they were alright. Did I get that?

Mike: Yes.

Linda: Is there more?

Mike: I know I get more angry than most would about this, and I used to scream like a nut when you were late, but what I really want you to get is how scary it is for me when you are late. If I let myself think about and feel this, it feels like my world would come to an end if something would happen to you. It's just like I felt when I didn't know if my parents were coming back. It was really unfair and disrespectful that they wouldn't call me when they were late. And they didn't understand why I felt so upset.

Linda: (*mirroring*) So, If I'm getting this right, you are remembering how scared you were when your parents came home late and didn't call. They didn't understand how upset you were, and that felt disrespectful. It seems like if something happened to me, your world would come to an end. When I don't call when I'm going to be late, it feels really scary. Did I get that?

Mike: You did.

Linda: (*validating and empathizing*) It really makes sense to me that you'd be scared when I was late, because you felt so scared when your parents did this to you when you were a kid. They depended on you at a young age, and yet they didn't show you respect when they were late or acknowledge that you had feelings about the responsibility you had. I can imagine this would make you feel angry, disrespected, and resentful that they did not take you seriously.

Mike: Yes, thanks. I have a Behavior Change Request if you're able to listen to it.

Linda: I can hear that now.

Mike: Okay. If you're going to be more than 15 minutes late, I would like you to call me 10 minutes before your expected time home. If I'm having a feeling about it—angry, negative, or frustrated—I'd like to be able to talk about it briefly on the phone using Couples Dialogue. I would like for you to do this 60 percent of the time you are late.

Linda: (*mirroring*) So if I am getting this, 60 percent of the time that I know I'm going to be more than 15 minutes late, you'd like for me to call you at least 10 minutes before my scheduled time home. If you are having a feeling about my being late, you would like to take a minute and have me use Dialogue to understand that feeling. Did I get that?

Mike: Yes you did. Thanks.

Mike and Linda did not come to this calm way of listening to each other over night. They experienced many volatile times in their marriage. Through their practice and failures in learning the dialogue process, they are able to create a safe space to hear each other. Prior to learning Couples Dialogue, a conversation regarding the above situation would have erupted into a major fight. Linda's childhood wound would have immediately been brought up since Mike's urgency about Linda's timeliness would tap into her feeling of being smothered, just like she felt growing up with intrusive parents and siblings. Linda undoubtedly needs to talk about how Mike's need to know her whereabouts taps into her memories of her parents planning her days and telling her who could be her friends. But for now, Linda was able to listen to Mike and hold her anxiety until they could create a safe place and time for her to be mirrored and validated. That time could be now, if Mike felt safe, or in a couple of days when they could schedule another dialogue session.

THE GREMLINS UNDER THE BEHAVIOR

To understand why Couples Dialogue works, I will describe some of the underlying fuel for frustrations. Frustrations are not necessarily fueled by problems or behaviors, but by developmental lags and wounds that make the behaviors very important. For some couples we know that a partner's chronic lateness is sometimes annoying but not grounds for a fight. For others, it is a very big issue that often results in disillusionment, anger, and feelings of abandonment. The problem may be resolved, but the fear still remains. Couples Dialogue is not just about problem solving or insight, although that may occur. The work you are doing with the couple, which includes Couples Dialogue, is about developmental growth. When couples are able to grow developmentally, they deal with the problem *and* the underlying fear.

Developmental stages are built-in impulses of the psyche. Pediatrician T. Berry Brazelton (1992) likes to call them "touchpoints." These impulses or touchpoints are the times in a developing child's life when the child will enter into the next level of development. Caretaker behavior toward the child at these touchpoints will determine how successful the child's emergence will be.

In the first stage of attachment, the infants need someone to attach to, whereas in the second stage of exploration children need support to explore and to differentiate. Once children pass through these two stages, they can differentiate and form an identity, or self, in the third stage if they receive mirroring. They can become competent in the fourth stage, provided they receive praise. Finally, children can develop concern for others in the fifth stage if they receive support from friends and family. This will allow them to form intimate relationships as adolescents. Parental awareness of self as well as child—indeed good parenting skills—support these developmental impulses, and much of this support occurs through the dialogue process between parent and child.

However, most people are not raised by aware, or conscious, parents. Experience tells us that most parents are probably wounded somewhere in their own childhood and are unaware of the effect their upbringing has on their parenting skills. These wounds usually keep them from giving their children what they need to fully develop—encouraging the developmental impulses. If attachments are disrupted and exploration/differentiation issues are not supported, a developmental wound occurs which results in the child getting stuck in a symbiotic stage of development; the child is unable to form an identity, feel competent, or express concern for others in a full way. The wound creates self-absorption.

Self-absorption is what we typically do when we are in pain. Imagine yourself on a tall mountain peak with a beautiful vista. The view is overwhelming, but suddenly you cut your foot on a sharp rock. What becomes the focus of your thoughts, the vista or your painful foot? For most people, the painful foot becomes most relevant while the views and other people become secondary. You become self-absorbed naturally. All you want is for others to see that you need help. Even with the beautiful view, you hope that they'll become symbiotic with your needs. And who could blame you?

According to Imago Theory, influenced by Erikson (1959) and Mahler et al. (1975), when children are unable to get past their natural developmental impulse, they develop a lag, and yet they still desire to have this impulse satisfied. In essence, while the developmental engine is still running, the transmission has been stopped. Therefore, such children have a difficult time moving forward—learning the skills necessary towards developing a complete self. Rather than fully appreciating the wonders of the world, they begin to pay attention to their own pain of not being able to complete their development. They begin to adapt and to make up their own way of living, hoping that others will see things through their eyes.

When these children grow up, they will not necessarily stand out in the crowd. Most will not be thought of as odd or different or in need of any help. They may be described by parents, adults, and other significant people in their lives as clingers, isolators, controlling, dizzy, competitive, unsure, loners, caretakers, conforming, or rebellious. They are children of all sizes, shapes, and colors. Regardless, they share one thing in common: their developmental needs could not be fully met. And in truth, it is almost impossible to fully meet the needs of any child. In other words, these are children who will grow up to be us. And when these children grow up they will marry someone who is equally self-absorbed. Subconsciously, they will hope their partner will meet the needs that their parents were unable to.

Self-absorption is the state that most couples present in therapy. They will both want you to see their point. Their motto for marriage becomes, "You and I are one and I am the one." The biggest problem with this motto is that both partners are saying, "I am the one," and this is where conflicts and impasses occur. As my wife likes to say about us sometimes, "One bone, two hungry dogs." When this happens, you lose the awareness of the "otherness of the other," and the power struggle begins.

Couples therapy has traditionally dealt with this through negotiation or behavior change—having both partners give in a little or having one partner give up his or her goal of being the one. In more traditional therapy—for example, a cognitive type—they might be told that their thinking is flawed and they need to change the way they think about their problems. However, the problem with this traditional therapy—although research shows that it does work for a short period of time—is that it does not address the underlying problem of the unmet developmental needs that cause symbiosis and self-absorption. This is the real fuel for the conflict, and Couples Dialogue is able to get to these deeper issues.

WHAT DOES COUPLES DIALOGUE DO?

Basically, the three-part dialogue process contributes to connection and differentiation. Mirroring is a way of making contact. Validation is a way of creating equality, while empathy is a means of being able to transcend the self and become involved in the other. It is when a person can transcend his or her "self" and his or her own pain to listen to the thoughts and feelings of the other that he or she can fully connect with another. When the other person reciprocates, the act becomes healing. There are four areas that Couples Dialogue works on simultaneously, which we will now look at in more detail.

Couples Dialogue Fosters "Connection"

Probably the most common phrase heard by a couples therapist who is working with a new couple is, "We just don't communicate." For example, he will then begin to tell you how she does not understand him or his point of view. She will tell you how he watches too much TV or reads the newspaper and does not listen to her. He might tell you how she spends time on the phone or is more concerned about the children than what he has to say. And although you will see some couples who do not talk, you are more likely to witness those who talk endlessly with each other as they defend their points of view. What might be a more accurate phrase for these couples is, "We just don't connect."

Connecting with another is a "fine line." One side of the line is described as too close—a smothering feeling permeates the interaction.

Judy: I'm really upset about losing that contract at work.

Jeff: You knew that would probably happen.

Judy: Yeah, but it is different when you finally hear it.

Jeff: I don't know why. You should have been prepared for it. That's what I do and it really makes the letdown easier. You should try it, so you don't get so freaked out.

The other side of the line is described as distant—a lack of connection permeates this interaction.

Judy: I'm really upset about losing that contract at work.

Jeff: Yeah, well I'm sure you will get over it. Have you thought about what we are going to do about the trip next week?

Judy: I should have been prepared, but it really is different when you hear it.

Jeff: I really need to know because there is a softball game scheduled on that Saturday.

Couples Dialogue seems to straddle the line—connection and interest in the other permeates these interactions.

Judy: I'm really upset about losing that contract at work.

Jeff: So if I am hearing you correctly, you are really upset about losing that contract at work. Is there more?

Judy: I should prepare myself for these letdowns because there is always a chance that you can lose these things. It just seems worse when you hear the final news.

Jeff: So you are saying you should expect this news and prepare yourself because that is the nature of your business. You are also aware that the news of the final disposition of the contract always brings about some intense feelings for you. I can understand that. It makes sense that bad news brings out bad feelings. I imagine you feel sad, shocked, and tired from all the work you put into this project and then finding out you were turned down.

Judy: Yes, you got it.

Dialogue assures connection at the right distance. The process of mirroring lets the sending partners know that they were heard by the receiving partners because they hear back their own words. It lets them know that what was heard by the receiver was what they said. It lets them know that there were no distractions or distortions in their words and their partner at least *heard* the message. At the same time, it keeps the receiving partner from going into a defensive mode and from attempting to invalidate what the sender said in an attempt to win an argument or prevent differentiation.

Validation lets the senders know that they make at least some sense to the receiver and that they are not "crazy." When receiving partners cut the sending partners off or don't take the time to make sense of the partner's message, they create a sense of instability in the sending partner. Senders may feel crazy, but basically they feel cut off or separated from the other. Validation allows the sending partner to feel connected through the act of making sense to the other. When a person is told that he or she makes sense, the other person becomes a part of his or her world at least for a brief period of time. They become connected through an understanding by the other.

When receivers validate, they probably understand that the sender is feeling what was said. The act of guessing what the sender may be feeling is another way of promoting connection. Typically, in a diatribe partners are so tuned into their own feelings, they miss the fact that the other person has feelings. To guess what the other may be feeling is a way of transcending the self to understand the other. In order for receivers to step out of the feelings momentarily, they have to experience and understand the feelings of the other. The therapist should strive for this way of connecting in Couples Dialogue. For a person to step out of his or her own feelings momentarily and to experience and understand the feelings of the other is the true state of empathy. It is differentiation with integrity.

Couples Dialogue Fosters Differentiation With Integrity

There are many ways of being differentiated as a couple. Couples who live parallel lives and who have their own friends and activities are differentiated. Couples who stamp their feet and say that they are going to pursue an activity or a growth experience because they have the right to are differentiated. Partners who finally get frustrated enough to say, "I'm tired of you not following through on your promises. I am going to start doing these things for myself"—and do just that—are differentiated. But none of these couples are in a relationship with each other. I consider them to be differentiated on a physical level—a type of differentiation where each partner has little consideration for the other.

Differentiation with integrity is different. It is an evolved differentiation that occurs on a spiritual level. Its goal is a partner who fully understands the other, while at the same time maintaining a sense of self. It allows the sending partner to be who she is, while the receiving partner remains who he is. These partners realize that the unrealistic mental picture of the significant other that they've been carrying around all these years—how the other ought to be—is what has been causing a lot of trouble. Finally, it is having the guts to provide a safe place for the partners to reveal to each other who they really are, even though it does not fit the other's mental picture. Even bolder differentiation with integrity is being able to stay in the relationship even though the prints don't match. This is being able to love one another beyond mere physical attraction. It is being able to love beyond what one partner can do for the other. This is a level of love that simply asks, "what can I do for you to make your journey safe and productive?"

During the writing of this book, I had the sad experience of losing my grandmother. She and my grandfather had been married 58 years, so it was no surprise when my grandfather passed away 6 months later. I was fortunate to have had the opportunity to interview them about their life together only several months before her death. Their love story was different in that they each weighed more than 300 pounds for most of their lives. When they first met, they were both over 200 pounds. They began their marriage loving each other on a level beyond mere physical attraction.

Theirs was by no means a perfect marriage, but it was one that depended on the two of them working together everyday. You see, their weight prevented them from reaching their feet. So everyday, they would take turns sitting in their recliners while they helped each other to put on their shoes. Each day, they would also run a shower for each other, scrubbing each other's backs and washing each other's feet. And, yes, they were very dependent on one another, but they never seemed to mind because it was reciprocal.

When my siblings and I were children, we'd be amazed to hear our grandparents say how beautiful the other was. In plain truth, they would not be considered attractive by today's standards, but they were not looking at outward appearances. Through their connection, they were able to see how special each other's heart was. Their many hours together working side-by-side in their New Orleans restaurant gave them an understanding of each other that many couples only dream about. Because of the many hours they spent talking, they knew about each other's developmental wounds. And knowing each other's pain from childhood made the other even more special and understood. I believe that this understanding created differentiation with integrity.

Differentiation with integrity occurs when the couple sees and appreciates the uniqueness in the other, and it allows that uniqueness to take root and flourish. It is appreciating the uniqueness of a person's physical attributes, skills, and goals. But it is also appreciating the uniqueness of the partner's feelings, his or her interpretations of a situation, and his or her past and present circumstances. When partners learn to appreciate that there are two realities in the relationship, they experience a differentiation from each other and, if they do it in Couples Dialogue, they continue to experience it in "connection."

It is easy to say that most couples cannot truly experience this type of transcended self and, thus, differentiation with integrity. I have heard therapists say that they are happy if couples just talk rationally about paying bills—that understanding the other's wounds is beyond the scope of their couples work. But the heart of Imago Therapy is helping couples to experience this deep way of relating. It is most important to their growth and healing. In the therapy sessions, couples need to be given the opportunity to experience each other as spiritual beings whose progress is being hampered by patterns created by unmet needs in their development. And to get to this spiritual, transcended, differentiated self, people have to get past the wounds that hold them in place. Couples Dialogue allows the couple to hold each other in connection while differentiating so that they can appreciate the uniqueness of the other. Like a piece of art, it is others' appreciation of our uniqueness that makes us priceless.

Couples Dialogue Heals Developmental Wounds

To get to the spiritual level attainable in marriage, a couple has to get through the developmental stages they are each stuck in from their childhoods. By mastering the communication skill of Couples Dialogue, the empathy necessary to healing developmental wounds will be developed. As mentioned earlier in this chapter, an individual's developmental wounds can be compared to a car with a running engine and a broken transmission. The energy to move on is there, but the ability to go forward is hampered. It was hampered at childhood when the necessary encouragement to move on to the next level of development was not provided by early caretakers. The energy to move on is then brought into the love relationship with the hopes that the partner will give the support and validation needed to move on to the next stage.

As previously mentioned in reference to Brazelton's (1992) work, children move through developmental touchpoints by means of a supportive dialogue process with caretakers. For example, a conscious parent will encourage a child's differentiation at about age 2 by saying things like, "Look at how big you are getting that you can turn on the TV!" or "Look at how smart you are that you can figure out that puzzle! You look so happy about that!" At age 4, the conscious parent will instill competence in the child by saying things like, "Look at how you planted those flowers in the garden! You must feel very proud!" If the child feels it is okay to differentiate, form an identity, or become competent apart from the parent, he or she will spend some time acquiring that skill and then move on to the next developmental step. Since the developmental growth for the child happens in a connection with the parent, the child will experience differentiation without losing contact.

Imago Relationship Theory sees marriage as Nature's way of giving individuals a second chance to have their developmental impulses noticed, practiced, and mastered. The process of Couples Dialogue is the perfect way to have that occur in connection. Couples Dialogue fixes the transmission and allows both partners to move on in their development. When receiving partners hear the pain around senders' needs, the senders are finally understood. When they are finally understood, the energy they have used for years in trying to get their partners to understand them can now be channeled into action. They can step out of the box and out of the limited behaviors they have lived with for years. They can take chances to differentiate, find a strong identity, develop competence, or become intimate with friends.

Receiving partners can then take advantage of the energy they have been using to defend themselves by encouraging their significant other toward developmental growth. And, of course, this will be a difficult process for receiving partners to go through because it will require them to stretch. But since empathy has now entered into the relationship, they are now able to understand the purpose for changing their behavior toward their partner, which possibly makes it easier to change.

Couples enter into a difficult period as they begin to change behaviors in an effort to heal their own developmental wounds. At the same time, they begin a partnership to work toward healing their partner's developmental wounds. Although this period of time is often described as challenging by the couple, the Couples Dialogue process gives them their main safety and communication tool. I have found that if a couple can stay in the dialogue process, they can make it through any tough situation—usually with a new understanding of the partner and his or her needs.

Couples Dialogue Bridges the Gender-Communications Gap

It's no secret that men and women have a difficult time communicating with each other. In his best-selling book, *Men Are From Mars, Women Are From Venus*, (1992) John Gray offers the sexes advice towards understanding why they cannot communicate with someone of the opposite sex. It is as if we speak two different dialects of the same language—things don't translate. The work of Deborah Tannen (1990) and other sociolinguists reveals that men's communication typically revolves around reporting facts, while women's communication is typically around forming community and seeking commonality.

This language difference appears to be learned in the culture in which people are raised; it is socialized in them via their family; just as important, it is reinforced on the playground. Boys learn at an early age to pass facts on the game and stats on the players. Girls learn nurturing and noncompetitive games, developing a language of inclusion around their play. These differences in childhood cause them to play at opposite ends of the playground, where they develop different cultures, different interests, and different ways of expressing themselves. Then, somewhere around 13 years of age, long after the patterns are entrenched, they decide to get back together and fall in love.

Even age 13 almost seems too late. Boys and girls are very different. Boys can become very competitive or rebellious. It has been observed that girls will give up some of their intellectual advantage in an effort to fit in with their crowd and not appear smarter than the boys (Miller, 1976). Hierarchies evolve as everyone begins to take his or her place in the intimate relationships that are about to begin within the structure that our present patriarchal society allows. Gender differences in communication now become entrenched and seem to be "just the way things are."

"Men are pigs!" "If women would just think!" "Men wouldn't know a feeling if it hit them in the nose." "You can't understand women!" The battle of the sexes begins. Even those who are not so verbal about the differences often wonder if their partners can ever understand their plight as a man or a woman. Similar to what one goes through in the stages of loss, a couple will first experience shock that their partner can't understand them. Then perhaps they'll go into denial at the lack of understanding of their ideas. This will be followed by a period of anger as the partners complain to each other that they are not taking the time to understand things from their point of view. Finally, disillusionment sets in, and again—like at the playground—the sexes separate and spend most of their time with their own gender.

But is this difference necessary just because it seems natural? And is it enough just to understand that the other gender is different and that we have to learn to live with it? I don't think so, and I believe Couples Dialogue is a key to bridging the gap between the sexes. Mirroring allows the couple to grasp the facts of what is being communicated. Validation allows both genders to know that they make sense to the other. And empathy, typically a stretch for men, helps couples learn that feelings are a part of communication. Dialogue gives us a common language. Although awkward at first, we Imago therapists have found that it is a language that both men and women can master. It has aspects of both gender styles that allow both sexes to grasp it as a useful tool to understanding the other. Couples Dialogue is a language that respects the best aspects of each gender's style.

Understanding gender-communications differences is helpful, but it is clearly not the goal. Understanding may relieve symptoms, but it more or less allows the differences to continue and, worse, become more accepted and a part of our culture. Gender-communication differences need to be healed, and certainly the best place to start is when children are young. But how do we teach children a healthy communication style? Through their parents. If couples are able to communicate with each other in a way that models what they truly hear, and if they are able to understand each other, their children will learn this new pattern.

We have seen and heard from couples who have used Couples Dialogue regularly. Not only do they say that it has improved their relationship, but also it has changed their children. This is especially true when they use the dialogue process with their children. They report that the children seem calmer and more respectful. Their children appear to develop an empathy for others and have a deeper respect for nature. Amazingly, the genders play with each other with more understanding and less conflict. In other words, children who observe and are spoken to in a dialogue process seem to have a smaller gender-communications difference. In the future, they will be "better fish in the stream."

But what is so great about connecting, differentiating, healing wounds, and healing differences? The Greeks understood this idea. Plato even wrote an allegory to address just that in the *Symposium*.

It seems that, long ago, human beings were a composite of both men and women. They had one head with two faces, four arms, four legs, two hearts, and two sets of genitals. In this state, they were very powerful and strong because they were complete. They were so powerful, in fact, that they became a threat to the gods. There was some talk among the gods about destroying human beings, but then the gods wondered who would be left to worship them. Zeus thought deeply about this and finally came up with a solution. He proclaimed, "Men shall continue to exist, but they shall be cut in two. Then they will be diminished in strength, so we need not fear them." Zeus began the process of splitting the humans in two and asked Apollo to make the wound invisible. The two halves were then sent in different directions to spend the rest of their lives searching for their other half to restore their wholeness.

When we are whole, we are stronger. When we are connected to another, we have companionship and understanding in our endeavors. When we are differentiated with integrity, we can accomplish things with support. When we can heal our wounds, we can be less self-absorbed and look out at the possibilities. When we can communicate with the other gender, our differences are outweighed by our similarities. Relationships are a path to healing, wholeness, and a deep spiritual life. The vehicle to move us along the path is Couples Dialogue.

3

SESSION ONE

The Cosmic Journey, the Brain, and Couples Dialogue

SUGGESTED TIME FRAME

Connecting with the couple	10 minutes
"The Cosmic Journey and the Brain" Lecture	15 minutes
Having a typical disagreement	5 minutes
Teaching Couples Dialogue	25 minutes
Assigning homework	5 minutes

GOALS

1. To create a safe environment so the couple can follow your instructions for the next 6 or more weeks.

2. To teach the couple the brain's function in their typical frustrations and arguments and to emphasize the importance of safety in a relationship by letting them experience a nonproductive and productive transaction.

3. To teach the couple Couples Dialogue and emphasize that this communications tool can transform their marriage if they use it in all conflict situations.

CONNECTION: AN IMPORTANT GOAL OF THE FIRST SESSION

The main goal of the first session is to establish a strong connection with the couple. If the connection is weak, the couple may not return, and you will have been of little help to them. As you know, in a short-term model, you do not have the luxury of spending several weeks getting to know your clients. What's more, in the first session, not only will you be connecting with them and giving a short lecture, you will be teaching them the most important skill they are to learn in the six weeks: Couples Dialogue. This leaves you with about 15 minutes to make small talk, during which you'll be learning about their marriage and assuring them that—with their commitment to the therapy—you can be of help to them.

If this sounds overwhelming, think back to the last party you attended when you met someone new. If you were relaxed at the time, you probably found out volumes about that person in just a few minutes. Moreover, if you were friendly, your new acquaintance was able to tell others, "I just met the nicest person!" Most of us have this capacity to "connect" if we create a safe and relaxed environment. Unfortunately, most of us were trained to be observers in the therapy session rather than to be active participants in our client's growth and learning. So, I'll next discuss the art of connecting.

The Art of Connecting

Not long ago, I read a newspaper article about Willa Shallit, an artist and daughter of movie critic Gene Shallit. Willa creates a unique form of art that she calls "Life Mask." Centuries ago, people of prominence often commissioned masks to be done of themselves immediately upon their death to serve as a permanent record of their facial features. Willa creates her masks of famous people while they are alive to capture their "essence." She has created masks of movie stars, famous politicians, and Olympic stars—even five presidents! According to this unconventional artist, the easy part is doing the mask; the hardest part is getting her subjects in a mood that will capture their essence and beliefs for the seven minutes it takes to make the mold. What they are thinking and feeling during that time makes a difference in how the mask turns out!

Imagine how our mask would turn out if it were done during a first session with a client. We put on our "professional face"—possibly with a furrowed brow—as we search for that ever-elusive diagnosis of our "patient." If we could see that three-dimensional mask, how would it look? Friendly? Safe? Nurturing? Or would it look serious, judgmental, or businesslike? How we appear does make a difference, because *our face is our password into the minds and hearts of others.*

In this session, you will be teaching couples about their brains and about the need to create safety in their relationships. You will be explaining and discussing the "reptilian" brain and its concern with survival and safety. And, because the couples' reptilian brains will be ever on the alert with you, it will be important for you to both look safe and be safe if you are to make a positive impact. Just as Willa Shallit needed time to capture the right mood for her masks, I need a few minutes to get you in the right mood, to enable you to approach a couple with your "essence" rather than with your "mask."

When couples come to us for therapy, they are not looking to be judged. They already feel defeated, because they have not lived up to the "happily ever after" myth that permeates our society. They are usually looking for some guidance as well as relief from the pain they are experiencing. They may enter your office loudly, hoping you will see right off the bat that the partner is "crazy"; but what most will tell you is that they want things to be different and less painful. They need you to act as a nonjudgmental, unconditionally loving grandparent. This is not to say that you should take them home for a hot meal; rather, it means that you should see yourself as a guide.

In our graduate programs, most of us were trained in the disease-medical model. The most popular class in my graduate program was "Introduction to Psychopathology," in which we learned about symptoms and diagnoses. I clearly remember the day when my classmates and I sat around after class and tried to diagnose ourselves (which I understand to be a very common practice among graduate students). We then went into our practicums and diagnosed everyone we came across. We tried to find out what was "wrong" with them. The only thing that was wrong, however, was that we had turned a tool into a weapon.

For these six weeks, with your client-couples, I'd like you to put your weapon down. We already know what's wrong: two people are unhappy with each other. Most will envision you as their last glimmer of hope, and they need your skills and empathy—not your diagnosis. The material in this book will work to some degree for everyone who comes through your door, with two exceptions. If one partner appears psychotic, I would recommend a medical opinion. Likewise, if one partner is a substance abuser, the couple should deal with the drug or alcohol problem *first*, and then return for the couples work. Although we have tried to work with substance abusers as a couple—before recovery begins—with the idea that the relationship may actually be precipitating the abuse, this therapy simply does not work in the short term. Rather, it only seems to cause more pain to the nonabusing partner—and that's the last thing he or she needs. This therapy is very effective, however, when conducted in conjunction with a long-term recovery program which includes regular participation in recovery support groups (Alcoholics Anonymous, Narcotics Anonymous, Al-anon).

The first means of tapping your essence is to become nonjudgmental and to envision yourself as working with people—not "patients." If, however, you are unable to see yourself not working in a disease model, how should you view yourself? What *is* your role in this therapy?

Helper and Healer

During one of my workshop presentations, I came down with a terrible headache. As I tried to continue with my talk despite my discomfort, the pain became an increasing nuisance. Fortunately for me, among those attending the workshop were three chiropractors. Thinking I'd try something new, I asked one of them—Dr. Michael Coppola—if he could take care of the headache. We went to a separate room where he pressed on my back and neck, and then he very gently "cracked" my neck. In minutes, my headache was gone—and without medication! I asked him about this, and his reply has since provided me with an analogy for what I see as the therapist's role in these six sessions.

Dr. Coppola explained that the nerves coming out of our spinal cord are like hoses that deliver the messages from our brain. When our spine is out of place, it squeezes the hose—just as you might do with your water hose to stop the flow. Squeezing the nerves prevents vital information from getting to where it needs to get to keep the body healthy. The human body comes ready equipped with everything, including every drug it needs, to stay healthy. With these drugs already inside of us, all that our bodies really require are clear pathways to deliver this internal medicine. Dr. Coppola described his role as that of an adjuster who makes sure that the pathways are clear and that the "hoses" are not being squeezed. Chiropractors, you see, help the body to help itself.

"That's what I do!" I thought to myself. Couples can heal themselves, but their pathways are blocked. Messages aren't getting through, and major headaches are occurring: for example, his not coming home on time has become a "pain in her neck"; she spends money while he "breaks his back" at work; he or she is "a pain in the. . . ." Well, you get the idea. This couple needs an adjustment! Your job is to give them the information and skills that will change how they see each other and open their communication pathways. If you can do this, the relationship has everything in it to keep the healing going. Like the chiropractor who helps the body, the therapist helps the couple to help themselves.

By now, you should be thinking of yourself as a nonjudgmental facilitator of health. If you are able to let this concept become your mantra, the essence you'll need to do this work will come through. That essence can be summed up in one word: safety. The creation of safety in couples work cannot be overemphasized and will continue to be a major topic throughout this work. It is, after all, what made you likable at your last party. It is also what allows others to trust you enough to reveal themselves to you and to believe what you are saying is true.

Later in this first session, you will be giving a lecture about the brain in which you will discuss the oldest part of the brain, referred to as the reptilian brain. As previously discussed, the primary function of the reptilian brain is to keep you alive by warning you of dangerous situations. When it is dangerous, the reptilian brain will tell you to fight, run, freeze, hide, or submit. When our clients are being resistant with us, what we usually don't see is that—in some way—we've made it unsafe for them, and their brains are doing exactly what they have been designed to do when a situation is dangerous.

They may *fight* us and tell us that we don't know what we're talking about, or they may not follow our instructions, or they may leave therapy. At times, they may *freeze* in the session and stare right through us as we offer them advice. If, for instance, you are an Employee Assistance Professional whose office is located on-site, you may begin to notice that they avoid or *hide* from you. Or maybe they'll finally *give in* to you if you confront them or "rag" them enough. Traditionally, we have labeled this "resistance" and placed the blame on the client; however, maybe we should take a closer look at our own methods. People are scared when they come to see us. Make it safe, and they will work with you. We know this to be true, because the other part of survival in the reptilian brain relates to a "safe" situation. When a situation is safe, our brains prompt us to play, nurture, mate, work, and be creative. If you can set this tone of safety in the sessions, chances are the couple will go home and do what we all do when it is safe: play, nurture, mate, work, and be creative. Sounds like a good relationship to me!

ABOUT THE LECTURE

After spending about 15 minutes getting to know the couple, you are going to take another 20 minutes going over what the next six weeks will entail and you will present a lecture: "The Cosmic Journey and the Brain." Although some authorities may question the appropriateness of giving a physics and biology lecture in a couples session, there are several reasons for presenting this lecture—one of which is that it grabs the couple's attention.

Typically when a couple comes to therapy, one is the "dragger," and the other is the "dragee." Dragees are the ones who think they can figure out problems on their own—that they don't need therapy. The lecture on the brain often appeals to them and, as a result, draws them into the therapy. If you can draw in the dragee, you will usually be able to make headway. As for the other partner, and his or her possible lack of interest, don't worry. There will be plenty to pull the couple into the work as you progress with the sessions.

A second reason for this lecture is to show the couple that there is an actual place in the brain that is responsible for both their defensiveness and their responses to frustrations. In this chapter, I've included a picture of the brain and labeled its parts so that you can show couples exactly where these brain functions are located. (In my office, I use a plastic model of a brain which I purchased at a science store, and I've colored the three parts of the brain so couples can see them in 3-D.) It is also useful to emphasize the need for safety in the relationship, so that our brain will not become defensive and "protect" us. Again, emotional safety is the real number one in this work, and all the processes you teach will be those emphasizing safety and empathy. When a couple becomes defensive in sessions, I know they are sensing danger, and I will say things to them such as "get safe" or "your old brain is responding." Because they have seen the brain model, they can immediately picture that part of the brain that is defending itself. They can experience what I am saying.

And this brings me to the third reason for the brain lecture as well as all of the work for the next five weeks: *couples need to experience what you say.* A big advantage that we humans have over other animals is our ability to "symbolize" what we experience. For instance, we can attend a lecture on the basics of golf and afterwards have a symbolic understanding of golf. Then we can go to a golf course, take a few swings, and have an experience of what we learned symbolically. At that point, we may be ready to hear about the best ways to get out of a sand trap, and then we could go back to the golf course and work in a sand trap to experience what we had been taught. Each session, therefore, contains a lecture or symbol and an exercise or experience of the symbol. The first session's symbol is the brain, and the couple will experience what you have presented in the lecture by performing the exercise. This process is designed to help them retain the information long after the session is over.

Each session will conclude with the assignment of homework. Give the couple a copy of the homework sheet, and review it with them prior to ending the session. Emphasize the importance of the homework; this work cannot be done in an hour a week, but will take a commitment on their part. Be sure to let them know that since you intend to check the homework, they should bring their completed sheet back with them for the next session. You should find that most couples will cooperate with you.

LECTURE ONE: *THE COSMIC JOURNEY AND THE BRAIN*

Note. If you suspect that the couple might be uncomfortable with the "Cosmic Journey" part of this lecture, or if you feel uncomfortable with it yourself, it is perfectly appropriate to leave it out. Although a paradigm shift to a relational view is hoped for in work with couples using Imago Therapy, it is not important that we change everyone's world view or offend their values. In cases where I suspect the couple may be uncomfortable with that section because of their religious beliefs, I will begin with the Brain lecture. I will usually start it something like this:

> I want to start by telling you something that when I first heard it, I was shocked. And that is, inside your head you have not one, but three very distinct and separate brains!

This brief introduction to the brain lecture usually pulls the couple into what you will say, and they become very attentive for the 15 minutes it takes for you to explain the brain functions to them. I also suggest that you give them "The Three Parts of the Brain," shown on p. 63 and located in the Homework/Handouts.

To understand where we are going, we have to understand where we came from. Scientists are now telling us that about 15 billion years ago, everything as we know it existed in a dot of matter about the size of the period at the end of a sentence. And it existed in a gigantic void. One day (give or take a few hundred years), this dot of matter inflated to about the size of a grapefruit and then exploded in a giant "Big Bang." When things blew up, they blew out as particles—and there you have us, in our most basic form! We are debris and shrapnel from this original explosion.

To explain further, if you explode a firecracker, the paper from the firecracker expands out and, at the same time, is pulled down by gravity. In a void, the gravity expands out rather than down, so the debris from the Big Bang keeps on spreading. Every atom in our body was once in that tiny dot, and every atom in our body was once a part of that original explosion and has traveled the 15 billion years to where it is today. So, if we are shrapnel from this original explosion, what we really are is energy. A bomb exploding would spew out hot metal. A dot exploding in a void would spew out particles that gather to form stars, that gather to form galaxies, that form solar systems composed of planets—with at least one which has developed life. What a miracle!

How can everything in the universe come out of a dot? Modern physics has given us the answer that relates to our basic composition: we are 99.99 percent space! Our bodies are made up of billions of atoms, all composed of a nucleus (a neutron and a proton) and encircled by electrons. These electrons are minute and encircle the nucleus at great speeds. As a matter of fact, they circle a billion times every billionth of a second! And everything you see, including your own body, is teeming with the energy from these billions and billions of spinning electrons.

Despite all we know about atoms, no one has ever seen one. They are too small, and we have no instruments capable of enlarging them enough to make them visible. We can only see them based on what they do—which has launched the whole field of Quantum Physics. If we were able to develop a model to enable us to see an atom in scale, we would need to make the model 14 stories high—just to be able to see the nucleus! To put this in perspective, if we enlarged an atom to the size of Yankee Stadium, the nucleus would be the size of a baseball sitting in center field; the electrons would be the size of gnats flying in the upper decks of the stadium; and the rest of the atom would be made up of nothing but space. Furthermore, if we took all of the space out of our bodies, what we would have left would be a million times smaller than a grain of sand!

So why have I started out this discussion with a physics lesson? Because I want you to get the picture that things aren't always what they seem, and that what we basically are is energy—energy from this original explosion, which means that we all have a common source. And that makes us a combination of three things:

1. **Neutral Pulsating Energy.** "Neutral," because we are neither good nor bad; "Pulsating," in that our life-sustaining energy expresses itself as a pulse; and "Energy" from the original explosion.

2. **Interconnected Neutral Pulsating Energy.** We are a node of energy, and we are connected to other nodes of energy. None of us can get through life alone; we can only get through if we are connected to other nodes of energy.

3. **We Are as Old as the Universe.** Every atom in our bodies existed at least 15 billion years ago. What has happened to the energy from this original explosion is really quite miraculous. Over the 15 billion years of expansion, particle collection and explosions, stars, solar systems, and galaxies formed. And our solar system formed a planet that could sustain life: the Earth. This is really quite impressive, because everything had to be just right for life to form. There had to be the right temperature and combination of elements. The atmosphere had to have the right combinations to sustain life. And, somehow, Earth did it! Life began to form, first as plants, and then as one-celled animals, and eventually—millions of years later—along came man and woman.

One of the best places to look at how this evolutionary process occurred in animals is to look at our own brains. For years, we've looked at brains as "left and right," but we should also be looking at them from back to front. I say this because, inside your head, you have three brains! I'd better explain.

In the base of the brain, we have the reptilian brain. We share this part of the brain with all animals, including alligators and lizards. The reptilian brain takes care of those things we don't usually think about: heartbeat, digestion, and breathing. It also is concerned with survival, and—if it's dangerous—it will help us to respond in one of five basic ways: fight (dogs growling or biting); flight (packs of zebras running from the lion); freeze/play dead (the deer that freezes, hoping the hunter will pass it by); submit (wolves never fight to the death, but only until one gives up and exposes its neck); or hide (animals that run into holes). Since we also have a reptilian part of the brain, we see these as the basic survival skills of couples. Couples will fight, flee (leave a situation), play dead (stare through their partners), submit ("Okay, whatever you want, just stop the nagging!"), or hide (go to another room).

On the other hand, if it is safe, there are three things we will do: we will play, we will nurture, or we will mate. Remember when you first met your partner? Remember how you played, nurtured each other and—if you were like most—mated?

We all have these survival mechanisms in us, and we use them in our relationships. They are located in the oldest part of the brain and are shared with all animals, with the difference being similar to the difference between a sparkplug in a VW and one in a Mercedes: same function, but bigger spark in the Mercedes.

As animals evolved, a second part of the brain developed known as the mammalian brain. This part developed when animals began living in groups and began to take care of and feed their young (mammalian brain/mammary gland). It's also the place in the brain where feelings are stored. The fact that all mammals experience some feelings and live in groups is because of this very part of the brain. So, if you've ever said to yourself, "I do not feel," that's simply not true, because there is a whole part of the brain that is dedicated to feelings. You may be cut off from this part, but you are quite capable of feeling.

Several million years ago, a third part of the brain developed called the cerebral cortex or the logical part of the brain. Humans have this part of the brain, monkeys to a smaller extent, and dolphins to an even greater extent than humans. The cerebral cortex is five times bigger than the other two parts combined and this is where all logical processes take place: speech, writing, math, and logical thought. Because this part of the brain is so much larger than the other two, it was once thought to be the most important part of the brain, with the other two parts serving as a sort of appendix—with little functional use.

We now know that all three parts work together simultaneously. If you open a door and see a Doberman pinscher baring its teeth, and the dog is drooling, growling, and has its ears back, the logical brain says, "That's a Doberman." The mammalian brain says, "I feel scared," while the reptilian brain says, "Run!" or "Freeze!" But, if you open the door and you see your favorite Aunt Betty standing there with a big apple pie, your logical brain says, "That's Aunt Betty"; your mammalian brain says, "I feel good when she is around. She makes me happy"; and your reptilian brain says, "Let's play!" So these parts of the brain all work together and, for the most part, they are concerned with survival.

Another way we react to danger is by either constricting (freezing, submitting, hiding) or exploding (fighting, fleeing). And we've found that, although this can change, people typically favor either constricting behaviors or exploding behaviors. How this relates to couples is that the constrictor and the exploder always marry each other.

It is important to know that we are structured to work this way. It's just how we work. When we tell our spouse to "quit screaming" or to "quit running away," we are asking that person to stop an adaptation to danger.

At this point, I am going to stop this story, and we'll pick it up here next week. What I would like to do now is to show you an exercise that will make what I just told you come alive and make more sense to you.

COUPLES DIALOGUE

You are about to teach the couple the most important tool any couple can learn: the Couples Dialogue. This is the tool that will help the couple learn how to fully hear one another. Even if the couple should leave and never come back to therapy, their marriage will improve if they use this tool. Couples Dialogue begins to teach the idea of emotional safety and the technique of fully hearing each other. It also clearly illustrates the brain's function in communication and how the brain will defend itself when it is feeling threatened. I will cover Couples Dialogue in detail here, but also refer to the Exercise Map (Exhibit 3.1)—a shortened "map" version outlining the steps. You should begin this exercise only *after* you have given the lecture on the brain and have fully emphasized how, when it is dangerous, we will fight, flee, play dead/freeze, hide, or submit.

Minimizers, Maximizers, and the Old Brain

Begin by asking the couple to have a typical 3-minute argument or frustration, and assure them that you *will* stop it in 3 minutes. At first this will be uncomfortable for them; but keep it safe, wait it out, and they will produce a 3-minute exchange.

Typically, what you will hear is two people trying to get their points across. If you listen and watch closely, you will see that what they are doing falls into one of the five categories: fight, flight, play dead/freeze, hide, or submit. Each will seem to want to win or keep the other one quiet. You will also see an energy exchange we call "minimizing and maximizing." All couples are comprised of someone who minimizes the problem ("It's not that bad" or "If you will just stop that, it will go away") and someone who maximizes the problem ("You are the most awful person in the world!" or "You always do this to me!"). When this exchange occurs in a back-and-forth manner, they are *not* hearing each other:

Partner 1: You know every time your parents come over they cause trouble, and we wind up not talking to each other for weeks!

Partner 2: It's not that bad. They're just excited to see us.

Partner 1: The last time they came over, we didn't talk for a week!

Partner 2: You're exaggerating. It was only three days, and it was just a misunderstanding.

Partner 1: I am not exaggerating! It was not a misunderstanding—your mother told me a lie.

Partner 2: But I talked to her, and it's all straightened out now.

Exhibit 3.1. Session One Exercise Map

Sender	Receiver
Have a usual frustration or argument for 3 minutes.	Respond as usual for 3 minutes.

Therapist watches this process, and then asks:
Is this typical? Did you fight? Flee? Play dead or freeze? Hide? Submit? Did you feel heard? Could you feel your old brain defending itself? (Both sender and receiver respond to these questions.)

Now let the couple know that you are going to show them a new way to communicate using Couples Dialogue.

Sender	Receiver
Send frustration in two to three sentences.	Find a "Safe Place" in your mind. Mirror what you heard: "I heard you say. . . ." "If I got it right, you said. . . ."
Acknowledge that partner heard it correctly and state what Receiver may have missed.	
Repeat the mirroring one or two more times on the same subject.	Mirror back what you may have missed. Mirror back until you have heard the Sender's message. Validate the Sender's statement: "I can understand that." "You make sense to me because. . . ." Empathize with your partner: "I imagine that makes you feel. . . ." Pick three feelings your partner may be feeling (this is only a guess).

Have the couple talk about what they just did and how it feels different. Find out if the Sender felt heard. Ask the Receiver if he or she learned anything different about his or her partner. Did the energy go up or did it stay the same?

Compare the process to pedals on a bike: "You have to wait until your partner's pedal is all the way down before you can start to push your pedal down." Then have the couple switch the process so the other partner can have the experience of doing the dialogue process and of feeling fully heard.

After the exchange, ask the question, "Is this typical?" The couple will usually tell you, "Yes, but at home it is louder"—which is understandable since, at this point, they've only known you for about 30 minutes. Now ask them, "What do you think just happened?" and keep them focused on process, not content. You are trying to find out if they felt **heard** and **understood** by each other. Most couples will say "no."

At this point, you want to make the couple very aware of how their old brain was at work during their frustration. Ask them about their argument, and ask them if they used fight. How about flight? Did they play dead or freeze? Submit? Hide? Even in short exchanges, three of these defenses are typically used. Ask them who seems to have maximized the problem? Who minimized the problem? Let them know that this is *typical* and that *all* couples have someone who minimizes *and* someone who maximizes an argument. What you are giving the couple is the idea that there are patterns to arguments.

Once you have gone over the argument they've just demonstrated, let the couple know that you now want them to learn a new way to communicate. Hand out the Couples Dialogue sheet and Feelings List, and let them know that you are going to teach them a three-step communication process. This is the basic tool in Imago Therapy, and—if the couple uses it—their relationship will change. If they do not, their relationship will stay the same.

Mirroring

Let the couple decide who will be the "sender" and who will be the "receiver" of the frustration. Since you are going to be asking the sender to send the same frustration in about two to three sentences, you have to do some work with the receiver. Let receivers know that they have to make it safe for the senders—and for themselves. Tell them to think of a "safe place" in their minds where they can mentally place themselves so that the old brain is not triggered. Once the receiver is feeling somewhat safe, the couple can then begin the process.

After the senders state the frustration in three sentences, the receivers—instead of responding as usual—are asked to "mirror" what they heard. Mirroring is the receiver repeating to the sender what the sender said *as the sender said it*—not as the receiver wanted to hear it. The receiver should start the sentence with something like: "I heard you say . . ." or "If I'm hearing you correctly you said . . ." or "If I got it right, you said. . . ." It is important that receivers mirror back *what they heard* and not how they wanted to hear it. They should finish each mirroring with the question, "Did I get that?" If the sender says yes, the receiver should ask, "Is there more?" Many couples want to ask that question as, "Is there any more?" In this form, the question discourages additional dialogue and should be restated as, "Is there more?"

Quite often, it will take receivers several tries before they get the mirror accurately, and that's usually because what is being said is not safe and the brain wants to respond defensively. Be patient and continue to encourage them to try again and mirror back as they heard it. Likewise, senders may have to send the same message several times before they feel the message was fully heard. The sender will be the final judge of this.

As a way of anchoring the brain lecture that you've just completed, alert receivers as to how their "old brain" is responding to the message when they are not able to "get it" correctly. Usually they will tell you, "I cannot hear this because I happen to have something to say about it." Encourage them to get back into their safe place so that they can fully hear their partner. Tell the couple, "It's more important to *hear* than to win."

You want them to fully understand the lecture on the brain by having them actually experience its principles through this demonstration. If they can feel their defenses going up, they can recognize what it is they need to control in order to fully hear their partner.

The senders should send two to three "rounds" of sentences they would like to have mirrored back to them. The receivers mirror back as they heard it. Once the message is fully heard and mirrored, you can move into *validation*.

Validation

Validation is a way of saying "I can see that you can see it that way." It is not agreement, although agreement might occur. It is understanding that the other possesses a particular thought or experience. The receiving partner might simply say, "I can see that" or "You make sense to me." The receiver can also expand on the validation, for example: "I can see how when I come home late you would get worried, because sometimes things happen to people that make them come home late—or worse." At this stage, there should be no explanations or apologies. The receiver should only be hearing and validating the sender.

The importance of validation is that most of us have had many *invalidating* experiences in our lifetime. As perplexing as it is for the little child who says "I'm cold!" and is told "You can't be cold—it's warm in here," invalidation can be confusing. When one partner responds too quickly, the other partner may feel invalidated, and the defensive processes begin.

Empathy

The third step is to develop empathy between the couple. Once the receiver has heard and validated the sender he or she needs to understand the feelings behind what the sender has said. Ask the receiver to guess how the sender might be feeling. He or she might say "So I imagine you might feel . . . (alone, scared, and abandoned)." I usually have receivers pick three feelings to give them the idea that we can have several feelings at the same time.

Again, you want the couple to experience what they learned and to process the experience. Ask them if this was different from what they usually do when they discuss their frustrations. Find out how they felt about what the other was saying. Ask them if they felt heard and if they felt they understood their partner differently. Help them *experience* the difference through their use of Couples Dialogue.

Taking Turns

Now, of course, there is the other side of the frustration. The receivers have patiently—or, at least, under instruction—awaited their turn. I usually explain the process like this: "First of all, you have to always keep in mind that it is not important to win. It is important to *hear* and to *be heard*. And the way to think about this is to think of pedals on a bike. The senders send their message or "pedal." They pedal, pedal, pedal, pedal (I make a pedaling motion with my hands and demonstrate one pedal going down) until the pedal gets to the bottom. When the sender has fully pedaled, or said what he or she needed to say—and the receiver has mirrored, validated, and empathized with him or her—the receiver then gets a chance to pedal until he or she is fully heard, validated, and empathized by the partner.

At this point in the session, have the couple switch to give both partners the experience of using the Couples Dialogue. Make it safe and nurture them through it, because it's both different and difficult. Make the analogy that it's like brushing your teeth with the opposite hand: at first it feels awkward and clumsy, but after a while you get it, and it becomes as natural as the old way of brushing. Keep in mind that couples may start to complain that this new process takes too long, and that their old way seemed quicker. Assure them that, in the long run, Couples Dialogue is actually more efficient, because they will feel heard and understood more quickly, which means they don't have to return to the same argument as often!

Once you have shown the couple the process and given them the experience of using the Dialogue, you should stress to them the importance of completing the homework you are about to give them. The homework has been designed to first help them learn the process; it then gives them at least five days of using the Dialogue in everyday situations. Make sure the couple understand that you not only expect them to do the homework, but that you will be checking it!

DAVE AND DIANA: A CASE STUDY

Throughout this book, we will follow the session-to-session progress of a couple, Dave and Diana. Dave and Diana will be used to illustrate what is supposed to happen each week when you are presented with a cooperative couple who complete the homework assignments. Dave and Diana's story is taken from an actual couple seen in the six-session format. All identifying information has been changed to protect their confidentiality.

Dave is a 49-year-old engineer and has been married to Diana, 40, for 15 years. They met at a local bar where Diana said she became interested in him because he was older and was in a secure profession. Dave and Diana said that their early marriage was filled with fun activities and Diana said she felt secure with an older man taking care of her. She said, "Our relationship was based on mutuality, but that seems to be buried deep right now." They married soon after they met and gave birth to a son who is 12 now.

Problems began to arise several years into the marriage. Both Dave and Diana were drinking heavily and she began to binge eat. Diana began to attend a recovery program for overeaters nine years ago and both decided that their alcohol consumption had become a problem and began recovery through Alcoholics Anonymous six years ago. For these six years they have been sober and regularly attend A.A. meetings.

Although their habits improved, their marriage had not followed. Dave and Diana grew cold and distant from each other. They passed mean remarks between themselves and avoided each other as often as they could. They were proud in describing themselves as "civil" about their fights, usually not raising their voices so they would not upset their son.

Although Dave and Diana were very bitter, they wanted to stay together to raise their son. They also said that underneath it all, they were still friends. The relationship began to affect their work, and they often found themselves daydreaming, being late, and, most recently, missing work days. Both of their employers noticed and made mention of the changes in private meetings. Their time in A.A. also allowed them to be open to looking inward and admitting their responsibility to the marriage, their jobs, and the problems they were experiencing. They had utilized all the resources they knew of and decided to seek professional help.

Initial Outcome Measures

As is the case with many managed-care clients, Dave and Diana were given outcome tracking assessments to chart their progress in the therapy. The measures used were COMPASS (Howard, Brill, Lueger, & O'Mahoney, 1992), to chart their individual progress, and the Marital Satisfaction Inventory (Snyder, 1981), to chart improvement in the marriage. Outcome tests are used in managed care as a baseline for client distress and as a way of directing treatment to the particular problem. They are also being used to make sure clients are making progress in the treatment. The tests were given before Session One and will be repeated after the sixth session.

COMPASS is a valid and reliable self-report inventory used by many large companies to track client progress and need for treatment. It measures Well-being, Symptoms, and Life Functioning and uses these scores

TABLE 3.1
COMPASS Scores of Diana and Dave

	Diana	Dave
Well-being	43	46
(Normal Range: Above 83)		
(Severe Range: Below 17)		
Symptoms	27	68
(Normal Range: Below 17)		
(Severe Range: Above 83)		
Life Functioning	13	10
(Normal Range: Above 83)		
(Severe Range: Below 17)		
Mental Health Index	41	25
(Normal Range: Above 83)		
(Severe Range: Below 17)		

to arrive at an overall Mental Health Index. Dave and Diana's scores are listed in Table 3.1.

These scores indicate that Dave and Diana are experiencing considerable individual distress and are in need of treatment. The stresses they are experiencing are especially problematic in the area of their everyday life functioning as both scored in the severe range.

This information was validated by the Marital Satisfaction Inventory, a 280-question valid and reliable self-report inventory that profiles 11 areas commonly reported in couples in marital distress. Generally speaking, T-Scores of 50 to 65 are indications of moderate to severe levels of distress, and T-Scores above 65 indicate severe levels of distress. Dave and Diana were especially high in Global Distress (T = 64 and 71, respectively), Disagreement about finances (T = 67 and 68, respectively) and Sexual Dissatisfaction (T = 64 and 66, respectively). Diana also scored high in the area of Effective Communication, how well she feels understood in the marriage, with a T-Score of 68.

DAVE AND DIANA: SESSION ONE

Both Dave and Diana were pleasant and contemplative in the first session. After a 10-minute greeting, they were presented with an overview of the therapy and the brain lecture. They were both interested and immediately recalled times where they used the mechanisms of fight, flight, playing dead, freezing, hiding, or submitting. As instructed, they were able to engage in a 3-minute frustration diatribe that proved illustrative of their communication style and defensive posture. Because of their time in A.A., over the years they have talked about personal growth, which seems evident in the following excerpt of their conversation:

Dave: Yesterday when we were talking and you said to me "I'm losing compassion here and the energy has changed and I'm feeling the anger." I did not want to be there. I did not want to answer because you were right. It angered me more to know you knew me. I felt very fearful.

Diana: But it really hurts me when you offer me one thing then take it back.

Dave: But I started in the right vein. And I meant that. That much I meant. I was there. But then a switch turned and I did not want to be there.

Diana: It's scary for me when you do that. You hit below the belt when you told me that I had not changed at all when I've been working so hard on my self. It makes me angry and it is not fair. To tell me you are going to be there and then you hit below the belt. It feels very scary and it's not okay.

Dave: (*interrupting*) But . . . go ahead.

Diana: You need to own some of your own stuff.

Dave: I'm trying to own my own stuff. I don't know what turns that switch for me. I just know the switch was turned. I'm totally unaware of when things change until you tell me and then I get angry because you have to point it out to me.

Diana: And I keep putting it out to you when I see it and you tell me, "Oh, I'm glad you pointed it out to me" after I get in all this trouble saying things to you. So I don't even want to tell you. I tell you and you yell at me, get angry, or leave me, so I just say that I don't want to risk telling you what I see anymore. I don't want to be your friend. It makes me want to just leave and go away because when I risk to be honest with you, you either put me down or go away. I feel like I am never going to get what I want unless I ask for it, which may not be right, but it is how I feel. So I say it and I get so mad when you say "I'm so glad you said something, hon." BLAH! I want to kick you. I don't want to have to be the one to say something to you.

Dave: It seems as though we need that. After I have time to think about it, I can come back and talk about it. But at first, I can't. I just get mad. I'm getting better at it. Before I could not even come back and say anything.

Diana: That's true, you are getting better. But when you do it, I feel so betrayed.

This is a typical argument heard in marriages with one partner aware of problems in the marriage and the other unaware until it is pointed out, who then becomes angry when it is pointed out. What is interesting is that although Dave and Diana are very insightful, they are not listening to each other. They are not having what would be called a dialogue, but rather a diatribe. This is very typical in couples as one is speaking and the other is beginning to think about what to say to defend him- or herself. The missing ingredients are safety and a dialogue process.

Dave and Diana were then guided in the Couples-Dialogue process. When Diana was able to get herself safe and made her body and mind willing to listen, her features changed. Her face softened and she seemed more inviting and less defensive. She was now leaning in toward Dave and her voice softened. She was able, with some assistance from the therapist, to mirror back Dave's words and match his affect, which appeared to get sadder as he talked. By listening, she was able to learn things about Dave that she had not understood before.

Dave revealed to her that he felt intimidated by her because she was able to figure things out faster than he could. He felt that she was smarter than he was about things and that made him feel inadequate. Dave was able to tell Diana that her ability to do that reminded him of growing up with his father, who never told him he was smart. He said, "My father was always telling me what was wrong and never that I did a good job." At that point, Dave became tearful and Diana was able to mirror back his words and his affect. She was also able to validate that she understood his logic on this and guess that he might feel inadequate, scared, and hurt.

At this point, the Couples Dialogue went to a deeper level:

Dave: I start to feel the inadequacies and I'm going to get mad at you for bringing them up . . . when I really want to get mad at my father.

Diana: (*mirroring*) So, if I am getting that right, you said that when you feel the inadequacies, you get mad at me for bringing them up, when you really want to get mad at your father. Is there more?

Dave: (*crying*) And I don't like that because I am a good person.

Diana: (*mirroring*) (*softly*) And you don't like that because you are a good person. Is there more?

Dave: I'm afraid to put that anger out on my father, he can't understand. (*sobbing*) He won't understand.

Diana: (*mirroring*) So, if I'm hearing you correctly, you are afraid to put out your anger on your father because he won't try to understand. Is there more?

Dave: He would shut down. He would not be there. And I feel in our relationship, you won't go away.

Therapist: Stay safe.

Diana: (*mirroring*) And you feel your father would shut down and could not be there for you. In our relationship, you know I won't go away.

Therapist: Can you validate that?

Diana: (*validation and empathy*) I can understand that. I understand that your dad would go away. I can understand that I am a safe place for you. I can imagine how angry you feel toward your dad and how hurt you feel toward your dad.

Dave: It feels so scary inside. It's hard to reconcile between the man and the child. I did not deal with it then and it's hard to deal with it at 49.

Diana: (*mirroring*) It's hard to deal with these feelings from childhood at 49.

Dave: It's very hard. It's hard to accept.

Diana: (*mirroring*) It's hard to accept. The things your father did were not very nice and I wish he would not have done . . .

Therapist: Stay with what he says, Diana.

Dave: I want to run because it is easier.

Diana: (*mirroring*) You want to run because it is easier.

Therapist: And that's what you did as a child.

Dave: Oh yeah! I just ran outside. I just got away and did not learn to deal with things.

Diana: (*mirroring*) So if I am getting this, as a child, you would run from the conflict and you did not learn to deal with things.

Therapist: Can you validate that?

Diana: (*validation and empathy*) I sure can. I imagine it feels scary out there too. It feels scary and hopeless.

Dave was able to begin the process of understanding how his present patterns with Diana may have had their roots in his childhood. His pattern of shutting down, running away, and getting angry may have started in his relationship with his father. Diana was able to understand that much of Dave's present behavior patterns may have had their roots in early childhood wounding with his father. This allowed her to feel less like he was doing this behavior to hurt her and more like there was a deeper source to Dave's hurt and his response to his hurt. She is now able to listen with empathy when she knows that she is safe and the attack is not totally directed at her. At the same time, Dave is instructed that as he becomes more conscious of the source of his pain, he has to gain more control of his behavior. Just because Diana understands his behavior does not mean that he has the right to subject her to it as he has been doing. Now, rather than acting out his wounds, he has to take responsibility to dialogue the wounds with Diana.

At this point in the session, Diana had some things that she wanted to say. They were instructed to switch roles with Dave getting safe and being the receiver to listen to Diana, the sender. She began by saying how sad she feels about now being heard by Dave.

Diana: I feel afraid because if I don't say it right, you won't get it. That reminds me of when I was a kid, when (*sobbing*) my father would say what a lazy tongue I have. It is scary for me to actually have you hear and see me right now. It feels like I want to go away right now.

Dave: (*mirroring, validation, and empathy*) It reminds you of when you were a kid and your father would say you have a lazy tongue. I can see that it is scary for you to have me see and hear you at the same time and it feels like you want to go away. It makes sense to me and I imagine you feel scared.

Diana: I feel scared and I want to go away. I did that as a kid when I did not want others to see me. It's not safe to be seen or paid too much attention to. But then I wanted someone to notice me. It's too scary to want too much attention. I need you to know how scary it is for you to notice me or not notice me.

Dave: (*mirroring*) So you are saying as a kid, you did not want to be noticed because it was not safe. You did not want to be noticed, but at the same time you do want to be noticed. You want me to understand how scary it is for me to notice you or not notice you. Did I get that?

Diana: (*tearfully*) Yes.

Dave: (*validation and empathy*) I can see how scary it is for you. I can imagine you are scared and sad.

At the end of the first session, Dave and Diana were now seeing the pain each other had from their childhoods. They now possessed a tool, Couples Dialogue, that they can use to hear each other and they've also had the experience of using the skill in the session. This tool and their experience of safety allowed them a few moments of empathy for each other and allowed them to reach past their anger and see the pain their partner is experiencing. To reinforce this, Dave and Diana were assigned homework (an illustration of the homework is shown on p. 63) so they could practice this new skill and reinstate caring behaviors with each other.

HANDOUT INSTRUCTIONS FOR THE THERAPIST

SESSION ONE

In Session One, each partner will leave with four pages of handouts.

1. The Three Parts of the Brain

Show this page to the couple while you are presenting the brain lecture. This will make the lecture seem more realistic to them and easier to follow rather than having to visualize it as you are talking. It is best to allow them to take a copy of this sheet home so they might find time to discuss the lecture further.

2. Couples Dialogue

This page can be given to the couple while you are teaching them the dialogue process or at the end of the session after they have learned it. I have found that some partners will need the sheet while they are practicing the dialogue: it is such a new way of communicating for them that they have difficulty following the steps. If this is the case, you may find that the couple's first experience at dialogue may sound rote and will continue to do so until the three parts of the dialogue process become integrated. In other cases, you will be able to lead couples in a spontaneous dialogue and the sheet will serve as a reminder of the parts to use for their homework.

3. Feelings List

Hand this list to the couple with the Couples Dialogue sheet. It is especially useful to the partner who is not familiar with feeling words. You may find that he or she will search the list for just the right words and that is perfectly appropriate until the feeling words become a part of his or her vocabulary. This list, although useful, should not be considered complete as there are numerous other words that express feelings.

4. Homework Instructions for Session One

This page should be handed out at the end of the session and explained to the couple. Between Sessions One and Two, practicing the dialogue is of utmost importance. This homework is designed to help the couple get over the awkward stage of learning the dialogue process so they can move forward into more serious issues. In order to check how often the couple practiced, have them check the days in which they completed the assigned task in the boxes at the bottom of the page.

Emphasizing caring behaviors is also important: negative behaviors the couple have exhibited towards each other have to be replaced by positive behaviors. Research by Gottman (1979) shows that stable marriages exhibit five positive behaviors (in the form of compliments, gifts, or affirmations) for every negative behavior (in the form of criticisms, ignoring, nonsupportive behavior). It is important for couples to place importance on positive behaviors, even if tentative at first. This homework assignment will ease the couple into adding caring behaviors into their relationship.

The Three Parts of the Brain*

Logical — Cerebral Cortex
Speech, Writing,
Use of Tools, Math,
Logical Processes, Time

Mammalian — Limbic System
Emotions and Living
in Relationships

Reptilian — Brain Stem
Basic Life Support including
Breathing, Heartbeat, Digestion
and Other Internal Organ Functions

Survival: If something is dangerous, we will fight, flee, play dead or freeze, hide or submit. If it is safe, we will play with it, nurture it, mate with it, work or be creative.

*Based on MacLean (1964).

Couples Dialogue

The following communication tool is the basis for healing in Imago Relationship Therapy. If you and your partner learn and practice this one skill regularly, you will stop the reinjuring process and begin to open the way for conscious healing.

1. MIRRORING

I heard you say . . . or

If I am hearing you correctly, you said . . .

Then:

Did I get that?

Is there more?

Repeat this process in two to three rounds of mirroring and then validate.

2. VALIDATING

Remember, validating is not agreeing. Validating is saying, "I can see how YOU would see it that way. From your perspective, you make sense."

Say something like:

I can understand that.

That makes sense to me because . . . (*Keep this short.*)

3. EMPATHIZING

That must make you feel . . . (*Pick three feelings from the Feelings List. Feelings are one word, not phrases.*)

Feelings List

Abandoned	Despair	Hateful	Nervous	Shocked
Adequate	Destructive	Heavenly	Nice	Silly
Adamant	Determined	Helpful	Nutty	Skeptical
Affectionate	Different	Helpless		Sneaky
Agony	Diffident	High	Obnoxious	Sorrowful
Almighty	Diminished	Homesick	Obsessed	Sorry
Ambivalent	Discontented	Honored	Odd	Spiteful
Angry	Distracted	Horrible	Opposed	Startled
Annoyed	Distraught	Hurt	Outraged	Stingy
Anxious	Disturbed	Hysterical	Overwhelmed	Strange
Apathetic	Divided			Stuffed
Astounded	Dominated	Ignored	Pained	Stunned
Awed	Dubious	Immortal	Panicked	Stupified
		Imposed upon	Parsimonious	Stupid
Bad	Eager	Impressed	Peaceful	Suffering
Beautiful	Ecstatic	Infatuated	Persecuted	Sure
Betrayed	Electrified	Infuriated	Petrified	Sympathetic
Bitter	Empty	Intimidated	Pity	
Blissful	Enchanted	Isolated	Pleasant	Talkative
Bold	Energetic		Pleased	Tempted
Bored	Enervated	Jealous	Precarious	Tenacious
Brave	Envious	Joyous	Pressured	Tense
Burdened	Evil	Jumpy	Pretty	Tentative
	Exasperated		Prim	Tenuous
Calm	Excited	Keen	Prissy	Terrible
Capable	Exhausted	Kicky	Proud	Terrified
Captivated		Kind		Threatened
Challenged	Fascinated		Quarrelsome	Thwarted
Charmed	Fearful	Laconic	Queer	Tired
Cheated	Flustered	Lazy		Trapped
Cheerful	Foolish	Lecherous	Rage	Troubled
Childish	Frantic	Left out	Refreshed	
Clever	Free	Licentious	Rejected	Ugly
Combative	Frightened	Lonely	Relaxed	Uneasy
Competitive	Full	Longing	Relieved	Unsettled
Condemned	Fury	Loving(love)	Remorse	
Confused		Low	Restless	Vehement
Conspicuous	Gay	Lustful	Reverent	Violent
Contented	Glad		Rewarded	Vital
Contrite	Good	Mad	Righteous	Vulnerable
Cruel	Gratified	Maudlin		Vivacious
Crushed	Greedy	Mean	Sad	
Culpable	Grief	Melancholy	Satisfied	Wicked
	Groovy	Miserable	Scared	Wonderful
Deceitful	Guilty	Mystical	Screwed up	Weepy
Defeated	Gullible		Servile	Worry(ied)
Delighted		Naughty	Settled	
Desirous	Happy	Needy	Sexy	Zany

HOMEWORK INSTRUCTIONS FOR SESSION ONE

1. When you speak to each other over the next 48 hours, talk using Couples Dialogue only.
   Example:

Partner 1: "Could you pass the salt?"

Partner 2: "I heard you say, 'Could you pass the salt?' I can understand that. That makes sense to me. I imagine that makes you feel dry, anticipating, and wanting."

The idea of this part of the homework is to learn the process. Have fun with it and learn at the same time. Nothing will get solved at this point—nor is it supposed to. You're learning a skill that at first doesn't seem natural—*but it's the most important skill couples can learn!* After the first two days, return to your normal way of talking, but be sure to use Couples Dialogue for 30 minutes a day on more serious issues. Remember, you are just learning this skill, and you are not expected to be perfect at it yet. Bring back any problems you've experienced with this process to the next session.

2. Three times a day for one minute each (i.e., 3 minutes per day), think a nice thing about your partner. Be sure to sustain that thought for an entire minute.

3. One time per day, say a nice thing to your partner.

HOME EXERCISE SESSION ONE	Day 1	Day 2	Day 3	Day 4	Day 5	Day 6	Day 7
1. Dialogue							
2. Think a Nice Thing (3× per day)							
3. Say a Nice thing (1× per day)							

Thought for the Week:

When it is dangerous, we will fight, flee, play dead or freeze, hide or submit. When it is safe, we will play, nurture, mate, work, or be creative.

4

SESSION TWO

Development, Childhood Wounds, and Mate Selection

SUGGESTED TIME FRAME

Checking homework	5 minutes
Watching couple practice Couples Dialogue	10 minutes
"Development and Childhood Wounds" Lecture	20 minutes
Guided imagery	20 minutes
Assigning homework	5 minutes

GOALS

1. To get the couple accustomed to the idea that you check the homework each week.

2. To check that the couple are hearing each other fully, using the Couples Dialogue.

3. To educate the couple on how their early childhood affects their choice of whom they pick as a partner.

4. To help the couple begin to gather memories from their childhood to begin the process of consciously understanding the purpose of their relationship.

STARTING THE SESSION

Last week, you met and connected with the couple, presented a lecture on the brain, and introduced them to the most used and useful tool in Imago work: the Couples Dialogue. The homework you assigned was designed to help the couple learn the process and become familiar with the three parts of Couples Dialogue. Because couples commonly feel awkward during their initial attempts at practicing Couples Dialogue on their own, in this session you first need to make sure that they understand the process. In doing so, you will reinforce the message that you *do* check homework. You will also stress the importance of doing the homework, since Imago work cannot be successful if limited to merely an hour a week in your office.

To check on the homework assignment, ask the couple to discuss a frustration they've been having while using Couples Dialogue. To begin the dialogue process, remember to have one of them get into his or her "safe place" and have the other send a frustration in two to three sentences. The sending partner should continue this process until he or she feels fully heard and understood. Then flip the process, and have the listening partner talk until he or she feels fully heard and understood. This part of the session should take about 15 to 20 minutes and is completed when you feel each partner has absorbed the process and has had an experience of feeling heard and understood.

ABOUT THE LECTURE

This week's lecture, "Development and Childhood Wounds," will introduce the couple to the idea that their childhood played an important part in the selection of their mate. It will be important for you to keep this lecture simple, since you will be taking the mystery out of psychological development. Babies and young children have needs that, when fulfilled, give them a sense of self-esteem and well-being. If a child's needs are not met, a longing occurs (a "wound"), and he or she develops an adaptation. We've seen similar adaptations in the plant world: if a plant is not receiving an ample supply of water, it will lose its bottom leaves in order to supply what little water there is to the top leaves. In other words, we do what it takes to survive. This isn't good enough for Nature, however. Nature wants us to work things out and, to help us accomplish this, places us with people who have similar wounds so we can heal together.

But why do we end up with mates who have similar wounds? Wouldn't it make more sense if we placed ourselves with those who could give us *exactly* what we need, so we could finally get what we've been longing for since childhood? If we need to be held, why don't we find someone who is affectionate rather than a withholder? If we need praise, why don't we end up with a mate who can give praise unconditionally? Instead, Nature puts us with mates who seem least likely to be able to give us what we need—mates who were wounded in childhood at precisely the same place in which we were wounded! Nature, rather than handing us a seemingly logical or sensible solution, opts for a "two-for-one" solution in healing human development wounds. By learning how to give our partners what they need, we heal ourselves and them in the process. By helping our partners, we are finally able to grow and reclaim the lost part of ourselves. This is what we see happening in Imago Therapy.

This lecture is designed to help the couple find out where they are. It will help them see that they are wounded—or developmentally arrested—in the same place; moreover, it will help them to realize that they need to see each other as allies rather than as enemies. The lecture will also help the couple realize that they are both equally wounded, and it will encourage them to aid each other in their healing. Whereas the first session gave the couple a tool for communicating, the second session begins the process of the couple working *together*. They will see that their relationship has a purpose.

On a final note, the stories in the childhood and development lecture come from my own personal experience. You are welcome to use them, change them to fit your needs, or—better yet—add your own. Stories and examples always heighten and enliven the presentations, because they give the listener an experience of what you are telling them.

ABOUT THE GUIDED IMAGERY

The third part of this session is a 20-minute guided imagery exercise. The idea of the guided imagery is to help the couple quiet themselves and begin to recall memories of their childhoods. If you have absolutely run out of time in this session or are totally uncomfortable with doing an imagery, you can give the couple the related paperwork, and ask them to complete it at home—preferably in a quiet place. Assigning the paperwork as homework will be effective, but I've found that doing the corresponding imagery during the session evokes deeper memories. It also gives the couple a sense that they did this work together. Some couples find a guided imagery to be painful; others enjoy the 20 minutes of relaxation. (Be sure to have a box of tissues nearby!)

If you have never done a guided imagery before, first be sure to read through the version presented in this chapter to familiarize yourself with its content. When you are actually doing the imagery, you should soften your voice and read the material very slowly to create a relaxed environment. The relaxation can be heightened by playing the right background music. If you wish to incorporate music, I highly recommend *Structures from Silence* by Steve Roach*—29 minutes of music which should bring even the most high-strung person into a relaxed state. You can also order an excellent guided imagery tape from the Institute for Imago Relationship Therapy (see Resources at the end of the book). After the imagery, distribute and explain the homework sheets and request that the couple bring them to the next session. The questions listed on the sheets match the imagery, and you will need the completed forms to conduct the next week's session.

Note: This session tends to be the longest session and the hardest to fit into an hour's time frame. One way to carve out some more time is to audiotape your guided imagery and assign it as homework. Tell the couple to find a quiet place and 30 minutes to listen to the tape and then complete the forms. This allows you to spend more time with the couple in dialogue.

---

*Published by Celestial Harmonies, P.O. Box 673, Wilton, CT 06897.

LECTURE TWO: DEVELOPMENT AND CHILDHOOD WOUNDS

Last week we talked about where we came from to get a picture of where we are headed. We said that we came out of a dot of matter some 15 billion years ago and that what we basically are is energy from the Big Bang. Over these 15 billion years, this energy formed stars and planets and solar systems and galaxies. And our planet formed life, and this life has evolved over time. We looked at the evolutionary process evident in our own brain and said that the oldest part of our brain, the reptilian brain, is there primarily to keep us alive. It's very evident when we have frustrations with each other that the old brain's "defenses" will kick in to keep us alive. So, when we are frustrated with each other, we will fight, flee, play dead or freeze, submit or hide. We also promised to pick up the story from this point—and it starts when we are born.

When you get here, you are whole—you're not yet developed, but you are whole. You have everything you need to make a "whole" person, or put another way, you have potential. Similarly, the acorn has everything it needs to make an oak tree except one thing: the environment. The environment determines how the acorn will grow. So, too, will the environment determine how a person will grow.

And the environment that we have constructed thus far has been one that limits and constricts our babies.

THE STAGES OF DEVELOPMENT

So now I want to discuss what happens after we are born and what is meant by childhood wounds, and I'll do this by talking about development.

The *Attachment Stage* spans from birth to 2 years of age. During this stage, the child wants only to be attached to a caretaker and needs the basics of availability and warmth. The child's main objective during this time is to grow and survive. We know this from studies of monkeys in which baby monkeys were taken from their mothers. These babies were then given a choice of a "mother" made of wire with a bottle stuck in the breast area or a wire monkey covered with fur, making it somewhat warmer and softer than the bare wire. The baby monkeys consistently went to the fur-covered mother. Babies, you see, need availability and warmth. Problems arise when there has been poor holding or when a parent is not available.

Marianne and I met in graduate school and did some work at Charity Hospital in New Orleans. Charity was one of the largest hospitals in the world. It is 19 stories tall, and its emergency room treats over 1000 people a day. There are 7000 babies born each year at Charity. One of the projects we worked on during this time dealt with infant psychiatry. Mostly what we did was to show mothers how to hold their babies correctly, because we were finding that many of the young mothers tended to hold their babies away from their bodies. We would teach them to hold them in toward their heart and chest. Essentially what we were doing was helping these children avoid severe emotional malnutrition.

When a child receives poor holding or has a parent who is unavailable to them at this age, a developmental wound occurs. As a direct result, one of two things can happen: the child can either become a *Clinger* ("I never got held so, when I finally do get held, I'm never going to let go!") or become an *Avoider* ("I never got held, and I don't want to be held because it would hurt too much, and I don't need it anyway"). An injury at this point in development produces a hurt that, in turn, produces a character adaptation to keep the person from feeling the hurt.

If children get what they need at each developmental stage, they'll move on to the next. The second stage of development is that of *Exploration* (2 to 3 years). In this stage, a child needs two things: to be able to explore and to have someone to come back to.

During the Christmas holidays, Alex, our 2-year-old, was thrilled to be able to explore the decorations around the house. We would sit in the kitchen as he would run into the living room to look at the Christmas tree, and he would gleefully return to us and say, "Christmas Tree! Christmas Tree!" Then he would take us to see the tree so that we could get as excited as he was. Alex needed to be able to explore, and he needed to have his parents present to tell them about his exploration.

Problems arise for kids who never get the chance to explore, or, when they do, there's no one around to come back to (for example, a child goes into another room, and a parent takes that time to go do laundry. When the child returns, there's no one for him to share his excitement with.) When this happens regularly over a period of time, the child begins to experience a sense of abandonment.

If children do not get what they need at this stage, again one of two personalities can develop. The child can become a *Fuser* ("No one was there for me to get excited with when I saw something interesting, so—now that I am older—if no one gets excited about my ideas, I'm going to scream until they do get excited") or an *Isolator* ("I never got any space or was allowed to explore when I was little, so no one is going to hold me down now").

If children's needs are met at this stage, they move on to the next stage which occurs at 3–4 years: the stage of *Identity*. This is a fun stage during which kids are reaching the end of being babies and are starting to find a sense of self. And what they do at this stage is experiment with a variety of selves.

Alex wakes up in the morning now and is a different animal each morning. Sometimes he wakes up and is a cat, and he says, "Meow," and expects us to pet him. Sometimes he wakes up and barks like a dog, and when we bend down he licks us.

What a childs needs at this stage is to be mirrored. So when Alex acts like a cat, his parents say, "What a nice kitty!" When he licks them, they say, "What a nice puppy!" Children at this stage need to know that others can see them in the very way that they are presenting themselves.

When Cory was 3 years old, one of the things he learned to do well was to put on his mother's makeup. And he was good at it! He would get the lipstick just right and put rouge on his cheekbones—just like a pro. Then he would look me straight in the eye and say, "Daddy, I'm beautiful!" At that moment, I could have really hurt him. I could have said (as probably most of us heard as children), "Boys don't wear makeup! Only girls wear makeup!" Had I said that to him, I would have run the risk of wounding him permanently. Instead, I said, "You are beautiful! Look at the way you have that makeup on so beautifully! You are so pretty!" He does not wear makeup at age 7, but at age 3, it was important to him to try on different roles.

From the two preceding examples, we can see that Cory and Alex were both experimenting with roles and beginning the formation of their identities. They needed someone to "see" them. So if their parents had said to them, "Boys don't do that!" or 'You're not a cat!" they may have developed *Rigid* personalities. This would manifest itself in rigid behaviors: that is, things are "supposed" to be *this* way or *that* way. On the other hand, if their parents did not acknowledge their behavior at all and simply walked past them as they were calling attention to their roles, the boys may have developed *Diffuse* personalities. People with diffuse personalities report feeling "invisible"—as though they don't matter.

Now, if kids get what they need at the Identity Stage they move on—at about age 4 (usually through 6 years of age)—to the stage of *Power and Competence.* At this stage, they're possibly attending preschool and beginning to do things outside the home. And that's what this stage is all about: becoming competent outside of the home, in school as well as with other people. This is the time when you'll find children proudly coming home armed with things they've done at school or done with friends. What they need at this stage is *praise, affirmation* and *mirroring.* For example, if a child brings home a picture she's done at school and says, "Look what I drew!" she needs her parent to say, "Look how wonderful—I love the way you've colored this picture! You must be very proud of it! I know I am!" In a nutshell, the child needs to be praised. Problems occur when children hear, "It's good, but it's out of the lines, and flowers aren't green—let's get it straight" or when they don't hear any comment at all. If either of these situations occur, you get someone who is *Competitive* ("No one saw what I did when I was little, so now I'll show them just how smart/athletic/creative I can be") or someone who is a *Passive/Manipulator* ("I never do anything right anyway—so why even bother").

Having received what they needed at the Power and Competence Stage, children now move on to the next stage of *Concern* at the ages of 6 to 9 years. This is another fun stage during which they're now playing outside of the home and developing friendships. There are three things they need to master at this stage. First, they need to find friends; then, they need to find a best friend (and you hear kids all the time saying, "This is my best friend!"); and last comes what we call "third party is a threat." That is, kids have a best friend, and one day they notice that there's this other kid across the street with a better set of trucks than their so-called "best" friend has. Mind you, all parties take notice, and now a jealousy takes place, often resulting in a fight and a switching of best friends. This is a perfectly normal process at this age: kids learning about relationships.

The problem occurs when a child is having a difficult time making friends at this age. Perhaps he or she looks different or thinks differently. Or possibly he or she has received little encouragement from the parents to go out and be with friends. If this happens, a child may learn that in order to make friends he or she has to become a *Caretaker* ("If I take care of them and do what they need, they will like me. They really need me"). Or the child may learn that it's too painful to make friends and so becomes a *Loner.* ("I can't make friends, so I'll just stay by myself and read books. I don't really need anyone.")

I have now given you examples of emotional injuries that happen at particular stages of children's development. What do you think happens to these children when they get older? Ready for this? They marry each other! The Avoider marries the Clinger. The Isolator marries the Fuser. The Rigid person marries the Diffuse. The Competitor marries the Passive/Manipulator, and the Loner marries the Caretaker.

Think about some of your friends' marriages. Can you picture some who would fit in this model? (*Spend a minute with the couple, processing some marriages they know and how they might fit into this model.*) Can you figure out where your marriage fits into this model? (*Spend another minute with the couple to help them figure out their wounds. Some couples are able to get this right away and some need time to think about it. If they need time, let them know that they will probably figure it out over the course of the work.*)

MINIMIZERS AND MAXIMIZERS

People usually marry those who are injured at the same developmental stage as they are. They also marry those who have opposite character adaptations and energy expressions. Imago Therapy terms these opposite characteristics as *Minimizer* and *Maximizer*. Let's go back to our Big Bang premise, keep in mind that we are energy from this original explosion, and understand that we all come into being with this energy. During our development, our caretakers socialize us in such a way that either they tell us to hold in or bind up our energy (such as in the idea that boys don't feel), or they do not recognize our energy—in which case our energy becomes boundless. So, we either learn to "minimize" our energy, or we "maximize" it. *Minimizers and Maximizers* marry each other. That's why fights usually sound like this:

Partner 1: What you did is absolutely unforgivable!

Partner 2: It's not that bad.

Partner 1: You are always late!

Partner 2: I was late once and you keep bringing it up.

By seeing to it that we not only marry people who are wounded in the same place as we are, but also who have opposite energy levels, is Nature's way of satisfying a need to heal itself.

How does Nature pull this off? Nature, it appears, has set up a process by which two mutilated, broken, and repressed individuals meet in order to try to recover what they are missing. So here we have two innocent and supposedly incompatible people who are forced to meet for reasons that are beyond their comprehension or, for that matter, knowledge. And Romantic Love sets in.

If you knew beforehand all the horrible traits your partner has, would you have agreed to marry? Welcome to Romantic Love! Romantic Love is "Nature's anesthesia." Nature says, "When two incompatible people meet, I'm going to make them believe they are happy. Then, I'm going to rip the blinders off!" Romantic Love is Nature's trick to bring two incompatible people together for the purpose of healing each other. This is not to say that you have what your partner needs. Rather, what your partner needs is what you also lack and need to grow into.

GUIDED IMAGERY: FINDING YOUR IMAGO

What I am saying will make more sense to you next week when we finish the exercise I am going to start with you now. I want to do a guided imagery which will help you access memories from your childhood. First, I want to tell you what a guided imagery is, and what it is not.

A guided imagery is a way to relax so that you can access your memories more clearly. It is not hypnosis! You will be fully awake the whole time. You may use your imagination to visualize the things I will say, or you may choose not to visualize at all. You may find that it makes you feel sad, and that would be all right. The more information you can gather from the imagery, the better the results will be for you. At the end of the imagery, I will give you some instructions on what to do with your memories. I will ask you to bring this back with you next week, so we can put what you will have written into a formula and discover the real reason the two of you fell in love.

Guided Imagery

So begin to relax, and go into yourself. Let your consciousness be on your breathing and on the sound of the music.

Take a deep breath inside your chest and diaphragm, and hold it to the count of four, and slowly let it out to the count of eight.

Letting go, letting down. Letting all the cares and troubles and tensions of the day fall away.

Now, do it again. A deep breath into your diaphragm, and holding it, and slowly letting it go to the count of eight, and letting all the tensions fall away. Feel all the tensions leave your body. Your head and neck. Chest and shoulders. Feel the tension leave your stomach and hips, legs and calves. Your feet and toes. All the tension washed away by a relaxing flow.

Now, in this relaxed state, the word "safe" appears in your mind as a light. And the light shines down upon you in a warm and golden glow. The light begins to flow around and touches you and bathes you in safety. And in this place of warm safety, you feel totally relaxed and safe.

Now I want you to hold that feeling of relaxation and safety and follow the light as it brings into your awareness your childhood home while feeling totally safe. Become aware of the surroundings: the smells, textures, and things of your childhood home. I want you to begin to become aware of your female caretaker. Become aware of the woman, the caretaker, nurturer of your life. Be there with your x-ray vision in her heart and in her mind. Be aware of her feelings and her thoughts. As a child, let yourself remember and experience her feelings: angry, joyful, depressed, guilty, happy, excited. Positives and negatives. See your mothering caretaker's feelings and record them in your mind.

Now see her traits. You can see into your mother's body and mind and describe her in adjectives: relaxed, tense, rigid, confused, caring, absent, preoccupied, or present. Let yourself recall and construct adjectives of your mothering caretaker. Positives and negatives.

And now, relive the behaviors between you and your mother: fishing, cooking, pushing you away, screaming and yelling, ignoring you when she was drunk, had died, was ill, or playing with you every day. Positive and negative behaviors with your primary female caretaker.

Now ask your female caretaker to sit down with you. Eyeball to eyeball, and say to her, "Mom, the thing that you do that hurts me the most is . . . ," and tell her what she does that hurts you the most, that wounds you the most. Say to her, "What I wanted from you and never got was. . . ." And tell her what you needed. Tell her about your pain with her.

And remember now your recurring frustrations with her. And remember how you felt and what you did when frustrated. Left the house, got quiet, yelled, talked with friends.

Now shift with her, and tell her the positives. Tell her, "Mom, your shining moment with me was . . . ," and tell her what she did that was wonderful.

And now I would like you to let your mothering image fade, and bring into your mind your fathering image. The man, the masculine, your male caretaker. Be there with your x-ray vision in his heart and in his mind. Be aware of his feelings and his thoughts. As a child, let yourself remember and experience his feelings: angry, joyful, depressed, guilty, happy, excited. Positives and negatives. See your fathering caretaker's feelings and record them in your mind.

Now see his traits. You can see into your father's body and mind and describe him in adjectives: relaxed, tense, rigid, confused, caring, hardworking, strict, absent, preoccupied, or present. Let yourself recall and construct adjectives of your fathering caretaker. Positives and negatives.

And now, relive the behaviors between you and your father: fishing, cooking, pushing you away, screaming and yelling, ignoring you when he was drunk, had died, was ill, and playing with you every day. Positive and negative behaviors with your primary male caretaker.

Now, ask your male caretaker to sit down with you. Eyeball to eyeball, and say to him, "Dad, the thing that you do that hurts me the most is . . . ," and tell him what he does that hurts you the most, that wounds you the most. Say to him, "What I wanted from you and never got was. . . ." And tell him what you needed. Tell him about your pain with him.

And remember now your frustrating times with your father. And remember how you felt and what you did: yelled, left the house, brooded, gave in.

Now shift with him and tell him the positives. Tell him, "Dad, your shining moment with me was . . . ," and tell him what he did that was wonderful. Now I would like you to let your fathering image fade.

And now look around in your mind and see anyone else who may have been responsible for your welfare or touched you in significant ways, both painful and caring. Grandmother, uncle, aunt, teacher, minister, or rabbi. See them and their traits in the same ways as you did your male and female caretakers. Positives and negatives.

Now let the place of childhood fade . . . and you find yourself on a path with all of your memories. And you continue on a path to the light beyond. At the edge where the light is, you find a vehicle of your choice to return you to this place and time and in this room. At the count of 5 to 1 you will be here alert and awake. At the count of 1, you will be ready for instructions on what to do with your memories: 5-4-3-2-1 here in this room, alert and awake with your memories.

DAVE AND DIANA: SESSION TWO

Dave and Diana were noticeably more relaxed in the second session. The session began by checking the homework assigned in the first session. Diana said that she was out of town for a few days, so they were not able to practice every day. They reported that the issues they chose to dialogue about were highly charged and it was difficult to stay within the dialogue parameters.

However, they felt encouraged since they were able to stay in the room, which they have not been able to do in the past. Dave talked about how during a heated part of the dialogue, he remembered Session One's lecture about the brain and the fight/flight response. He said that as he felt like leaving, he asked his self what he was so afraid of at the moment, and by doing this, he was able to calm down and consciously stay in the room. His big insight was, "Safety is acknowledging the reptilian part of the brain and then moving on."

Dave and Diana were then asked to practice the dialogue process and Dave volunteered to be the receiver first. He noticeably took 30 seconds in the session to close his eyes and make his self feel safe. He then let Diana know he was able to hear her. Diana chose to work some more on the previous session's issue of being too scared to be noticed. She let him know that she was scared to deal with this subject. She added that she was scared to talk to him about any of her issues because they were so loaded. Dave was able to mirror this back. She told him that she feels like she drags them down as a couple because she is so serious and Dave mirrored. She told Dave that she felt too overwhelmed and too scared to talk. Rather than rescue Diana, as he might have done in the past, Dave mirrored and validated Diana. Diana visibly exhaled and began to talk.

Diana: When we were little, we only had so much time to talk, so I had to get it in fast. (*sobbing*) It would make me really nervous because I did not know if I would say the right thing. I couldn't get it out fast enough. I was always so scared to talk. (*sobbing deeply*) My father always told me I had a lazy tongue. He was never there to listen to me.

Dave: So if I'm hearing you correctly, when you were little, you only had so much time to talk and you had to talk fast. You did not know if you would say the right thing and you could not get it out fast enough. Your father told you you had a lazy tongue and he was never there to listen to you. Did I get that?

Diana: Yes and he would always correct me. (*sobbing deeply*) Everyone would say, "What did you say?" They could not hear me.

Dave: Your father always corrected you and everyone would ask what you said. They could not hear you. I can understand that. You make a lot of sense to me. I imagine you felt sad, alone, and misunderstood.

Diana: I always felt that my tongue was twisted and wouldn't talk right. I always feel that way when I have to say something specific.

Dave: So your tongue felt twisted and wouldn't talk right. You still feel that way when you have to say something specific.

Diana: It was so frustrating because I don't know how to explain it. It was like I did not have a tongue in my mouth. It could not come out. I could not be understood!

Therapist: But I felt it very strongly.

Diana: I did! I felt my feelings. I felt my words. I felt my truth! But people did not understand. People did not understand my truth. This is too much of a subject. It's too big!

Therapist: Mirror that, Dave.

Dave: This subject feels too big. It's too much.

Diana: Yes, it's taking up too much time. I'm not allowed to have this much time. Somebody's going to get mad.

Dave: So it feels like it's taking up too much time and somebody's going to get mad because you are not allowed to have this much time.

Diana: It was so frustrating. It was like being mute. I could not get it out. No one understood. It was so frustrating (*sobbing*).

Dave: It was like being mute. No one understood. It was so frustrating. I can really understand that and I imagine that you would feel frustrated, not understood, sad, and invisible.

Diana: Yes.

Dave was able to hold Diana as she sobbed. It was obvious that his compassion was now out and being directed at Diana's pain. Dave had managed to keep his self safe and allow Diana to go past her anger and fear to the sadness underneath. This allowed Diana to be fully expressive and be understood clearly by Dave—a healing experience for Diana. At this point in the therapy, there was no attempt to assist Dave in "fixing" what was going on for Diana. Dave was simply being taught to listen with empathy. They stayed in the moment until Diana felt fully held and contained by Dave.

For the next 20 minutes, the therapist presented the development lecture to Dave and Diana. In this lecture, they were able to discover where they may have been wounded in their development. After some discussion, they were able to place their wound in the Power and Competence Stage. Dave saw himself as competitive, which is why he reacts so harshly when Diana calls attention to problems in the relationship and in activities he is participating in. He felt that this makes sense since his father always picked out what he did wrong and never told him that he did a good job, as discussed in the first session.

Diana felt that she used passive and manipulative means to get Dave to do things for her. She felt that this also made sense when her lack of praise is considered. Her father also told her that she could not do anything right. Hearing this as often as she did as a child, Diana began to believe it and often looked for Dave to rescue her, which because of his competitive nature, he always readily did in his own self-righteous sort of way.

Then the therapist told Dave and Diana that they were going to experience a process that will begin to make the lecture even more relevant. The experience they were about to go through was the guided imagery designed to help them gather information about their childhood. They were able to quiet themselves and go through the imagery with some noticeable tears. The therapist then gave Dave and Diana the homework sheets (illustrated on p. 80) designed to help them organize their memories and they were told to bring the sheets back for the next session. In addition, the therapist instructed them to continue their dialogues, especially around the childhood memories they just touched on in the imagery. And last, they were asked to learn at least one new thing about the other person's childhood through their dialogue.

HANDOUT INSTRUCTIONS FOR THE THERAPIST

SESSION TWO

The second session consists of three handouts totaling five pages.

1. Couples Developmental Scale

Give this scale to the couple prior to doing the development lecture. This will allow them to follow along and give them the opportunity to discuss the scale in their dialogues assigned for homework. It is a good idea to have a copy for yourself and to use it as a prompter for your lecture. It is designed to match what you will say to the couple and should be able to guide you in your presentation to them.

2. Instructions to the Couple for Finding Your Imago and Childhood Frustrations/Positive Memories of Childhood Sheets

This handout actually consists of three pages: Instructions to the Couple, a page entitled Finding Your Imago that is recognizable from the large heart on it, and a page that says Childhood Frustrations and Positive Memories of Childhood. These sheets will be used by the couple to organize their memories from the guided imagery. You should emphasize to the couple that they should write as much as possible to get the best results from this exercise. Let them know that they will get the surprise ending in the next session and should spend this week writing down their memories. The instruction sheet and the information on each page should be sufficient in helping the couple fulfill this task; however, it is suggested that you review it with them following the guided imagery.

Emphasize to them that they are writing down the traits of their early childhood caretakers. Some couples have confused the exercise and have written down information on themselves or their partner. Some may complain that they have no memories from childhood or that they are all good memories. Work with these clients to help them generate a little information. As they see how this works—and that it is not about parent bashing, but rather about understanding the journey—they usually begin to cooperate. Also, the best way to learn how to help the couple fill out the sheets is to fill one out on yourself. Take some time to do that prior to seeing couples. You might just find it interesting!

3. Homework Instructions for Session Two

Each partner should receive one of these sheets to keep track of the homework. The emphasis should be on filling out the forms thoroughly and bringing them back to the next session. This is important since much of the next session is based on the results of these forms.

The couple should continue practicing the dialogue process a minimum of three times a week. Following the guided imagery, they should have a lot to dialogue about concerning their childhoods. Suggest to them that they dialogue this week about how they experienced the imagery and also about their childhoods.

Couples Developmental Scale

Minimizer

	Attachment	Exploration	Identity	Power and Competence	Concern
Minimizer	Avoider	Isolator	Rigid	Competitive	Loner
Normal Development	0 to 2 years	2 to 3 years	3 to 4 years	4 to 6 years	6 to 9 years
Needs:	Availability and warmth	To be able to explore / To be able to come back and tell someone	Mirroring	Praise / Affirmation / Mirroring	To find friends / To find a best friend / Third party is a threat
Problems:	Poor holding / Not available	Cannot explore / Shamed when returned or no one to return to	No mirroring / Poor mirroring	Partial mirroring / Shaming	Unable to find friend / Poor modeling
Maximizer	Clinger	Fuser	Diffuse	Passive/Manipulator	Caretaker

Maximizer

Finding Your Imago

In a relaxed and safe state, recall your childhood memories of your caretakers. It is important that you think as a child and recall your caretakers as they were when you were a child and not as they are today. On the top section of the figure below, list the positive characteristics of each caretaker. On the bottom, list all of the negative characteristics of your caretakers. Use adjectives such as "warm," "strong," "cold," "distant," and/or phrases such as "never there," "always there," "not dependable," "not available emotionally."

(B)

Female +   Male +

Female −   Male −

(A)

(C) What I wanted and needed most as a child was _____

_____

Childhood Frustrations

In the left column below, list any recurring childhood frustrations such as "did not get listened to," "no one knew I was being hurt," "had to take care of parents or siblings." On the right, list how you responded to these frustrations. This should be how you felt AND your behavioral response (i.e., what you did.).

Frustrations	Response(s)
	(E)

Positive Memories of Childhood

On the left column below, list your positive memories of childhood. This can be specific memories such as "going to the shore in 1960" or "the annual picnic at grandma's house." On the right, list the feelings you associated with each memory.

Memories	Feelings
	(D)

INSTRUCTIONS FOR HOMEWORK SESSION TWO

1. Fill out the two pages given to you with the information you recalled in the guided imagery. Be thorough and complete in filling these out. Remember to bring them back to the next session.

2. Using Couples Dialogue, talk about your childhood memories, both positive and negative, for 30 minutes each, three times this week.

3. Continue thinking a nice thought about each other three times a day for 1 minute and say a nice thing to each other once a day.

HOME EXERCISE SESSION TWO	Day 1	Day 2	Day 3	Day 4	Day 5	Day 6	Day 7
1. Fill Out Memory Forms							
2. Dialogue About Childhood (3× this week)							
3. Think a Nice Thought (3× per day) and Say a Nice Thing (1× per day)							

Thought for the Week:

Emotional safety is the real number one!

5

SESSION THREE

Developing Empathy and Reimaging the Partners

SUGGESTED TIME FRAME

Couple uses dialogue about childhood while therapist fills out the My Imago sheets	15 minutes
Processing the My Imago sheets	10 minutes
"Reimaging Your Partner—Developing Empathy" Lecture	5 minutes
Parent-Child Dialogue	15 minutes
Holding Lecture	3 minutes
The Holding Exercise	10 minutes
Assigning homework	2 minutes

GOALS

1. To confirm that the couple now fully understands the dialogue process.

2. To use the Imago forms so that each member of the couple can visually see that his or her choice of partner was unconscious and based on positive and negative traits of his or her early childhood caretakers.

3. To begin the process of helping the couple understand that they are allies rather than enemies.

4. To use specific processes to help the couple begin developing empathy for each other.

STARTING THE SESSION

This session involves more work on experiential processes, with considerably less time spent on giving a lecture to the couple. Begin this session by filling out the My Imago sheets for each partner with the information the couple have brought back from their homework assignment (see below). While you are filling out these forms, ask the couple to do a Couples Dialogue on their childhoods or some other important topic of their choice. It will take you about 7 to 10 minutes to fill out the forms, so this will give the couple time to experience Couples Dialogue in your presence once again. As you are filling out their My Imago forms, keep an ear open to make sure they are doing Couples Dialogue correctly. Correct them when necessary.

FILLING OUT THE "MY IMAGO" FORM

To complete each partner's My Imago sheet, ask the couple for each partner's Finding Your Imago and Childhood Frustrations/Positive Memories of Childhood sheets which, again, they should have done for homework. If they have only written down a few things, you may want to take a minute to help them come up with more traits, frustrations, and so on. The more they've written down, the better.

The My Imago form consists of five sentence stems, each ending with a letter from A to E. These letters will correspond to the same letters found on the Finding Your Imago and Childhood Frustrations/Positive Memories of Childhood forms. You will·now move the information from the Finding Your Imago and Childhood Frustrations/Positive Memories of Childhood forms (family and childhood) over to each partner's My Imago form.

For example, move every description on the Finding Your Imago form under (A), which are the negative traits of early caretakers, over to the sentence stem on the My Imago form marked (A). You can mix up the traits of each caretaker, because the Imago is a mixture of traits of all the early caretakers. Continue this process until all five sentence stems are filled in. Don't bother correcting for grammar or tense. The purpose of this analysis is to show the couple that traits of their parents can be found in their spouse. In effect, the couple have recreated their childhoods by selecting a spouse who has the traits of early caretakers!

USING THE IMAGO WORK-UP

When you have finished filling out each partner's My Imago sheet, you will share them with the couple. Since this session deals with empathy and with developing empathetic feelings between the partners, begin by taking actions that create the right mood—such as softening your voice—to help them stay in a "feeling" mode. Encourage the couple to listen and discourage questions at this time. Listening adds to empathy, whereas asking questions brings on thinking and tends to create a cognitive mode.

As a way of introducing your reading of the My Imago sheets, tell the couple the following:

> Last week you pulled together memories of your childhood caretakers and wrote those memories on these forms. I have taken your memories about your childhood caretakers and have put them into a formula about your partner. Most of the things will fit; some will not. Listen as I read them, and see what fits.

Read each partner's My Imago sheets slowly. You may want to read them twice, so that the couple can fully grasp them. Most couples will say the picture fits. Every once in a while, you will get a couple who will say nothing fits. Ask them to give it a day or two. In many cases, (I estimate 80 percent) couples agree that My Imago is an accurate description. The remaining couples will be able to see its accuracy later on. For the partner who says "nothing fits," ask if *any* traits fit him or her. Sometimes rather than projecting parental traits on the partner, we will take on the traits ourselves. •

ABOUT THE LECTURE

This session has two short lectures designed to help the couple begin to think about the importance of empathy in the relationship. Empathic connection is the missing ingredient in most relationships. As mentioned in the chapter on Couples Dialogue, pain causes people to look inward at their suffering and to pull others into their way of seeing things in an attempt to lessen the pain. Empathy cannot be present in these symbiotic relationships. We also cannot heal our own pain. If a wound was caused in a relationship, it can best be healed in a relationship. This healing occurs through empathy.

Luckily, if the therapist can help the couple create a safe environment, empathy seems to be an easy state to recreate. The lectures are designed to create a curiosity about the processes the couple will learn in the session. They are designed to soften the couple to the experience of the Parent-Child Dialogue and the Holding Exercise. To complement this process, it is best to soften your voice as you present these lectures. Use your self to help the couple ease into these sometimes scary, but highly beneficial, empathic experiences.

LECTURE THREE: REIMAGING YOUR PARTNER— DEVELOPING EMPATHY

So, Nature seems to have brought together two totally incompatible people for a purpose. And that purpose is to recreate the scene from our childhood, so that we can finally get *now* what we did not get then and, thus, move on. The problem is that, up until this point, you have seen each other as enemies and have not co-operated with Nature. When we do not cooperate with Nature, it's not safe. And when it's not safe we will fight, flee, play dead or freeze, hide, or submit. It's only natural!

So how do you cooperate with Nature? You have to see your purpose in each other's lives. You are each other's healers. You are the surrogate parent for each other—whom Nature has chosen to give your partner what he or she needs to grow. And, to see that, you have to reimage your partner as an ally rather than as an enemy.

THE THREE TYPES OF LOVE

One of the problems with our language is that we have only one word for love: L-O-V-E [spell out]. The ancient Greeks had three words that best sum up the process we've been talking about. The first word is **Eros**, or Romantic Love. It's that sort of drug-induced, knock-you-down, the-sun-rises-and-sets-on-you kind of love. But, basically, it's an attraction. This is how Nature first gets two people together, and it's usually short-lived. You probably experienced it when you first met, and maybe with others before that.

A second word for love—and the one most important to what we are doing now—is **Agape** [pronunciation: Ah-gah-pay). This word actually evolved out of war. You see, when the generals of ancient Greece grew tired of the fighting that was occurring in their country, they sought a way to stop war. After putting their heads together, they came up with the word Agape, which—literally translated—means "when you are in my territory, I will make you safe."

The Greeks realized that the reason it was so easy to kill is that they had made the enemy a "nonhuman." And we do this all the time in our wars: we bombed the "Nips" and killed the "Gooks" and feared the "Reds." And we find it's easy to kill when we do not know each soldier as a person. So the Greeks' idea was to make their enemies human, and—rather than kill them when they came onto Greek soil—they made them safe. Agape love, therefore, is a transformative love. It takes our enemies and makes them our allies.

If we can maintain agape long enough, we can attain the third type of love: **Philia**—as in **Phila**delphia. This is a brotherly type of love in which two people enjoy desireless valuing, empathetic communication, joy, and an overall feeling of being fully alive. It's not an "icky" type of brotherly love, but one of care and concern about the other—one in which two people work together for each other's common good. But, in order to arrive at philia, you have to go through agape. You have to transform your partner from an enemy to an ally. And the way to do this is through empathy.

EMPATHY

Empathy is something that we all probably had when we were younger, but lost when we were told to look out only for ourselves. Empathy is being able to see things through the other's eyes. It's using your heart to feel what another is feeling.

A young woman once told me a story that took place one afternoon when she was sitting in front of the TV while *Lassie* was on. She wasn't watching the show but was actually crying after having had a stressful day. At some point, her 7-year-old daughter walked into the room—only to see her mother crying. The girl looked at her mother and then looked at Lassie. And again she looked at her mother and looked at Lassie. Trying to make some sense out of this scenario, she finally went over to her mother, put her little arm around her and said softly, "I bet you had a friend named Lassie."

This was a true attempt at empathy. She may not have had the picture right, but the little girl attempted to understand her mother's pain. (Actually, she made her mother laugh so much, that afterward the woman felt much better.) And to reimage our partner, we first need to empathize. So we are now going to do two exercises that should help you begin to reestablish empathy with each other.

PARENT-CHILD DIALOGUE

This exercise is designed to help couples begin the process of reestablishing empathy. It is based on the idea that Nature has set couples up to be surrogate parents to each other, so that they can finally get what they did not get as children. If this is the case, then it might be possible for partners to speak directly to their parents through their partner to express some of these needs. In turn, the receiving partners will know their partner's hurt directly and empathetically. In this session, you will only have time for one partner to do this exercise; the other will do it as homework.

Have the couple sit facing each other, with one partner choosing to be the partner-as-parent—or receiver—for the exercise. Let the receiver know that your instructions will have to be followed carefully, and that he or she should listen *from the heart*. Ask the sending partner if he or she would rather talk to Mother or Father or perhaps to another significant caretaker. Then tell the partner-as-parent (the receiver) to ask the following question: "I am your mother/father/significant caretaker. What was it like to live with me?" It is important that the question remain simple and open, so that the sending partner can talk expressively. The only other thing the partner-as-parent is permitted to say is, "Tell me more about that." Saying anything else will only serve to bring the sending partner into a cognitive mode and should, therefore, be stopped. (Cognitive material will be covered in Session Five as a Behavior Change Request.)

The sending partner should be allowed to talk freely for about 10 minutes, always keeping in mind that he or she is talking to the parent of choice. At the appropriate time, ask the partner-as-parent to ask this second question: "I am your mother/father/significant caretaker. What did you need from me that you did not get?" Again, let the sending partner speak freely, and be sure to keep the couple in a quiet and empathetic mode.

At the end of this exercise, couples are typically quiet and will appear somewhat more connected. Although you should be keeping your questions to a minimum, you may want to ask the receiver if he or she can now see the sending partner's pain. You may also want to ask the receiver-partner-as-parent if at any time it felt as though the sending partner was actually talking to him or her instead of to a parent. Get ready, because many receivers will report that what the sending partner expressed as a need from the designated parent *is exactly what that sending partner has been asking of him or her for years!* For example, the sender may have said to his or her "parent" during the exercise, "I needed you to spend more time with me," and the receiver has been hearing his or her partner say for years, "You never spend enough time with me." Help the couple make the connection that, once again, Nature has recreated that scene from childhood to enable the pain to resurface and, this time around, allowed the pain to be handled in a better way. Listening and understanding with empathy is a new opportunity to handle the pain better—at long last!

At this point, when the couple are feeling closer and a bit more understanding of each other's and their own childhoods, let them know that you're going to show them one more exercise to heighten this feeling.

THE HOLDING EXERCISE

Start this exercise with the following brief lecture:
Remember when I told you that there are three parts to the brain? Well, I lied—sort of. There are actually four parts, the fourth being the heart. I'll explain. If you take a brain cell and put it on a petri dish, do you know what happens? It dies right away. A brain cell cannot live apart from the other cells. But if you take a heart cell and put it on a petri dish, do you know what it does? It doesn't die right away, but continues to beat (you see, each cell does what the organ is designed to do—so a heart cell beats). And then this heart cell begins to beat wildly or goes into fibrulation. Finally, it dies from beating too wildly.

Now, if you take two heart cells and put them on a petri dish—close to each other, but not touching—can you guess what happens? At first, they too begin to beat wildly, but then something strange occurs. The cells find each other through the space and begin to beat together. Somehow, through some kind of particle or wave energy, they find each other!

If this happens with two cells, what happens when you put billions of cells next to each other? We believe that this same kind of heart communication occurs between a mother and a child. Whether they are left- or right-handed, mothers universally hold their babies in the left arm—on the side where the heart is located. So in this holding exercise, we recreate this scene, so that you can feel safe and in sync with each other. It's the most vulnerable, yet safest position we know.

THE HOLDING POSITION (see Figure 5.1)

At this point, have the partner who was the "parent" or receiver in the Parent-Child Dialogue sit on the floor against either a wall or a sturdy piece of furniture, if possible (a chair with arms will not work). Be sure that he or she has back support. Position the person to sit with the right leg straight while bending the left leg up. The sending partner will sit on the receiving partner's right, hip-to-hip, and facing the opposite way with his or her arms folded in front. Then tell the sending partner to fall to his or her right and into the receiving partner's left arm. Think of a mother holding a baby, and you should get the idea. The sending partner should not be holding him or

Figure 5.1. Correct Position for the Holding Exercise

herself up but should be fully supported by the receiving partner (babies do not hold themselves up!). The couple should be as close as possible, with their faces about 6 inches apart.

You may have to work with the couple for a few minutes to get the "hold" somewhat comfortable. Make adjustments for those with injuries or for those whose weight makes the hold difficult. For some—especially men—the holding position can be awkward at first, so be reassuring, and let them know they're doing fine.

Once you have the hold down, let the sender know that he or she is no longer talking to parents but to his or her partner in the present tense. Have the person being held say, "When I was a little (girl, boy) . . ." and have him or her talk about childhood while staying in this hold position. Let the holder (receiver) know that he or she can only say "tell me more about that," or he or she can mirror back feelings, such as "that must have made you feel sad and lonely." The idea is for holders to keep senders in their feelings. If the couple are feeling connected, this should enable the holder to see and understand the sender's feelings and to feel nurturing towards the sender. Allow the couple to stay in this position as time permits. Again, since both partners will not have the time within the session to do this, assign the switch over as homework. If you feel comfortable, you can allow the couple to stay in this position while you talk about the homework.

DAVE AND DIANA: SESSION THREE

Dave and Diana returned to the third session with their homework in hand. They immediately offered that they felt "better" this week. Dave said that he was experiencing more awareness. He said that he really became aware of his childhood and how it relates to his marriage. He said, "My mother really succumbed to my father. Her world revolved around him and I was the same way. I really felt my mother's fear. It helped me to see why I have such a hard time getting in touch with my emotions. My life has been run by fear."

Diana added that she became very aware of her passive role. She said, "I watched what I do to give things away. That's what it feels like." She also observed that it was easier to do the sad work in the office with the therapist than it was to do it at home. She wondered with the therapist if that was typical. The therapist assured her that it was typical, but that the goal of the therapy was to enable the couple to do the work at home with each other. The idea of the homework was to help them feel comfortable doing the work at home.

It was now time for the therapist to put the information from the homework assigned in Session Two into their respective My Imago sheets. While the therapist worked on transcribing the information, he instructed Dave and Diana to dialogue about an issue of their choice.

Diana: I find it easier to let you be the spokesperson, to let you speak first. I always hope that it is you who has the conversation when we socialize.

Dave: So if I am hearing you right, you are saying that you prefer that I am the spokesperson when we socialize and you hope that it is me who has the conversation when we socialize. Did I get that?

Diana: Yes. It amazes me how much I lean on you as a couple. I wish I could get out of there as an individual, but I hide behind you.

Dave: So you are amazed at how much you lean on me and you wish you could step out as an individual, but you hide behind me. Did I get that?

Diana: Yes. I feel frustrated, angry at myself. But it comes out as anger toward you. I want the words and the courage, although it does not seem like I have that.

Dave: So you get frustrated and angry at yourself, but it comes out at me. You want the words and courage, but it does not seem like I have that. Is there anything I can do?

Therapist: (*softly*) Just mirror it. Don't try to fix it. She just needs you to hear it right now.

Diana: Yes, what you can do is just hear it. That's what I need.

Dave: So you just need me to hear it. Did I get that?

Diana: Yes.

Dave: Is there more?

Diana: Yes, because when you fix it, that just seeds the thought that I can not do it.

Dave: So when I fix it, it just seeds that you cannot do it. Did I get that?

Diana: Then I become like that little girl who could not do anything. My father had to fix it.

Dave: So if I'm hearing that right, when I try to fix it, you become like that little girl who could not do anything and your father had to fix it for you. Did I get that?

Diana: Yes. I want to be grown-up!

Dave: So you want to be grown-up.

Diana: It's scary.

Dave: And it's scary.

Diana: It's hard to step out and just be me. The reason I come home and isolate so badly is because I know I have to be me up there.

Dave: So when you come home and isolate it is because you know you have to spend some time being you up there. I can understand this. It makes a lot of sense to me. I would imagine you feel sad, lonely, and hidden.

Diana: Yes.

Dave and Diana seemed to understand the dialogue process now and were getting quite proficient in it. Dave was able to maintain his safety and listen to Diana's pain and understand her hope of being a "grown up." He also understood how sad and lonely she felt in trying to be herself. Their empathy is beginning to flow for each other and they were now listening to each other rather than lashing back and getting stuck in their usual impasse.

It was now time for the therapist to read back to Dave and Diana their My Imago forms. The therapist told them that many of the things would fit, but some would not. He also asked them to consider if the traits that did not fit the partner were aspects of themselves. Diana's Imago form read:

> *I am trying to get a person who is:* always home, sad, angry, busy, scared, strict, confusing, distant, always distracted, explosive, hated crying or noises, and squelched fun noises.
>
> *To always be:* caring, loving, disciplined, consistent rules, make parties, financial provider.
>
> *So that I can get:* help to see that I am worthwhile. To be special, to count, to feel loved from the inside.

And feel: bonding, warmth, sharing, laughter, united, attention, seen and heard, surprised, appreciated.

I stop myself from getting this sometimes by: not telling anyone and fixing it myself; crying to get them to understand my discomfort; being hypervigilant; feeling all the time; becoming a fixer; do what they please and what I want does not count.

Diana readily agreed that most of these traits fit and was startled that the ones that did not fit Dave fit her so well. Some of the traits that she disliked so much in her parents, she had taken on herself. This was a very typical response to the results of this Imago form. Parents introject their traits, positive and negative, onto their children. Some are taken in by the children as their personality traits, while others are traits that are sought unconsciously in another person—the Imago match. Diana was now able to understand this concept through the My Imago exercise.

Now it was time to move on to Dave's My Imago form. He was equally startled by the accuracy of the results. Dave's read:

I am trying to get a person who is: not available emotionally; fearful of Dad; too strong to hold me; always bitching; never takes me anywhere; cold.

To always be: loving; available; a good housekeeper; smart about things; provide financially; strong; and keep the house repaired.

So that I can get: to be heard; listened to; and played with.

And feel: freedom to have fun; excitement; happy and free.

I stop myself from getting this sometimes by: playing with others or outside; always doing the right thing; crying so I can't be heard; holding in tears; not wanting to do anything; staying out of the way; feeling what I had to say was not worth it.

It was at this point that Dave began to cry. He said that it made him sad to know what he was missing and he lamented, "I know that I deserve it!" He was also able to see that his marriage was Nature's way of giving him a second chance to get what he needed. He was now able to understand that the impasses with Diana had a basis in his childhood. He was beginning to see that his marriage had a purpose, and he was ready to discover that purpose and begin the healing process.

This process would begin with the lecture on the three types of love and the loss of empathy. The therapist told them that empathy was necessary in a relationship, but it is a trait lost in most couples. Then he asked them to participate in the Parent-Child Dialogue as a way to reclaim their empathy for each other. They readily agreed.

Dave decided to be the sender and to talk to his mother in the exercise. The therapist asked them to close their eyes and he also asked Diana to imagine herself as Dave's mother who was going to listen to Dave with her heart this time. The therapist suggested to Dave to go back as far in his childhood as he thought he needed to and to talk to his mother as a little boy. Then the therapist asked them to open their eyes, and then he gave Diana a question to ask Dave with instructions to listen only.

Diana: I am your mother. What was it like to live with me?

Dave: It was empty . . . sad . . . like you were not there. I did not know you . . . you were always waiting for Dad . . . always working around the house. You never had time for me. You never talked to me. You never held me. (*crying*) You never hugged me. . . . You never told me you cared. . . . It wasn't very nice to be with you. (*sobbing deeply*) I was always scared. Did I do something to make you angry? Then you would start the drinking. I didn't like living with you . . . didn't like it. I was afraid, always afraid. Especially on the weekends. I never knew what you would do with the drinking. You were Jekyll and Hyde.

Why? Why? Tell me why? (*sobbing very deeply*)

Therapist: Let it come out.

Dave: Ohh . . . Oh, it hurts, it hurts! (*continues sobbing for a few minutes, Diana listens with empathy now*)

Therapist: Diana, ask Dave this question. I am your mother. What did you need from me that you did not get?

Diana: Dave, I am your mother. What did you need from me that you did not get?

Dave: I needed you to listen to me. I needed you to know I was here. I needed you to be calm. I needed you to be yourself, so I could be myself. I needed you to not be scared, so I was not scared. I needed you to hold me, hug me, tell me I'll be okay. To know you care. I know you know how. Why don't you just do it?

It was at this point that the process was switched to the Holding Exercise. The therapist asked Dave and Diana to close their eyes and come out of their roles. Now they were to be their adult selves for the process. Next the therapist gave a short and subtle lecture about holding (see p. 87) and he helped them into the Holding Position.

To get Dave started in the Holding Exercise, the therapist gave him the sentence stem "When I was a little boy . . ." to complete. The therapist instructed Diana to softly mirror back feelings as they came up: "I can see that you felt scared"; "So you felt all alone when your mother did not pay attention to you." It was very important that Diana not ask questions during the Holding Exercise because this would cause Dave to come out of his feelings and go into his logic. The idea of the Holding Exercise is for the person being held to reexperience feelings from his or her childhood in a very different way, in a place that is safe, nurturing, and empathetic. It is also a way to increase the knowledge of the receiving partner that the sending partner has wounds and unmet needs from childhood that are a source of great pain.

Dave and Diana were able to finish this 10-minute exercise in a safe and compassionate manner. Dave told Diana more about his childhood and she softly mirrored back his feelings. He began to look very comfortable in her arms. As is often the case with this subtle and personal exercise, actual dialogue was not heard by the therapist. The therapist spent the time maintaining the moment by providing a safe structure.

When Dave had been held long enough, they sat up and wiped each others tears. Diana asked a question often heard during this session: "What do I do when I hear him saying things to his mother that I have heard him say to me in the past?" Diana experienced a front-row view of the Imago. Couples fall in love with a person who has the positive and negative traits of their early childhood caretakers. They then begin to work out frustrations with their partners that have roots in their caretakers. These two exercises made this idea real to Dave and Diana. They had begun their conscious marriage.

HANDOUT INSTRUCTIONS FOR THE THERAPIST

SESSION THREE

There are three handout pages (illustrated on p. 96) to be given to the couple this week.

1. My Imago

This form should be filled out by the therapist while the couple is practicing dialogue. Ask them for their completed Finding Your Imago and Childhood Frustrations sheets from the last session. You will notice that there are five sentence stems on the My Imago sheet with a letter at the end in parentheses. These letters correspond to a letter next to a section of the Finding Your Imago and Childhood Frustrations/Positive Memories of Childhood sheets. Move all of the information next to the letter from the Finding Your Imago and Childhood Frustrations/Positive Memories of Childhood sheets to the end of the sentence stem with the corresponding letter on the My Imago sheet. For example, at the end of the sentence stem, "I am trying to get a person who is (A)," transcribe all of the negative traits of the early childhood caretakers from the Finding Your Imago sheet. You can mix the traits up from various caretakers since the Imago is a combination of all of the primary caretakers.

After you have completed all five sentence stems for each partner, read these back to them and let them discuss them briefly using dialogue prior to moving on to the lecture on "Reimaging Your Partner—Developing Empathy."

2. Parent-Child Dialogue

During the session, one partner will experience the Parent-Child dialogue with his or her partner acting as one of his or her parents. At the end of the session, give the couple the Parent-Child Dialogue sheet for homework. This sheet contains the two questions they will ask their partner in the role as their partner's parent. After they are through this process, they will move into the Holding Position to further dialogue their experiences.

3. Homework Instructions for Session Three

This sheet gives the instructions for homework following Session Three. Ask the couple to find some uninterrupted time to set a quiet mood in order to complete this work. They will each take a turn talking to his or her partner "parent" as described on the "Parent-Child Dialogue" sheet and then move into the Holding Position for further dialogue.

When they have completed the two processes, they should use the space provided on the sheet to write down their partner's wound and their own wound as they now understand it. Finally, they should find some time to dialogue about their wounds to increase empathy and understanding.

My Imago

Using the information from the Finding Your Imago and Childhood Frustrations/Positive Memories of Childhood sheets, complete the sentences below. The letters in parentheses correspond to these sheets and tell you from where to transcribe the information.

I am trying to get a person who is (A)_____

_____

_____

To always be (B) _____

_____

_____

So that I can get (C) _____

_____

_____

And feel (D) _____

_____

_____

I stop myself from getting this sometimes by (E) _____

_____

_____

SESSION THREE

HOMEWORK INSTRUCTIONS FOR SESSION THREE

1. Continue the Parent-Child Dialogue that we started in our session. You should spend 15 minutes on each parent. The listening partner should only ask the questions on the sheet and refrain from making other comments. He or she can invite dialogue, however, by saying "tell me more about that."

2. Do the Holding Exercise started in our session. Each partner should be held for 30 minutes. The holding partner should only mirror back softly the sender's feelings. The idea is to keep your partner in his or her emotions so that you can reimage your partner as wounded and give your partner what he or she did not get as a child. Asking questions pulls people out of their feelings and into their thoughts. Empathy will keep your partner in his or her feelings.

3. In the chart below, write down your partner's wound as you now understand it, and check it out with him or her using Couples Dialogue.

4. In the chart below, write down your wound and talk about it with your partner by using Couples Dialogue.

HOME EXERCISE SESSION THREE	Day 1	Day 2	Day 3	Day 4	Day 5	Day 6	Day 7
1. Parent-Child Dialogue (1× each)							
2. Holding Exercise (30 min. each)							
3. Write/Dialogue Partner's Wound (1× each)							
4. Write/Dialogue Your Wound (1× each)							

Thought for the Week:

> Frustrations are a little about now and a lot about the house you grew up in.

SESSION THREE

Parent–Child Dialogue

Ask your partner the following question and listen with empathy:

"I am your (mother/father/significant caretaker). What was it like to live with me?"

Then ask:

"I am your (mother/father/significant caretaker). What did you need from me that you did not get?"

First one partner talks to one parent, and at another time talks to the other parent. The receiving partner is an empathetic listener. DO NOT ASK QUESTIONS OTHER THAN THOSE ABOVE. Questions pull people out of their feelings and into their thoughts. You want to listen empathetically to your partner's words and feelings.

Then switch roles.

Spend about 20 minutes talking to each parent.

6

SESSION FOUR

Reromanticizing the Relationship

SUGGESTED TIME FRAME

Checking homework	10 minutes
"Reromanticizing the Relationship" Lecture	5 minutes
Caring Behaviors Exercise	20 minutes
Little Surprises Lecture	10 minutes
Belly Laughs Exercise	10 minutes
Assigning homework	5 minutes

GOALS

1. To check the level of empathy being developed between the partners.

2. To emphasize the importance of emotional safety and make the point that pleasure increases the sense of safety.

3. To create a list of caring behaviors and surprises that when done by one partner will make the other partner feel cared for and safe in the relationship.

4. To emphasize the importance of daily belly laughs as a way of increasing safety and a sense of well-being.

STARTING THE SESSION

In Session Three the couple worked on developing empathy and were given homework designed to reinforce this empathy. Typically, at this stage, the couple are beginning to see that to make things better, they have to work together. They are beginning to understand their purpose in each other's life, and they are beginning to see each other as wounded. Begin this session by checking their homework, and ask what they experienced as they did the work. You will, from time to time, have a couple who have had a bad experience with it or who will not have done the work at all. In either case, you may want to spend this session doing more work on empathy.

If the couple did do the homework, concentrate on enhancing safety in the relationship. After spending 10 to 15 minutes processing their experience from the previous session, present this week's lecture, "Reromanticizing Your Relationship." Since there is much to cover in this session, the lecture has been designed to be brief and is followed by three exercises that the couple will start this week, with the rest assigned as homework. Once again, emphasize the importance of their making the time for this work. As an added incentive, let them know that most couples will later report that they enjoyed this homework assignment in particular.

ABOUT THE LECTURE

There are several brief lectures in this session designed to help the couple begin to understand the importance of caring behaviors in the relationship. Caring behaviors cannot be overemphasized in any relationship. In a study by Gottman (1979), he found that healthy, long-term relationships had one thing in common: there was a constant ratio of five positive behaviors for every one negative behavior. This lecture and session is designed to give the couple the idea that there is a need to flood each other with positive, caring behaviors in addition to listening to each other using Couples Dialogue.

A point emphasized in the lectures is that the behaviors have to be pleasurable to the receiving partner. If the sending partner buys the receiving partner season tickets to the football game and the receiving partner does not like football, it is not a caring behavior. However, if they like the opera and they receive tickets to the opera, this is registered as a caring behavior. Again, you should stress understanding the other's needs, both in pain and in care. The Caring Behaviors Exercise creates a sense of safety in the relationship that allows the hard work to be done without fear of losing connection. When conducting this session, become a willing participant in helping the couple enjoy the processes.

LECTURE FOUR: REROMANTICIZING YOUR RELATIONSHIP

Over the past three weeks, you have learned the following: a communication skill, the importance of safety in the relationship, and that Nature seems to have brought you together for a reason. Also, if we learn to cooperate with Nature by having empathy for each other, then growth and healing can occur. For this to happen, the most important ingredient is not love, but emotional safety. Emotional safety is the *real* number one. It's the soil in which the seed of love grows. And you have to make it safe for your partner in order for him or her to get on with his or her healing.

Remember that when it is dangerous, our old brain feels like it's going to die, and it defends itself through fighting, fleeing, playing dead or freezing, hiding, or submitting. When it's safe, we will play, nurture, and mate, and this is what you would like to do a lot of in your relationship. So how do you increase safety? By increasing pleasure! Experiencing pleasure in your life actually releases chemicals in your brain that give a sense of well-being, and so you want to have these chemicals flowing as much as possible.

But there is a catch, and it can be summed up in one sentence: your partner is *not* you! Remember, I told you that there are *three* parts in the brain. On one of those parts is a small button that we call the "care receptor." In order for your partner to feel cared for, you have to hit that receptor head-on. And you know when you have done this, because they tell you so. They "gush" and say, "Thaannk Yoouu!" or "This is just what I needed!" But we spend a lot of time missing this receptor. A typical indication of this is in the gifts or behaviors we give to our partners. In many cases, what we are giving them is what we actually want for ourselves.

Most people have things around their house that they bought for their partners and which remain unused. Does this sound familiar? Our house is littered with things that we never asked each other for such as an aquarium, a stained glass studio, and a portable CD player. It wasn't until we got the idea that we have to *listen* to our partners that we started *hearing* what it is they really need in order to feel cared for. So what you have to do is come up with a list of Target Behaviors. And that's the first thing we are going to do today. Your partner is going to give you a list of behaviors that, if you do them, will make him or her feel cared for and feel safe with you as a result.

I'm going to get you started on this exercise today and have you finish it as homework. Then I am going to talk to you about two other ways in which you can bring safety into the relationship. The nice part about what we are going to start today is that it doesn't require growth. It requires you to restart behaviors you probably once did in the relationship but have stopped over time. You will also receive specific information about your partner on how he or she feels cared for by you.

CARING BEHAVIORS EXERCISE

Keep in mind that couples presently do some things in the relationship that make their partners feel cared for. Too often, however, they don't do them enough, or they don't realize how special their behavior is to their partner—either because they are never told or because they're not listening when the partner thanks them.

The Caring Behaviors List

"Hit My Care Button"

In the first part of the exercise, you will be helping the couple develop a list of behaviors that each partner does now which, when they are done, makes each of them feel loved and cared for—behaviors that hit their care buttons. This session should be light and fun-filled, so it helps if you go in with a carefree and playful attitude.

Start by having each partner list one or two behaviors that fit this description. When they are done, have them each read the list to the other partner, using the Couples Dialogue to mirror back what they heard and validate that the behavior is special. You want them to understand that caring behaviors allow the partner to feel cared for, to feel special, and to experience other positive feelings. When they are finished reading their lists, encourage them to do these special behaviors more often so that the partner may continue to feel cared for in the relationship. Instruct them to add more items to the list for homework so each partner will have additional caring behaviors to choose from.

"You Don't Send Me Flowers Anymore"

When couples are in their early romantic stage, they often do many behaviors that make their partner feel special, such as making tea, opening doors, giving back rubs, or cooking gourmet dinners. As relationships move into power-struggle stages, these behaviors are often forgotten. The second part of the Caring Behaviors Exercise is designed to resurrect the behaviors that once brought caring feelings.

Have the couple list behaviors that their partner once did that made them feel cared for and which, if they were done again, would make them feel cared for once again. Be careful to guard against the couple who may try to use this as a weapon to prove the point that "he/she's [the partner] changed."

The idea of this part of the exercise is to make the couple aware of their earlier caring behaviors and the positive effect these behaviors had on the relationship. Again, have the couple dialogue their list, and encourage them to reinstate these behaviors. Remind them that by doing so they will bring safety into the relationship. This will enable them to begin to work toward healing each other's childhood wounds. Safety has to become a promise in the relationship, and caring behaviors create safety. Additional behaviors should be added as homework to give each partner more choices.

"Go Ahead . . . Make My Day"

The third part of the Caring Behaviors List gives the couple the opportunity to ask for caring behaviors they have not asked for because of fear or embarrassment. Some couples may not have anything to put on this list, but this will give them the opportunity to do so in the event they have kept things to themselves—especially out of fear. Expect anything from the mild to the outrageous, and be sure to give the couple the opportunity to dialogue about this at home if they are too embarrassed to do so in the session. Additional items can also be added and dialogued as homework.

LITTLE SURPRISES EXERCISE

The Little Surprises Exercise is more of a lecture to encourage caring behaviors at home that come off as a surprise, and it goes like this:

So you have the Caring Behaviors List, and let's say one of the behaviors is getting a cup of tea. So you get your partner a cup of tea, and the next day you get him or her a cup of tea, and the next day you get him or her a cup of tea, and the next day you get him or her a cup of tea. Although this is certainly nice, what has happened to the "gift" of a cup of tea? It becomes routine. It's similar to having an ice cream cone. You know how great that first lick tastes, but as you get to the end of the ice cream cone, it doesn't taste as good as the first lick, and you wonder why you even indulged in the unnecessary calories. So the solution to this is to have a lot of first licks. And the way to do this with caring behaviors is with surprise.

You want to get in the habit of having a lot of surprises in your relationship that can range anywhere from an affectionate note slipped into a briefcase to an unexpected dinner. Again, keep in mind that the surprise has to be something that your partner wants. A way to figure out what he or she wants is to listen for what we rather romantically call "random droppings." These are comments you'll hear your partner say all the time, but which you probably don't pay much attention to. You might be going through the mall, and you'll hear her say. "Those are nice earrings" or "I want to get this book one day." Make a note of this, and go back and buy it for her as a surprise. You cannot go wrong because you heard her say she wanted it, and she'll enjoy being surprised.

As a matter of fact, make the commitment to surprise each other once a month. Just the anticipation of the surprise can keep you on a happy edge.

Work on this with the couple for a few minutes. Encourage them to start a list of behaviors that might happily surprise their partner. Have them make the commitment to surprise each other at least once a month.

BELLY LAUGHS EXERCISE

This exercise is usually a lot of fun. Often when couples come to therapy, they've already quit having fun in their relationship. If you ask them when was the last time they had a good laugh together, many of them cannot remember. But laughter really is a great medicine. A sustained belly laugh releases endorphins into the brain—natural drugs that create a sense of well-being. Since there are very few ways of releasing endorphins naturally, other than through extreme exercise or an orgasm, it's best you stick with belly laughs in your office. Let the couple know that through the release of endorphins they will experience a sense of well-being. And when they have this sense of well-being, they will feel safe.

If they have their own way of creating a belly laugh, they are welcome to use it. I will offer a few suggestions here. Some couples may find them silly, and that's okay! Just be sure to encourage them. By the way, it helps if you can begin to loosen up and have fun with them as well.

1. **Butteryfly Kiss.** The couple face each other and get close enough to put their eyes together so that when the blink they are tickling each other with their lashes.

2. **Suck and Blow.** Ask one partner to take out a license or a credit card. If you suck on the card, it will stick to your mouth. The object of the game is for them to suck and blow the card back and forth between each other. Their mouths should be less than a half-inch apart, and while one sucks the card, the other blows it to them. The fun enters into play when they drop the card—they end up kissing! (Therefore, I don't recommend that you demonstrate this with the couple: they'll figure it out.)

3. **I Can Do That.** Have the couple stand across from each other. Have one partner make a body motion and say, "I can do this. Can you do this?" The other partner does this motion, adds another, and says, "I can do that. Can you do this?" The next partner adds a motion and says the same, and the game continues until they cannot add a motion and are—at this point—laughing at the silliness.

Caution: Belly laughs are contagious, and you may find yourself laughing along with the couple. Enjoy!

At the conclusion of these three exercises, you will be explaining one more homework assignment (Mutual Relationship Vision), but also strongly encourage the couple to follow through on all homework and add caring behaviors to their daily routine.

MUTUAL RELATIONSHIP VISION HOMEWORK

The couple are going to come up with a Mutual Relationship Vision (shown on p. 110 and located in the Homework/Handouts) in which they will be writing down what their "dream" marriage would look like. Sometimes when we write things down as a goal, we can make them come true. In the first part of the assignment each partner is to write down on the "My Dream Relationship" Worksheet his or her own dream marriage. Instruct them to write in the present tense and to start out with the word "We." For example: "We take walks together three times a week" or "We are financially secure." To give them additional ideas and suggestions, hand out the sample sheet of John and Jane Doe's Dream Relationship.

After they have written down their individual visions, they are to come together and dialogue about their visions, combining the items on which they agree. Then they are to write these combined items down on the third sheet: Our Dream Relationship. This combined vision is very similar to the business plan of a small company. If it is written down, the couple can treat the vision as a goal. Encourage them to post the vision in an easily visible place and to review it monthly until they have attained their dream marriage.

DAVE AND DIANA: SESSION FOUR

When Dave and Diana returned for the fourth session, they were promised a little fun. The last three weeks had been productive, yet emotionally draining for them. In a marriage, all work and no play makes for a very dull relationship that feels unsafe to the partners. Again, Session Four is about reinstating caring behaviors and creating safety through pleasurable activities. First, however, the therapist had to check homework.

They were able to finish the Partner-as-Parent and Holding Exercises with each "parent" as instructed. Diana wished she had more time to work on the homework because she felt she learned a lot. She said, "The big thing I learned is that I have a hard time being held. I can let people hold me, but I am not always present as they do this. I learned a lot from that." She also noticed an increase in her empathy for Dave. She recalled that previously if Dave shut himself off from her when she offered to help him, she would say, "Fine!" and storm off. This week when he did that, she stayed with him and said to herself, "He needs to be loved right now." Dave said he recognized when Diana did that and appreciated it.

Dave said he had a positive experience in using the process with Diana as his father. He said when she asked the first question, "What was it like to live with me?" he had an experience that was mostly cognitive. When she asked him, "What did he need from Father that he did not get?" things became very emotional. He was able to say a lot of things to Diana that he wished he could have said to his father and felt like he got a lot off his chest. The most surprising part for Dave was when Diana held him. He said that he felt an excitement that was indescribable. He said, "It felt so freeing."

Dave and Diana both asked a very typical question for this stage of the therapy: "Will this get easier and safer to do outside of the office?" Dave and Diana were experiencing one of the downfalls of short-term therapy—the fear of losing the feeling of therapeutic support once the sessions are completed. The therapist reassured them that while this is a hard process, if they commit to doing the work they are being taught, things would get easier.

For several years the atmosphere at home had become unsafe and a place where mean remarks and distancing were prevalent. It was unrealistic of them to think that this atmosphere would change overnight, but they could do it over time if they committed to the processes they were learning, thereby creating safety on a conscious level. It was important to validate their fear, and at the same time, give them hope in the processes they are learning.

The lecture about the importance of safety in the relationship was presented, with its suggestion that one way to increase safety is to increase pleasure. In Session Four Dave and Diana learned three ways to create pleasure. They began by making their Caring Behaviors List of things they used to do for each other, of things that they do now for each other, and of things they fantasized doing for each other that would make each feel loved and cared for. The therapist asked them to begin the list by writing down two behaviors under each sentence fragment and then finish the list for homework. As part of the session, they engaged in Couples Dialogue about the two behaviors. The therapist then reminded that this dialogue was to be fun.

Dave: I love when you acknowledge things I've done without my bringing it up.

Diana: So if I am hearing you correctly, you love it when I acknowledge things you have done without having to point it out. Did I get that?

Dave: Yes. It makes me feel appreciated and worthy. As though I did not do it for the acknowledgment.

Diana: So when I acknowledge you, you feel like you did not do it for the acknowledgment and you feel appreciated and worthy. Can you tell me more about worthy?

Dave: Yeah. . . . Making me feel worthy lets me know that things are worth doing. It's knowing that I did it for me, partially, and not for someone else. Yet having it acknowledged gives it an extra plus.

Diana: So when I make you feel worthy, it lets you know that things are worth doing. You know that you did it for you and not because you felt like you had to do it for someone else. Having things acknowledged gives what you do an extra plus. Did I get that?

Dave: Yeah. It kind of lets me know that I did it without having to do it. I did it and it was accepted and appreciated. I never got that.

Diana: So being acknowledged without calling attention to what you did lets you know that you did it without having to do it. It was accepted and appreciated and you never got that as a kid.

Therapist: Can you validate that?

Diana: I can really validate that! I think it is really cool! You look happy and sound happy to share that with me.

Dave: You got it!

Therapist: Nice! Dave, are you ready to hear Diana's caring behavior?

Dave: Sure!

Diana: Okay. I feel loved and cared about when you come up behind me and hug me. It must feel safe because I really love when you do that.

Dave: So you really love and feel cared about when I come up behind you and hug you. It feels safe to you.

Diana: Yeah. As I said that, I realized that it must feel comfortable to me because I don't have to give anything back. I just receive. It's not like me having to hold you too. So in getting hugged that way, I feel that I am just in receiving.

Dave: So when I hug you from behind, it feels safe because you do not have to hug back. You are just in receiving and you feel loved and cared for. I can understand that and I imagine that you do feel safe and that you do feel cared for by me.

Diana: Yeah. It's safer for some reason.

Dave and Diana spent the next 25 minutes going over and dialoguing about the list they created. They were educating each other on behaviors that created safety and caring in their marriage. Dave and Diana learned that in a conscious marriage, caring behaviors are important, and it is equally important to give to the partner the caring behaviors that each needs in order to feel loved and cared about. Performing the behaviors as outlined in the Caring Behaviors List was essential.

The rest of the list would have to be developed as homework—a list of 15 to 20 behaviors that they wanted the partner to give to him or her in order to feel loved and cared for. The therapist instructed them to give the partner at least one caring behavior a day, even if they did not feel up to it. This simple act would begin to increase the safety in the relationship.

However, as we know, adding safety and pleasure to the relationship will take more work than engaging in caring behaviors. Pleasure seems to need variety; otherwise it becomes routine. The therapist suggested that they pepper their days with new experiences—"surprises." Surprises cause what we call "gush" reactions: "Oh, this is great! I love it." The therapist told them to try for the "It's just what I wanted!" reaction because that's what a good surprise does.

If Dave, the engineer, surprises Diana, the graphics artist, with a cellular phone, he might get a disappointing reaction. But if he purchases her the original work of art she had her eye on while on a recent shopping trip, he is more likely to get a gush reaction. Likewise, if Diana surprises Dave with tickets to the theater, she might get a mediocre reaction. However, if she gives him the gift of the latest game software for his computer, she will likely hear "It is just what I wanted!" They needed to listen to and observe what the other would enjoy as a surprise. They were to make a commitment to each other to surprise the other at least once a month.

For the next 10 minutes of the session, Dave and Diana experienced another method of creating safety and pleasure in their relationship: high-energy fun or belly laughs. The only rules is that there were no rules except for the activity to be pleasurable to both of them. And in this session, it was.

Dave and Diana played and laughed hard with each other. A quick game of "I Can Do That!" produced hilarious body movements and uncontrollable laughs. This was followed by a game of "Suck and Blow," which had both Dave and Diana holding their sides for few minutes.

When they completed their laugh, Dave and Diana passed a prolonged smile. They commented how it had been a long time since they had a good laugh together. They knew immediately that they had to do it more often and they were given instructions by the therapist to do just that. Belly laughs should happen once a day with a couple. Dave and Diana commented about how hard that would be to accomplish, but they recognized that they had to try.

A belly laugh may take 5 minutes or less and is a behavior that should be used to replace criticism. It is a behavior that creates a sense of pleasure and well-being and lets the reptilian brain relearn that the situation is safe. And when the reptilian brain learns this, it will let the person play, nurture, have sex, work, and be creative. Safety is something Dave and Diana now want to strive for in their marriage.

HANDOUT INSTRUCTIONS FOR THE THERAPIST

SESSION FOUR

Examples of the handouts are shown on p. 110.

1. Caring Behaviors List

This sheet should be given out following the Reromanticizing the Relationship lecture. The couple will begin work with you on this handout and will be given instructions to complete it for homework. The full instructions for this list can be found in the text under "Caring Behaviors Exercise." It is important for the couple to know that they should each have a fairly extensive list of caring behaviors to give to his or her partner, and they should also spend time dialoguing their lists in a safe, possibly romantic setting. The object is to give each other a long list of behavior choices; if any one behavior was performed, the partner would feel loved and cared about. At any point, more items can be added to the list.

2. Mutual Relationship Vision: Dream Relationship Worksheets

This handout consist of three pages that are given to the couple at the end of the session for homework. The first is the My Dream Relationship Worksheet, which is basically a sheet that each partner uses to record ideas concerning his or her "ideal" marriage. Ask the couple to write this in the present tense, as if they have this ideal marriage already, and tell them to begin each sentence with the pronoun. "We." Give them the second sheet, John and Jane Doe's Dream Relationship as an example.

After each has compiled large individual lists, instruct them to come together to dialogue their two lists in an effort to compile them into one list, Our Dream Relationship, if possible. Have them dialogue each of their hopes individually and, if there is agreement, place them on the blank sheet, Our Dream Relationship Worksheet. Upon completion, the couple should have about 15 items that would describe their ideal marriage. This list should be placed somewhere visible in the couple's home and reviewed at least once a month using Couples Dialogue to remind them of the direction they hope to take their relationship.

3. Homework Instructions for Session Four

This sheet should be given to the couple at the end of the session. It instructs them to complete the Caring Behaviors List. The couple should also be instructed to perform one of the caring behaviors daily in an effort to get them used to the importance of these behaviors in the relationship. They are also instructed to have at least three belly laughs or to participate in some high-energy-fun game (e.g., Not-it, Simon Says, Patty-cake. Finally, they are instructed to complete their Mutual Relationship Vision: Our Dream Relationship Worksheet) and post it somewhere visible. Be sure to remind the couple to keep track of the number of times they have performed each homework task by checking the list on the homework page.

Caring Behaviors List

"Hit My Care Button." The things you do now that "hit my care button" and make me feel loved and cared about are . . .

_____
_____
_____
_____
_____
_____

"You Don't Send Me Flowers Anymore." The things you used to do that "hit my care button" and made me feel loved and cared about are . . .

_____
_____
_____
_____
_____
_____
_____

"Go Ahead . . . Make My Day." There are some things that I always wanted to ask you to do that would make me feel cared about and loved, but I have been afraid to ask. (Some typical fears are being needy, outrageous, kinky, extravagant, perverted, disgusting, sentimental, or selfish.)

I am afraid of appearing . . .	But I will manage my fear and ask you to express your care and love by . . .

Mutual Relationship Vision: My Dream Relationship Worksheet

Working by yourself, write down in the space below all the things you would like in your relationship that would make it a perfect relationship. Start each sentence with the pronoun "We" and write each dream in the present tense as if you already have it.

_____
_____
_____
_____
_____
_____
_____
_____
_____
_____
_____
_____
_____
_____
_____
_____
_____
_____
_____
_____
_____
_____
_____
_____

Mutual Relationship Vision: Our Dream Relationship Worksheet

Working together, using the information from your Dream Relationship Worksheet, design your mutually agreed upon dream relationship. Start each line with "We" and write each dream in the present tense as if you already have it. If you have an item you do not agree upon, skip it. This exercise should be fun and filled with hope. When completed, talk about it using Couples Dialogue, place it in a conspicuous place, and read it together once a month.

Our Dream Relationship

_____
_____
_____
_____
_____
_____
_____
_____
_____
_____
_____
_____
_____
_____

HOMEWORK INSTRUCTIONS FOR SESSION FOUR

1. Complete the Caring Behaviors List we started in today's session. Make the list exhaustive and review it with your partner using Couples Dialogue.

2. Do at least one of the caring behaviors on your partner's list at least once a day. Remember, pleasure equals safety and you are trying to make the relationship safe. Caring behaviors change the atmosphere of the relationship which, in turn, will promote growth.

3. Have at least three belly laughs or high-energy fun activities this week, even if they are staged.

4. Work on your Mutual Relationship Vision this week. Go over it with your partner before the next session using Couples Dialogue. Post it somewhere visible and review monthly. Believe in it and it can happen.

HOME EXERCISE SESSION FOUR	Day 1	Day 2	Day 3	Day 4	Day 5	Day 6	Day 7
1. Complete and Review Caring List							
2. One Caring Behavior Daily							
3. Belly Laughs/High Energy Fun (3× per week)							
4. Complete Mutual Relationship Vision (Review 1× per month)							

Thought for the Week:

How do you increase Safety?
By Increasing Pleasure!

7

SESSION FIVE

Restructuring Frustrations

SUGGESTED TIME FRAME

Checking homework	5 minutes
"Blueprints for Growth" Lecture	15 minutes
Behavior Change Request Process	35 minutes
Assigning homework	5 minutes

GOALS

1. To emphasize to the couple the importance of safety in restructuring frustrations.

2. To make the point that frustrations are desires stated negatively.

3. To have the couple fully understand that their frustrations with each other correspond directly with parts of themselves that are "lost," and they are now being given the opportunity to reclaim these lost parts.

4. To have the couple understand the phrase, "Your partner has the blueprint for your growth" and that the sender's list of Behavior Change Requests being developed is the receiver's blueprint.

5. To emphasize that change is slow and not easy and that giving one's partner what is needed is healing to the partner and, at the same time, part of his or her lost self.

STARTING THE SESSION

Couples experience frustrations with each other every day. Some of these are minor, such as the annoyance that one partner may feel when the other forgets to put a dish away. Some are major, such as the agitation that one partner experiences when the other stays out all night. The problem is not that the couple have frustrations; on the contrary, frustrations can often be "mile markers" for growth, as we will show later. The problem is that couples, without even knowing what their frustrations are about, present them to each other in a way that they are each unable to hear. In this session, you will help the couple understand the real source of their frustrations, and you will teach them to phrase the frustrations in such a way that they can not only hear each other, but also can make a behavior change accordingly.

You will begin this session by checking the homework from the last session. Look over each partner's Caring Behaviors List to make sure there are enough behaviors listed so that the sending partner has ample choices. Ask them about their dialogue on the caring behaviors and then inquire about the belly laughs they had this week. After spending 5 minutes checking their homework, present this week's lecture.

ABOUT THE LECTURE

This is a very important lecture to help the couple understand that marriages are about personal growth and becoming "whole." Many couples observe that they have made no changes in behavior, yet, and in part, they are right. In Imago Therapy, we believe that you cannot change a behavior until you fully understand your partner's need for you to change the behavior. Otherwise, the change is coercive and typically short-lived. If, however, the receiving partner can understand the sending partner's need for a behavior change empathically, there is a more understanding attitude toward the changes. Added to that, if the receiving partner understands that by stretching into the new behavior requested by the sending partner he or she grows, too, the request begins to have a purpose and to make sense for his or her individual growth.

It has been said that opposites attract. But we have often seen couples where both partners like biking, hiking, the same breed of dogs, playing cards, or they both have brown hair and blue eyes! So it is not so much that couples have opposite traits or interests as it is that they have opposite ways of expressing themselves. The lecture emphasizes that the socialization process asks family members to give up certain ways of expressing themselves to live in a family—be it thinking, acting, feeling, or sensing. The process of romantic love and the power struggle has taught us that partners fall in love with the parts they were told to turn off in their childhood. To reach our full potential, we need all four ways of expressing ourselves. Partners in committed, conscious relationships can lead each other back to wholeness with full use of all expressive parts.

This lecture and exercise will help the couple understand that the places where the partner is most frustrated with him or her is the place that he or she most needs to develop. You will emphasize to the couple that the frustrations will need to be reworded so that the receiving partner can hear them—through desires and requests. These desires and requests will become the Blueprint for Growth for the receiving partner.

LECTURE FIVE: BLUEPRINTS FOR GROWTH

In the last session, we did some work that helped you feel safe in the relationship, and this is good because today is when the growth begins. You'll recall that we view relationships as a growth experience—but what are we trying to grow into?

Going back to the first session, we said that we are energy from that Big Bang of 15 billion years ago. Our energy, or potential, expresses itself in four ways: through our thinking, our actions, our feelings, and our "sensing." When we think, we are using and expressing our logical energy. When we act on something, we expend a physical energy. Our feelings represent an energy inside us and, when we sense, we try to understand the energy outside of ourselves, or what some might call intuition. Sensing people are also aware of their bodies.

When we are children, our parents usually discourage two of these energy expressions. They may say, "Don't think!" "That's a stupid idea!" "Girls don't think!" "Quit thinking!" or they may ignore our thoughts—and we might lose that means of expressing our energy. This doesn't mean that we cannot think; more likely, the main way we express ourselves may not be through our thinking. Think of the blind person whose hearing and feeling becomes sharper in order to compensate for the lack of sight.

When our parents reinforce the same messages over and over again, such as, "Don't do anything!" "You can't do anything right!" or "Just sit there, I'll do that!" or ignore our abilities we may lose our ability to do things. They may say, "Don't feel!" "Boys don't feel!" or "Don't feel that way!" or do not validate our feelings and we lose our energy expression of feeling. Or they may say, "Don't trust your gut!" "Who cares what you are sensing; we want to know what you think about this!" and we lose our ability to sense. Although we lose parts of ourselves, we adapt and are able to develop other abilities.

What do you think happens to these children when they get older? They marry each other! The Thinker/Doer marries the Senser/Feeler. Or the Thinker/Feeler marries the Doer/Senser. Or the Thinker/Senser marries the Doer/Feeler. And at first this is great! The Thinker/Doer sees the Senser/Feeler and says, "Oh, my gosh! She feels so deeply. I love how passionate she is about things." And the Feeler/Senser says, "He's so smart! He owns and manages three businesses!" And we fall in love with these parts that we're missing in ourselves.

Keep in mind that our gender is not necessarily a factor in determining which parts we're lacking. Men can be Sensers/Feelers, for instance, and women can be Thinkers/Doers. In our culture, however, we tend to socialize boys to think and do, and girls to feel and nurture. In truth, we need to socialize people to do all four, and to do so we have to reclaim those missing parts for ourselves so that we can at last be "whole"—having all four parts available to us as means of expressing our energy.

But what happens to those parts that we once loved in our partner? After a while, we actually begin to resent them! We start to say things like, "Quit feeling! You're so oversensitive!" Or we'll say, "You insensitive jerk! Why does everything have to be logical! Quit working so hard, and spend some time with me!" Why does this happen? Because the part our partner has and uses begins to "tickle" the very part we were told to turn off. You see, it's not that we don't have the part, we just don't use it as fully as our partner does. When our partner does too much and expects more out of us, that might tickle the acting part and go against the "don't **do**—you can't **do** anything right!" messages we received as children. In many cases, the only way we know to make the tickle stop is to scream at that part of our partner: "Quit **do**ing so much!" Similarly, maybe our partner's feelings stir up the part in us that was told not to feel, so we scream, "Quit feeling!" to keep the partner from making us anxious. But in truth, the part that we've been screaming at is *exactly the part we need to reclaim in ourselves in order for us to become "whole."*

How do we know what to do to reclaim these parts? Try listening, because your partner has been screaming it at you all along! And herein lies the problem: we cannot hear a scream. When someone screams at us our old brain becomes defensive, and we cannot take in what's being said. But if your partner has been screaming at you, "You insensitive jerk! Can't you feel?" chances are you need to reclaim your feelings. Likewise, if he or she had said, "This is nothing to cry about. Just think it through!" your thinking is probably your lost part.

This is one of Nature's little secrets: our partner has the blueprint for our growth. The trick is for the partner to present it to us in a way that we can hear, and that's what we are going to start today with the exercise. Before we begin, keep two things in mind: we're only going to *start* it today, the rest will be assigned as homework; and what we will be doing will not change your partner. It will, however, educate your partner about your needs in a way that he or she can hear. If your partner is able to "stretch" to do the behavior, he or she will be able to meet your needs and—as a bonus—will reclaim a part of himself or herself that had been lost. Today, you will begin the process of giving your partner the blueprint for his or her growth. In turn, you will receive your blueprint.

BEHAVIOR CHANGE REQUEST PROCESS

This exercise will teach couples how to take their frustrations and list them in a way that their partner can not only hear, but also can do something about. We believe that behind every frustration is a desire that needs to be expressed. If the frustration can be changed into a positive desire, it can usually be heard by the partner. The exercise will then go one step further by taking the list of desires and changing it into a list of specific Behavior Change Requests. Behavior Change Requests (BCRs) are positive, "doable" behaviors that—if done by the partner—will heal a wound or give that partner what he or she needs to grow.

But there *is* a catch! The behaviors that one asks of the partner are always the hardest for that partner to do. For instance, a partner may desire "I want you to understand my feelings with me" and give a BCR of "When I'm feeling sad, I'd like you to sit with me and hold me while I cry. I would like you to mirror back to me what it is that you suppose I am feeling." A request such as this would most likely be given to the partner who is the Thinker/Doer—a person who usually *runs* from such feelings. Thus, it's important to encourage the Thinker/Doer to do the BCR—to "stretch" into the part that has been turned off in his or her childhood.

Remember to tell couples that what their partner is giving them in this BCR list is their very own Blueprint for Growth. The requests on the list will be difficult for them to do, yet it is what their partner needs and *it is what they need to do* to reclaim the parts of themselves that have been turned off.

This is not to say that the BCR list should be considered a "have-to" list. On the contrary, it's actually a gift list! Couples don't *have* to do these behaviors for their partners; however, if they *do* do them, they'll give their partners what they need—and they themselves will grow. Keep in mind that growth is not mandatory. Growth can only come when we give it as a gift, without expecting anything in return. This is what we call *unconditional love*. When we give and expect something in return, that's not a gift at all—that's a trade.

Starting the Exercise

Your first task in this session will be to make a decision. Included in the handouts are two ways to conduct the Behavior Change Request Exercise. Use the Restructuring Negative Behaviors form for those couples you suspect may not be psychologically minded—who do not want to deal with deep feelings or childhood wounds. For those couples who understand the concepts you have delivered, are in touch with feelings, and understand how one person's behavior affects another, use the Restructuring Frustrations form. This form is more complete and tends to encourage the deeper feelings to be discussed during this session. This is the form of choice for most couples.

Frustration Ladder

In this session, you will have the couple get started in the work and assign the rest as homework. All couples, whether using the Restructuring Negative Behaviors or Restructuring Frustrations form, start with the Frustration Ladder. On it they will be ranking their frustrations from 1 to 10, with 10 being the mildest frustration. For this session, tell them to jot down two mild frustrations on lines 9 and 10; they will complete the rest at home. The purpose of the Frustration Ladder is to help the couple organize their frustrations in a visibly structured manner. They do not have to show the partner their list.

Restructuring Negative Behaviors Form

After the couple have written down their frustrations, work with them on changing these to a desire. For example, "I hate when you are late" can be changed to "I want you to be on time." It's much easier to *hear* a desire; for most couples, a desire does not signal the brain to become defensive. Have them write it down on the Restructuring Negative Behaviors form. Give them the Sample Restructuring Negative Behaviors form for reference.

Next, go a little further by taking the desire and making it a specific Behavior Change Request. The desire "I want you to be on time" more specifically becomes "I would like you to be home within 15 minutes of the time that you say you are going to be home. If you are going to be more than 15 minutes late, I would like you to pull over and call me to let me know. I would like you to do this 80 percent of the time." The reason for adding a percentage or stating how many times a week, and so on, is that you do not want to set the request up as a failure. Remember, requests are given as *gifts*, and the one giving the gift should not be set up to fail. The request should be written on the Restructuring Negative Behaviors form.

Now that the frustrations have been changed and written into a positive, measurable, and doable behavior, have each partner read his or her BCR using Couples Dialogue to discuss the request. Let receiving partners know that the behavior they will hear will likely push against their adaptation and they will feel uncomfortable hearing it. It is important for them to maintain their safety and mirror back so that the sending partners know they are being heard. At this point, they are not making a commitment to perform the behavior but are only committing to hearing the request and to understanding the sender's point of view on their need for the change.

The couple should be given the instructions to continue their lists for homework and dialogue several requests with the partner. This homework may cause tense moments, so tell the couple to deal with all feelings with Couples Dialogue.

Restructuring Frustrations Form

This form seems more complicated but flows in such a way that it gives a partner a deeper understanding of the other's frustration. It is also very convenient for the couple to dialogue and gives more choices of behavior changes for the receiving partner.

Hand the couple the Sample Restructuring Frustrations form to follow along, as well as several blank forms. Begin by having each partner pick a frustration from the Frustration Ladder and have them transfer it to Box 1 (write Frustrating Event) on the Restructuring Frustrations form.

Tell the couple that when Partner 1 behaves in this way, it causes Partner 2 to feel a certain way. Ask them to write down the feeling they experience when their partner behaves in this way in Box 2 (write Feeling Response). Remind them that feelings are one word and that a person can experience several feelings at one time.

When people experience a feeling, they will typically behave in a certain way. Have them write down their behavioral response to the feeling experienced in Box 3 (write Behavioral Response).

Tell the couple that people usually behave in certain ways because of an underlying fear. Ask them to take a moment to determine what their hidden fear is and write it in Box 4 (write Hidden Fear). It may take the couple a moment to think about this because this may be the first time they are hearing this information. When couples are given a moment to think, they recognize that they may react to the partner's lateness because they fear they will be left alone. In another scenario, they react to their partner's telling them what to do because they fear they will be smothered when the partner makes all of their decisions. In still another scenario, they have strong feelings when their work is not appreciated because they have fears of becoming invisible and ineffective.

At this point, the partners begin the process of changing the frustrations into desires. Recalling that a frustration is a desire stated negatively, have the couple convert their frustrations into desires that are worded positively and write them in Box 5 (Desire).

Finally, have the couple develop three positive and doable BCRs based on the desire and write them in the three boxes on the bottom of the Restructuring Frustrations form. All of the requests should relate to the frustration being addressed. The reason for three requests is to give the receiving partner a choice of behaviors they can change in order to positively affect the sender's desire. Also, when the couple have converted all ten frustrations on the Frustration Ladder into BCRs, this form gives them 30 behavior choices they can work on to meet the partner's needs and begin the process of reclaiming their lost parts.

After the couple have completed the Restructuring Frustrations form and you have checked to make sure that the behaviors are positive and doable, have each take a turn dialoguing their requests. Starting with Box 1, have them each dialogue one box at a time like in the example below:

Partner 1: I get frustrated when you come home late.

Partner 2: So if I am getting this right, you get frustrated when I come home late. Is there more?

Partner 1: Yes, it makes me feel scared and angry when you come home late.

Partner 2: So if I am hearing you correctly, you feel scared and angry when I get home late. Did I get that?

The couple should continue this format until they have dialogued the entire Restructuring Frustrations forms. You may not have time for both partners to dialogue their individual sheets. If that is the case, assign the rest for homework and also tell them to dialogue several more Restructuring Frustrations forms this week.

There is more to a BCR than seeking a change in behavior. What you will notice is that most of the requests on couples' lists are the hardest for their partners to do. The request of "calling if you are going to be late" may be difficult for someone who was overprotected or smothered as a child; it may, however, be made by someone who felt ignored or abandoned as a child. It's important that the couple connect the request to a wound or an area of needed growth. At this point, the empathy skills that were developed in Session Three will come in handy.

You'll also begin to notice that the requests correspond to an area of growth needed in the giving partner, such as the person who *feels* will ask his or her *Thinking* partner to listen to those feelings. This is very hard for the Thinker to do, but—by stretching into this behavior—he or she will gain the part that was turned off in childhood. You will never see a request by a Feeler for the Thinker to *think* more, nor will you see a request by a

Thinker for the Feeler to *feel* more. The couple's frustrations lie in the parts of each other that are turned off. The BCR list is one partner's blueprint for the other one's growth. If partners give the desired behavior, they will regain the part of themselves that was lost.

A very important point to emphasize is that couples should not expect changes overnight. Change takes place slowly—often over many years. If they try to do the behaviors all at once, the effects will be similar to a crash diet: it works for a while, but you wind up gaining back all the weight. The idea of this exercise is to educate couples about each other's needs and about the areas where they as a couple need growth. Sometimes the resistance to change is strong, and they'll each say, "I cannot do that!" Assure the couple that it is not that *they cannot* do the behavior change, but that they are responding to an *adaptation* that tells them they cannot do it. The key is stretching into the new behavior—to heal the wounds and bring about growth.

The session ends with the assignment of homework, with special emphasis on both the idea of *educating* one's partner and on the fact that change will not happen overnight. Finally, on the chart provided on the homework sheet, have the couple put a mark alongside that area of behavior that may need to be stretched into in order to accomplish the request that the partner wishes. This lets partners know where they might experience difficulty in doing a behavior, and it identifies that part of themselves they will be able to reclaim by doing the stretch.

DAVE AND DIANA: SESSION FIVE

The session started off with the therapist asking Dave and Diana about the homework. They immediately smiled and began to talk about their week in which they consciously gave each other small gifts and appreciations. They smiled as they told the therapist about how this changed the feeling in their house and how this makes them look forward to being home. They also talked about the three belly laughs they had this week.

In the fifth session it seemed like a good time to do a temperature check on Dave and Diana. Diana quickly stated that the work they were doing in their marriage had been seeping into other relationships—their son, friends, and colleagues. She said, "I am now honoring differences, even in other relationships. Rather than walking out on someone when we have differences, I hang in there and recognize that we are different. This has made a big difference in my marriage and in all my relationships." Dave added, "It is like they say, 'Marriage is work. If you want to be married, you have to work at it.' And that means acceptance of the parts of people you don't like."

Diana then summed up the changes she had experienced as, "We have made it safer. The safety we created is a good base to go out from. Before we did not have a base. I know my safety level is increasing and I find that makes a difference. Even though it is being challenged now because I am reaching out, I've made a base." Dave and Diana seemed well on their way to creating a safe and conscious marriage.

It is good that Dave and Diana have created that base of safety because Session Five tends to be quite a challenge to couples. This is the session in which they start to make changes. Up to this point, the therapy has not "fixed" anything. There has been no negotiation, compromises, or requests to act on frustrations. The sessions and the homework have been purposeful. To fix anything, Dave and Diana needed to learn to listen and to talk. They needed to learn to understand each other and the childhood drama that brought them to this point. They needed to develop empathy. Empathy for each other will allow Dave and Diana to make changes because they want to and because they understand that their partner's requests for change are really about growth. With empathy and understanding, Dave and Diana will not feel coerced.

The therapist lectured Dave and Diana on Blueprints for Growth—the four ways people use to express their energy or selves. Diana decided that she was the Feeler and Senser, while Dave determined that he was the Thinker and Doer. Their frustrations began to make sense to them when they recognized that their frustrations with each other tended to be around the lost parts of the other.

Diana tended to get frustrated because Dave did not understand her feelings and he seemed cold in his dealings with her. Seldom did she tell him that he does not think enough or do enough in a day. Dave's frustration with Diana, on the other hand, centered around Diana's tendency to not think things through, and he thought she was too emotional. He often wanted her to do something about her problems, but Dave never asked Diana to feel more or to use her intuition on a matter.

Through this lecture, Dave and Diana started to understand the idea that "your partner has the blueprint for your growth," and that the blueprint is buried in their frustrations with each other. Couples cannot hear a frustration because it calls up the reptilian brain, but in this session Dave and Diana were able to begin the process of turning their frustrations into desires. The therapist told them to remember that "a frustration is a desire stated negatively."

"I hate it when you are late" becomes "My desire is for you to be on time." "I hate it when you leave the refrigerator door open" becomes "My desire is for you to close the refrigerator door." Desires are easier to hear. To accomplish this, the therapist took them step by step through the Behavior Change Request Process.

They began with the Frustration Ladder. The therapist instructed each of them to write down two mild frustrations on each of their sheets. Again, the Frustration Ladder is used only to help the couple organize their frustrations to get a picture of the most annoying and least annoying traits that they find in each other. The therapist encouraged them to address the least annoying frustrations first and to wait several weeks or even months to go after the most annoying, or they will face certain disappointment. It was also important for them to know that they were only beginning the process of learning the BCR Process in this session and they were expected to finish the Frustration Ladder as well as the other accompanying forms for homework.

After Dave and Diana wrote down two frustrations each, the therapist explained, step-by-step, the form for Restructuring Frustrations. The therapist chose this form because Dave and Diana were eager participants who easily dealt with emotional issues. They worked quietly and diligently as they worked separately on their forms. The therapist took them through each block one at a time and then took time to check what they wrote. The therapist was looking to make sure that Dave and Diana wrote their requests in words that were positive, doable, measurable, and achievable. The therapist also looked for negative words such as "stop," "don't," and "not." Such words tend to activate the reptilian brain.

This is the time for the therapist to be picky because this first form becomes the model for the Restructuring forms that will be completed by the couple. If Dave and Diana completed the assignment in terms that were negative or indicated behaviors that were not achievable, chances are that all other forms would be completed in this negative manner and their behavior requests would become other sources of frustration, rather than the blueprint for growth. The therapist explained this pickiness to Dave and Diana, and they were willing participants in the effort to make sure that their statements were positive and the behavior requests were achievable.

At about 35 minutes into the session, Dave and Diana were ready to begin the dialogue process for their Behavior Change Requests. The therapist reminded them that the session was not about changing each other. Rather it was about educating the other person about the behavior he or she needed to do that would meet the needs, end the frustration, and at the same time create a new behavior that would produce growth for the receiving partner. In Session Five, they were beginning a process that would take years to accomplish, but would produce growth if they gave each other what they each respectively needed.

The therapist instructed Dave and Diana to dialogue, box by box, Diana's Restructuring Frustrations form (see Exhibit 7.1).

Diana: My frustration is when we are going somewhere, you are always uptight.

Dave: So you get frustrated when we are going somewhere and I am uptight. Did I get that?

Diana: Yes. It brings up a lot of emotions. First I get scared, then I get rigid inside, then I feel controlled and judged.

Dave: So you have lots of emotions about this. You feel scared, rigid, and uptight.

Diana: And controlled.

Dave: And controlled.

Exhibit 7.1 Restructuring Frustrations (Diana)

1. Write Frustrating Event
What you do that frustrates me is…

> What Actually Happened
>
> When we go somewhere and you are uptight when we are getting ready.

2. Write Feeling Response
And I then feel …

> Emotions—Feelings
>
> Scared
> Controlled
> Judged.

4. Write Hidden Fear
to hide my fear of…

> Fear Your Response Hide
>
> I fear that my scatteredness is coming out.

3. Write Behavioral Response
and what I do is…

> What You Actually Do
>
> get angry, uptight
> get distant from you

5. Hidden Desires
My desires from you are…

> Desire
>
> My desire is for you to acknowledge the time it takes for me to get ready and give me some credit.

To obtain my desires, I would like to request from you…

> **1. Behavior Change Request**
>
> For the next 2 months, I would like for you to tell me by noon in a dialogue process what your time needs are.

> **2. Behavior Change Request**
>
> 4 times this month, a half hour before we start getting ready to go somewhere, I would like to dialog about our feelings for the evening.

> **3. Behavior Change Request**
>
> For the next 2 months, if I am late, I would like for you to dialogue your frustration with me after we return so I can enjoy getting ready - 50% of the time.

Diana: It feels like you are judging me because I am not organized enough, so my fear is that my scatteredness is coming out.

Dave: So you are say . . . I'm confused.

Diana: I feel judged that you say that I'm not organized.

Dave: If I am getting that, you are saying that you feel judged when I say you are not organized.

Diana: And I have a fear that my scatteredness is coming out.

Dave: So you have a fear that your scatteredness is coming out.

Therapist: And that reminds me of my childhood.

Diana: Yeah. When I was a kid, I was not good enough. I was not doing something right.

Dave: So when you were a kid, you never felt good enough and it felt like you were always doing something wrong.

Diana: Yeah, and there are some other hard things to talk about such as why I had to be scattered in my family.

Dave: So there are some other reasons that are hard to talk about such as why you had to become scattered in your family to live there.

Diana: Yes. So I get angry and I tighten up. Then I get real distant from you.

Dave: If I am getting that, you get angry and tighten up. This causes you to get real distant from me.

Diana: And my desire is for you to acknowledge the time it takes me to get ready and give me some credit.

Dave: So your desire is for me to acknowledge the time it takes for you to get ready and give you some credit.

Diana: Yes. So my first request to you is, for the next two months, in a dialogue process four days a week, I would like you to tell me by noon what your needs are concerning time.

Dave: So you would like for me over the next two months to tell you by noon what my needs are about time. You would like me to do that four days a week.

Diana: Yeah. The second is four times this month, about a half hour before we start getting ready to go somewhere, I would like to dialogue about our feelings for the evening, feelings about going somewhere, and about our expectations for the evening.

Dave: So four times this month, a half hour before we start getting ready to go somewhere, you would like for us to dialogue about our feelings about going out and our expectations for the evening. Did I get that?

Diana: Yes.

Dave: (*to therapist*) Can we negotiate this? (*chuckles*)

Therapist: Not yet. Hear her request.

Diana: My third request is that for the next two months, if I am late, I would like for you to dialogue your frustration with me *after* we return and give me the time before going out to enjoy getting ready 50 percent of the time.

Dave: So for the next two months, if you are late, you would like for me to dialogue my frustration about your being late after we return so that you can enjoy getting ready. You would like for me to do this half of the time you are late. Did I get it?

Diana: Yes.

Therapist: Okay. Breathe out. (*They chuckle.*) Dave, that tenseness you are feeling is the request pushing on your adaptations. Diana is asking you to share your feelings and that's what is turned off in you.

Dave: Yeah, I really get that because I want to think this through.

Therapist: And for your growth, you will need to follow Diana's directive. Her requests are bringing you into your feelings. Can you commit to any one request?

Dave: I could do the midday one. I'll think about the others.

Dave and Diana had their first experience with restructuring their frustrations into achievable Behavior Change Requests. The frustration that Diana worked on in the session was now organized, defined, and written in such a way that Dave can respond. Over the next few weeks, they would fill out ten more Restructuring Frustration forms in an effort to organize their frustrations and educate each other in the areas of change needed for them to meet their needs. In the process, each partner will receive the blueprint for his or her growth, and thereby the blueprint for marital growth. If they follow through, Dave and Diana's marriage will become a vehicle for reclaiming their expressive parts that were lost in childhood.

HANDOUT INSTRUCTIONS FOR THE THERAPIST

Examples of handouts are shown on p. 128.

SESSION FIVE

This session requires you to copy many forms, but it is important because this is the session where behavior changes begin. You will need to make enough copies of the Restructuring Negative Behaviors forms or the Restructuring Frustrations forms for the couple so that they leave with some blank ones to make their own copies. Suggest that they make at least 20 copies so they can work on 10 behaviors each.

1. Socialization and Mate Selection

Use this form when you are presenting the Blueprint for Growth lecture to give the couple a visual portrayal of what you are saying. Each of the circles, which represent two people, has a section marked "Thinking," "Acting," "Feeling," and "Sensing." You will be delivering a lecture describing how to live in a family; members are typically asked to give up two ways of expressing themselves. For example, if you are talking about having to give up thinking, with phrases such as "Don't think," "That's a dumb idea," "Girls don't think," use a pen on the left circle and put a mark across "Thinking" to represent an area given up and used very little. Do the same to "Acting" on that circle to represent the partner being asked to turn that part off. When talking about Feeling and Sensing, cross out those sections on the other circle. The figure should now represent two people with only two ways of expressing themselves. Give the couple a minute to decide if this best represents them or if they are a different combination. For homework, tell the couple to take the form to dialogue about its significance in their relationship.

2. Behavior Change Request forms

There are three sheets that are used to help the couple through the Behavior Change Request Process. As explained earlier in the chapter, there are two ways to complete the BCR. Use the Restructuring Negative Behaviors form if you are short on time or if you suspect that the couple will only complete the minimum work necessary in their therapy. Use the Restructuring Frustrations forms for couples who are willing to take the time to do deeper emotional work and are willing to look at how their childhoods influenced their behavioral adaptations and their frustrations. You can give them both versions, but it is best to have them experience only one and use that same version for the remainder of their requests.

a. Frustration Ranking

The Frustration Ladder is used simply as a tool to help each partner organize his or her frustrations with their partner. Have each partner put their mildest frustration at Number 10 and work up to the most severe frustration. This page does not have to be shown to the partner, so you can give them permission to be honest in what they write. Because of time, they need only write one or two frustrations in the session and complete the rest for homework.

b. Restructuring Negative Behaviors

Give them a copy of the Restructuring Negative Behaviors sample as a guide. Then have the couple take a behavior from their frustration ladder and change it into a desire. Then have them change it into a positive, doable BCR. Then have the couple use dialogue to present and discuss each other's requests.

Restructuring Frustrations

Give the couple the Restructuring Frustrations sample as a guide. Have the couple pick one of their frustrations from the Frustration Ladder and place it in Box 1. From there, guide them through each box and give them time to write their feeling, response, fear, desire, and request. Again, this version gives the partner the opportunity to write three requests for each frustrating behavior. Remember that each of the sender's requests is a stretch for the receiver. It is important that the receiver is given choices since this work is not about setting him or her up to fail, but rather to stretch into new, growth-producing behaviors.

After at least one partner has written down the three BCRs, have the couple dialogue using the form as a guide. Each block is a natural stopping point for the sender to be mirrored by the receiver. Do not expect change in the session. The goal of the session is for the sending partner to educate the receiving partner, thereby creating the receiver's blueprint for growth.

3. Homework Instructions for Session Five

Give the homework sheet to the couple at the end of the session along with blank Restructuring Negative Behaviors or Restructuring Frustrations forms. The homework sheet will give them simple instructions on what they are to do to complete the forms and the dialogue—directions that you've already reviewed in the session.

Following the dialogue, the receiving partner should notice that the behavior requested is a stretch into one of his or her lost parts. For example, the sender may be asking the receiver to think more or listen to his or her feelings. To help the receiver clearly see that the sender has the blueprint for the receiver's growth, tell the receiver to put a number, or a check mark, in the box desired for monitoring stretching. For example, if the sender requests "I would like for you to listen to my feelings about school for 15 minutes using dialogue," the area requested for growth is feelings and the receiving partner should put a mark next to feelings on the monitoring box. What the couple will probably notice is that there are one or two areas of growth that the partner is requesting consistently. They may also notice that they have opposite requests.

Socialization and Mate Selection

We express our basic energy, or selves, through four functions:

Thinking • Feeling • Acting • Sensing

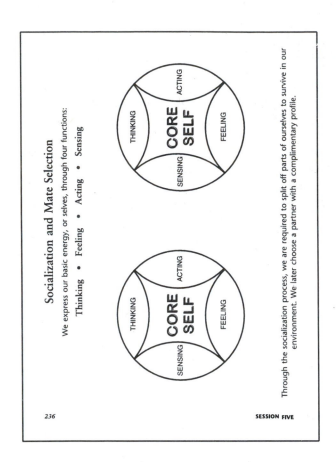

Through the socialization process, we are required to split off parts of ourselves to survive in our environment. We later choose a partner with a complimentary profile.

Frustration Ladder

Rank your frustrations from 1 to 10, with 1 being the most severe and 10 being the mildest. It is important to tackle the milder ones first. Trying to tackle the most severe ones will only result in failure and more frustration.

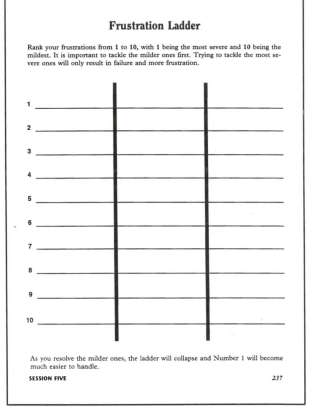

As you resolve the milder ones, the ladder will collapse and Number 1 will become much easier to handle.

Restructuring Frustrations

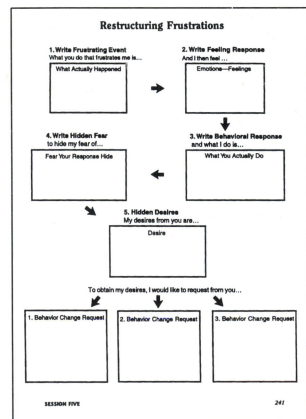

1. Write Frustrating Event
What you do that frustrates me is...

What Actually Happened

2. Write Feeling Response
And I then feel ...

Emotions—Feelings

4. Write Hidden Fear
to hide my fear of...

Fear Your Response Hide

3. Write Behavioral Response
and what I do is...

What You Actually Do

5. Hidden Desires
My desires from you are...

Desire

To obtain my desires, I would like to request from you...

1. Behavior Change Request

2. Behavior Change Request

3. Behavior Change Request

HOMEWORK INSTRUCTIONS FOR SESSION FIVE

1. Complete the Frustration Ladder, placing the mildest frustration at the bottom and the most difficult one at the top. When you begin to work on this, you will start with the mildest frustration first. You do not have to show your partner this form—so be exhaustive and honest.

2. If you've been give the form labelled Restructuring Negative Behaviors, change each frustration into your desire (column A). Then take each desire and change it into a Behavior Change Request (column B). Remember: Be positive, behavioral, and so specific that a stranger could figure out what you want and do it perfectly.

   The object of this homework is to begin to EDUCATE your partner about what you need and in the areas in which he or she needs to grow. Do not expect your partner to do these behaviors right away. Doing the behaviors will require your partner to stretch, which will require time. Also, keep in mind that your partner will only change as much as you do.

3. If you have been given the form labeled Restructuring Frustrations, write a frustration in Box 1 and then follow and answer the boxes on feelings, behaviors, fears, and desires as you did in the session with the therapist. This form asks the sending partner to write three Behavior Change Requests for the receiving partner regarding the sender's desire. This gives the receiving partner a choice of behaviors to give to the sending partner that will be accomplished only through growth on both of your parts.

4. Review your Behavior Change Request with your partner using Couples Dialogue. Stay very safe during this exercise because although some of the things on your partner's list may seem impossible, it is more likely that your partner is pushing you on an adaptation that you have developed. Our partner's requests are usually in the areas that we most need to grow into, and growth and change are never easy.

5. Monitor your stretching by observing that each Behavior Change Request will require a stretch into one of the areas you were told to turn off in childhood (Thinking, Acting, Feeling, or Sensing). After reviewing your partner's request using Couples Dialogue, decide which area will require growth in order to accomplish the request and place a check mark next to the appropriate area. You should discover that the request requires a stretch in one or two areas.

Monitoring Stretching—Area of Behavior Change Request			
Thinking ☐	Acting ☐	Feeling ☐	Sensing ☐

HOME EXERCISE SESSION FIVE	Day 1	Day 2	Day 3	Day 4	Day 5	Day 6	Day 7
1. Complete Frustration Ladder							
2. Change these frustrations to Behavior Change Requests							
3. Review Request (Use Couples Dialogue)							
4. Monitor Stretching							

Thought for the Week:

Your partner has the blueprint for your growth.

8

SESSION SIX

Resolving Rage

SUGGESTED TIME FRAME

Checking homework	10 minutes
"Appointments for Anger" Lecture	5 minutes
Container Process	35 minutes
Reviewing Follow-up Plan	10 minutes

GOALS

1. To thoroughly check that Behavior Requests were written in a positive manner with doable behaviors.

2. To emphasize that these behaviors may take years to accomplish but that doing so heals both partners.

3. To give the couple the experience of expressing anger and rage in a safe containment process.

4. To make sure that the couple fully understand that hurt underlies anger and that it is important to hear our partner's hurt.

5. To thoroughly review and to have the couple understand the importance of the follow-up plan.

AN OPTION

The plan for the sixth session offers you a flexible option. If carried out as planned, you will be spending the session helping the couple deal with rage in a structured process called the Container Process. However, in our use of the short-term format, we have found that many couples do not need such an intense session on anger or that the dialogue process has been sufficient at diffusing the anger experienced in their relationship. Many couples report that it would be better for them to spend the time solving problems. Also, some therapists are uncomfortable with the intensity of the Container Process. For these couples and the therapist, we recommend continuing with the Behavior Change Request work.

You will probably know a week ahead of time in what direction you will be taking this session. Angry couples will probably need to do the Container Process and those who have trouble working out their frustrations or who often come to impasses will probably do better working on Behavior Change Requests.

If you decide to work on BCRs, have the couple bring in several completed Restructuring Frustrations or Restructuring Negative Behaviors forms that were assigned as homework in Session Five. Spend the hour with the couple in Behavior Change Request dialogue.

If you have decided that the Restructuring Frustrations form is appropriate for the couple (rather than the less intense Restructuring Negative Behaviors), you would be using the boxes as a guideline for the flow of dialogue. For the couple open to the idea, you may want to add a step after the fourth box by giving them the sentence stem, "And what that reminds me of in my childhood is . . ." and having the receiver mirror it back. This additional step allows the receiver to understand that his or her frustrating behavior triggers something from the partner's childhood and begins to bring the sending partner's behavior into perspective. Tension around behavior changes tends to ease up when the person who has to make the change understands its importance to the person making the request.

If you decide to use the Restructuring Negative Behaviors form, have the couple present it to each other using dialogue as you did in the last session. Help them get accustomed to talking about their frustrations in the less-threatening desire to BCR format. Then, make sure they understand that Behavior Change Requests must be written in a positive, doable, and measurable fashion. Give the couple the experience of dialoguing their desires and educating each other through BCRs on the areas needed for individual growth.

After the establishment of safety, dialogue, and empathy, these Behavior Change Requests are the most important part of this work. After the fourth session many couples will observe that although they are hearing each other better, they still are not *doing* anything different. And that would be true. You cannot change anything unless you know what the purpose is for making the change. Otherwise, you are being coerced into the new behavior and resentment increases. Even though it might be "for your own good," coercion has a wounding effect. On the other hand, if the couple can develop empathy for each other and learn to hear each other's needs, it is easier for each partner to give the behavior changes and the receiver does not feel coerced.

STARTING THE SESSION

It is important that even if you decide to go on to the Container Process in this session, you take a few minutes to review the BCR assignment from Session Five and emphasize its importance. Look at the couple's Behavior Change Request list and make sure that the requests are stated as positive, doable behaviors. Remind them that the idea of compiling this list was to educate their partner with regard to their own needs, and—if they do the requests—they will reclaim a part of themselves lost in childhood. Briefly process this with the couple by asking them if they could feel the partner's requests as going against their own adaptations of not thinking, feeling, acting, or sensing. Ask them if they understand that through doing the behaviors they begin the process of reclaiming themselves.

After you have processed the BCRs for about 10 minutes, begin with this week's agenda. The lecture is very short because you will need the rest of the time to do the Container Process (which will take about 35 minutes), as well as to go over the follow-up program for those who are finishing therapy in six sessions. Session Six will incorporate everything you've taught the couple in previous sessions with the addition of the Container Process to deal with anger and rage.

ABOUT THE LECTURE

This lecture is designed to set up the Container Process that the couple will experience in the session. Most people are appropriately afraid of anger because it feels threatening. The reptilian brain interprets it that way and, therefore, goes into its fight, flight, playing dead, hiding, or submitting routine. Anger never gets fully resolved or heard because the situation calls for both parties to defend themselves. This lecture and exercise is about giving couples a new way to express and understand anger. Safety and empathy are again stressed as a way to understand the other.

There is an odd moment in the lecture in which you are asked to spontaneously scream. This may seem like a very strange thing to do in a therapy session, but it clarifies the point you are trying to make—anger should be expressed by appointment only. You could just describe this process to the couple, but going back to the learning process described in the first session, people learn best when they can experience what you say. Couples can clearly see and feel the difference between your spontaneous scream and when you ask for an appointment. Try it a couple of times with your couples to see if it gets more comfortable.

LECTURE SIX: APPOINTMENTS FOR ANGER

What do we do with anger and rage? I'm sure you've both been angry with each other at some time, and—if you're like most couples—your anger usually goes nowhere. There may be screaming and shouting, or one of you storms off and keeps the anger in—feeling that it's useless or dangerous to express your feelings. And, as usual, you don't hear each other. Typically, such a situation has become unsafe, and so the old brain takes over with fighting, fleeing, playing dead, freezing, hiding, or submitting.

But we've found that anger has a very important function in a relationship and, in fact, is another vital key to childhood wounds; however, we never hear the anger or allow it to do what it is intended to do, because we are too busy defending ourselves from it! This is similar to the theory behind the development of antiballistic missiles. Missiles, you see, are designed to do a job of sorts; so someone got smart and developed an antiballistic missile to knock the original missile out of the sky before it could do any destruction.

When our partner sends us an angry statement, we usually respond with a statement designed to take the punch out of it. If we let ourselves really listen to our partner's statement, however, we may find that it has a real purpose and a real meaning. We know that underneath anger there is always hurt, yet we seldom get the chance to hear our partner's hurt because of our own defense.

But how can you listen to your partner's anger? By appointment only! Sound crazy? Perhaps, but it's the safest, most productive way to deal with anger. And, as illustration of this, tell me what happens when I do this: **"Aaahhhhh!"** (At this point, therapist should **suddenly** scream loudly.) Could you feel yourself jump and get defensive? I know you probably thought I was crazy, but I wanted to get the point across that when we spring anger on our partner, we activate his or her old brain, and he or she has no choice but to become defensive.

Now what would happen if I first let you know that I had a need to scream and needed an appointment to scream—would you give me that appointment? Can you get yourselves safe so that I can scream? Are you safe? Ready?

"Aaahhhhh!" (Therapist again screams.) Could you feel the difference this time? Did you feel as defensive? If you did not feel as defensive this time, it is because you were ready for it, and you were safe. And you have to make that promise to each other. You have to promise that there will be **no** more, **no** more, **no** more spontaneous expressions of anger with each other—ever again! Anger will be expressed **by appointment only.**

If you can do this, then you will be able to *hear* what your partner's anger is about and *connect* it with his or her childhood wound. And to do this, we use a seven-step process called the Container Process.

THE CONTAINER PROCESS

At this point, you will lead the couple through a seven-step process. Although this exercise is probably the hardest of all to do, if you keep in mind that it includes all of the exercises you've taught the couple in the previous sessions—with the addition of "containment"—you should do well. Also remember that this process is more than likely a marked improvement over whatever it is that the couple have been doing at home. Anything that they can pick up from it will help them. It is safe, structured, and allows couples to push through their rage to the hurt that lies underneath.

The Container Process involves one partner listening with empathy to the other partner's anger—no matter how loud the anger is expressed. The receiving partner holds or becomes the *container* for the sending partner's anger. Although some may immediately view this as abusive, it is really the safest way to express anger. The safety is built into the structure you give to the Container Process as you help the receiving partner see that behind the anger, there is always a deep hurt that the sending partner needs to have heard.

It is more important that the couple learn the steps in this session rather than have a "good argument." They must leave with the idea that, from now on, all arguments must be done through the Container Process—or, in other words, *by appointment only*. Some may argue that this is difficult to do or that it takes the spontaneity out of arguing, but the fact remains that containment makes the rage more productive and safer. Furthermore, before they begin, the couple must agree to three basic rules: no hitting, no property damage, and no leaving until all seven steps have been completed.

Let the couple decide who is going to be the sending partner and who is going to be the receiving partner, and tell them that you will be guiding them through each step of the process. Have the sending partner make an appointment with the receiving partner, giving or confirming the appointment as soon as possible. Besides allowing the receiving partner time to "get safe," another reason for scheduling an appointment is that sometimes *now* is not the appropriate time to begin an argument. An example of an inappropriate time is when one partner is about to leave the house for work. In such an instance, an appointment should be made for the container to take place as soon as possible—and it is *very* important that they keep the scheduled appointment time.

It is also very important for the receiver to begin going to his or her safe place for the process. The receiver must stay safe during this process or the couple could get into their typical argument. Sometimes I will tell the receiver to remember that the anger is a little bit about *now* and a lot about the house in which his or her partner grew up. If the receiver wants to find out what that's all about, he or she must stay safe or the sender will not be able to get to that deeper level of hurt and thus remain angry.

The second step of the Container Process is for the sender to state in one or two sentences what the anger is about and for the receiver to mirror this back. Use only mirroring in this part, because its basic function is to let both partners know what the rage is about.

After the mirroring, instruct the receiving partner to get safe again and also indicate that he or she is only allowed to say, "Tell me more about that" or "Say that louder." Then ask the sender to explode his or her anger about the triggering event. Some can do this quite easily, and others will need some prodding from you, the therapist. You can ask the sending partner to begin slowly and to build up his or her anger. Be sure to remind the sender that the receiver is going to make it safe for him or her by listening to the sender's rage. You may also have to interject thoughts such as "I hate that!" or "It ticks me off!" and have the sender repeat them.

Think of yourself as "kick-starting" the rage. Once it gets going, let it go for 10 minutes or so—keeping the situation safe. The idea is for senders to fully express their anger or rage to enable them to get to the hurt that lies underneath. When you think that the anger has reached its height, you can throw in one of two lines: "And *that* hurts" or "And that reminds me of when I was a kid." This typically will shift the focus from the rage to the hurt or to the sadness underneath. When the receiving partner can see the sending partner's pain, the empathy he or she began to develop several sessions ago begins to return, and the receiver can begin to feel compassion for his or her partner's anger and hurt.

During the fourth step of the exercise, several things can happen. The sender may break into tears—an "implosion"—and should be brought into the holding position that you taught the couple several sessions ago. This should be done quickly and gently so the sender can stay in his or her emotional state. If you say anything other than "Could you please hold him/her?" you risk taking the couple out of this compassionate state. Move them into the holding position, and simply tell the sender to "sob it out" or "let those old sobs come."

Most of the time, you'll find that the session takes on a sad tone, but the sender will not be in tears. In that case, do the same thing and place the sender in the holding position so that he or she can talk about his or her underlying hurt. Sometimes this will deepen the hurt, and sometimes it will increase the compassion from the receiving partner. Either way, you will have helped the couple increase their empathy and understanding of each other's anger and rage.

After 5 to 10 minutes in this position, move to the fifth step: separation and rest. If the couple got into a full-blown container, which resulted in an implosion, the most common thing you will hear from the sending partner is how tired—yet relieved—he or she feels. This step may last but a moment as the couple gather themselves together, or it may be a short processing of what just transpired.

The sixth step is a Behavior Change Request made by the sending partner that is related to both the trigger and the wound. The sending partner will make three Behavior Change Requests which the receiver will mirror. The sender will later write those requests on the Container Record. The reason for this, you will recall, is that requests are gifts—they are *not* something that the receiver will be forced to do. The sender gives three requests, hoping for one. Typically, what you see is that the receiving partner is so touched by the partner's hurt that the receiver will make the effort to do all three. Make sure that the requests are stated positively and are related to the wound that the receiver saw in the Container Process.

The seventh step is *very* important. The couple just went through a very emotional exercise, and because of this, they may seem tired and drained. So the seventh step is for them to have a sustained belly laugh or high-energy fun. This is not to make light of what just happened but to bring energy back to them. They also have to rid themselves of some negative emotions; therefore, your aim is to help them fill themselves up with positive emotions. The sender will choose the activity, and the receiver must participate. Get them going, and just watch them have fun!

Be aware that the Container Process may not go as written, and the couple may resist or tell you, "We can't get into this." Your job is to show them the steps and give them an experience of the steps—no matter how small. It will be their choice whether to use the skill or to continue as usual. The Follow-up Plan (Chapter 9) is designed to slowly guide them into using the Container Process or a variation of it (the Container Transaction or Container Days) on a regular basis.

Variations of Containers

The entire Container Process lasts between 30 to 45 minutes, utilizes seven steps, and is used by the couple to deal with intense anger. There are two variations that will assist the couple in making the expression of anger safe and productive in their relationship.

The Container Transaction

There are times in any given week when frustrating events produce mild anger between partners. This period of mild anger may not have any connection to childhood, but may need a safe forum for expression. An example may be leaving shoes in the family room, leaving a dish out, or forgetting to pick up the dry cleaning—again. And although this may produce an angry feeling, the situation may not need a 30-minute process to deal with the feeling. For frustrating events that need more than Couples Dialogue, but less than the Container Process, we recommend the Container Transaction.

If you are working in six sessions, you will not have time for the couple to practice this process, so you will have to describe it to them. The steps are described on the handout entitled Using the Container. The first two steps are identical to the Container Process in that the sender will make an appointment and have the triggering frustration mirrored back to him or her by the receiver. The third step involves a short 3-minute explosion of the feelings regarding the event with the receiving partner listening from his or her safe place. The receiver then does a global mirror to let the sending partner know he or she was heard.

Following this mirror, the sender makes a Behavior Change Request about the triggering event and is mirrored by the receiver. The couple have the option of ending with a belly laugh, but it is always recommended. The entire Container Transaction should last about 5 minutes and the object is for the receiver to fully hear the sender's anger and understand it from the sender's point of view. This, of course, may cause corresponding feelings in the receiver and that should be discussed in the dialogue process.

Container Days

People learn through repetition, experience, and practice. Containers are not easy or natural for couples to do, so in an effort to anchor the skills, you may want to recommend Container Days.

Tell the couple that in an effort to have the Container Process become a natural part of their lives, you are recommending that they participate in Container Days for the next 90 days. On Monday, Wednesday, and Friday, one partner promises to be the container, or the receiver, of the anger of the other partner all day. This means that the containing partner makes himself or herself available all day to listen to the partner's anger in a safe, structured, and dialogical way. If the receiving partner experiences his or her own anger that day, he or she must make the commitment to hold it until the following day when the process switches—the other partner promises to be the container all day on Tuesday, Thursday, and Saturday. On Sunday, both partners are available for each other, but we recommend high-energy fun on Sunday.

For the sender, this means that on his or her designated day he or she can express anger. But the sender also has the option of not expressing anger on that day with the assurance that he or she will not have to listen to anger on that day from the receiving partner. Couples have found Container Days to be either expressive or peaceful depending on the sender's needs for that day. This process tends to be exciting for maximizing partners who know they will be fully heard that day and, at the same time, frustrating for them when they get angry on the day that is not theirs to send and they have to wait until the next day. The benefit here is that maximizing partners have to learn to contain themselves on the days they are the container and they develop some inner controls. Minimizers learn to express themselves as the fear of being overwhelmed by the other is removed.

This is often a difficult assignment for the couple to complete fully and they will make faces at you as you assign it. The excessiveness of this assignment is not unlike drug and alcohol support groups recommending 90 meetings in 90 days. Couples have to put as much time in improving their relationships as they did in avoiding them and being critical. Even if the couple have Container Days half of the time, this will be an improvement over how they have handled explosive situations in the past and they will be more effective in handling anger.

FOLLOW-UP PLAN

For couples completing therapy in the sixth session, you will also be reviewing the follow-up plan. Make a copy of the entire plan (located at the end of the Homework/Handouts) for the couple and review some of what they will be doing. More specific instructions and details about the plan are given in Chapter 9.

DAVE AND DIANA: SESSION SIX

Dave and Diana returned for Session Six in an upbeat mood. They spent the week working on the Behavior Change Request assignment and presented a few BCRs to each other. As Diana said, "We didn't work on the toughies." But that also gave her an important insight when she said, "I told Dave that I think it is good we did not do the tough ones. Maybe we need to tackle the easy ones first so we can gain experience to tackle the tough ones." This is an important concept for couples to understand in this work. Change is a lifelong process and it is far better to work on the milder frustrations so that you can gain the strength and experience needed to work on the tough ones. Change happens slowly over a long period of time; otherwise it is like a crash diet: you might lose the weight quickly, but you will gain it back quickly, plus a few extra pounds.

The therapist took a few minutes to check carefully Dave and Diana's written Restructuring Frustrations form. As is typical, there were a few BCRs that were written too generally or with negative words. They were coached to rewrite these requests into positive, doable, measurable, and time-limited behaviors. The therapist reminded them that Behavior Change Requests are not a way of telling each other that they have to change; rather it is a way of telling each other that these are the behaviors that will meet *my* needs and heal *my* wounds. And, each partner will grow into his or her lost parts if these behaviors are given as gifts. Diana commented, "It's a nice way to do this. It is really fair."

After about 10 minutes into the session, the therapist began the lecture about anger and rage. He commented how anger never seems to get anywhere and usually causes additional pain rather than healing and a sense of being understood. As is typical, the couple responded quizzically when they were told that anger should be expressed by appointment only. Dave asked, "If you are in the middle of anger, how can you stop and make an appointment?" The therapist mirrored and validated what Dave said and then did the scream demonstration. Through the demonstration the appointment idea made more sense to Dave and Diana and they then understood the need. They were also very realistic and admitted that this would be difficult.

The therapist then took Dave and Diana through the Container Process. Diana decided that she would be the sender and made an appointment with Dave. Dave was able to make himself safe and granted the appointment. Diana then told him in a few sentences what her anger was about and Dave was able to mirror. Diana identified her anger trigger as, "I'm angry when you get silent with me. It frustrates me because I feel I have no choices."

Dave then got safe again while Diana built up her anger for this transaction. The therapist instructed him to say only, "Tell me more about that" or "Say that louder." Throughout the transaction, Dave did his best to stay safe, to stay focused on Diana, and to listen to her with his heart and with empathy. The therapist told him that if he listened to the anger long enough and with his heart, there was a "prize" underneath, and that was the hidden reason for the anger.

Diana: (*in an angry tone*) When you pull away from me like that, it hurts because I don't feel like I have choices. I feel like you have gone away. It feels like you have abandoned me just when I need to express who I am. Unless things are comfortable, it feels like you go away. And I feel totally lost and I feel angry at you for doing that. (*angry*) You said you'd stay!

Therapist: Stay in your anger.

Dave: Tell me more about that.

Diana: (*angry*) You said you would stay. That's what you said when we got married, for better or for worse, and every time I show any sign of me being on my worse side, you leave. (*yelling*) And that hurts so bad and I get so angry because I don't know what to do. And I want to hurt you. And I want to hit you and I want to turn away from you to let you see how it feels. Every time I have something adverse to say . . . it makes me feel like my words aren't important. It's not fair! It's not nice!

Therapist: Say that louder.

Diana: (*screaming*) It's not fair! It's not nice! And I don't do it to you! I listen to all the garbage and it's not always nice. When I hear the anger and it comes out sideways, I listen to all of that. But when I have a little bit of anger, you run away from me! I'm not your mom and I am not scary!

Dave: Can you say that louder. (*still with a look of concern and maintaining his safety*)

Diana: (*screaming very loudly now*) I am not your mom and I am not scary! I am a nice person, but I have upset and angry feelings sometimes! And it is not okay to leave! I hate you when you leave me.

Therapist: (*softly to Dave*) Stay safe.

Diana: (*sounding angry and regressed*) I hate you when you leave me! It hurts so bad! I want to punish you so mean!

Dave: Can you tell me more.

Diana: It makes me feel choked up inside. It feels like when you leave me, you shove everything I want to say right back down my throat and I don't get to say what I mean. And I get so scared.

Therapist: (*mirroring*) I get so scared.

Diana: I get so scared to say anything. I get so scared to go forward and ever tell you that I don't agree with something. The only way I can have a relationship is to just agree, agree, agree! I have to stuff it!

Therapist: I'm tired of stuffing it.

Diana: I'm tired of stuffing it. I'm not going to anymore. I want freedom in my throat. It feels like it is all stuffed down all the time. I have a voice and I want to be heard! I want you to hear me!

Therapist: Louder.

Diana: I have a voice and I want you to hear me! I want you to give me time to express what I am trying to say! I don't want you to go away!

Dave: Tell me more about that.

Diana: You go away! You punish me! I'm not supposed to be punished for who I am! I am not supposed to be punished for being me!

Therapist: Louder.

Diana: I am not supposed to be punished for being me!

Therapist: Louder.

Diana: (*very loud and crying*) I'm not supposed. . . . I am a nice person! I am! And I get angry sometimes. I don't like things sometimes! And I don't get to tell you that! I can only show you the nice parts!

Therapist: And that reminds me of when I was a kid.

Diana: Ugh. (*crying*) They never wanted to hear anything. . . . Ahhh! . . . (*at this point, Diana let out several painful screams*) Ahhhh! . . . Ahhhh! . . . (*Dave looks on with empathy*)

Therapist: Can you give it language.

Diana: (*screaming*) I hate you Mom for making me so good! I hate you Dad for being so angry! Ahhh! . . .

Therapist: Tell Dave about it. Give it words.

Diana: (*sobbing*) I wanted time to be heard. To be able to say something not nice and not feel that they were going to hurt me, or walk away, or put me down. I just wanted to be heard for what I was feeling. It didn't matter. No negative feelings were ever allowed to be heard. They never wanted to know that part of me ever. I get so angry because I watch all the garbage going on. And that's why I just cry. And they put me down for that sometimes, but I can't stop it. I can't do anger. I'm so afraid they'll hurt me. I'm so afraid that you will hurt me if I get angry. I think they would hurt me if I expressed anger.

Therapist: And that hurts. Tell Dave about the hurt.

Diana: (*weeping*) It is so hard to only be a half a person. It is so hard to only come from the rules and what's right for everyone else. And the line. You don't cross the line. I feel like parts of me are dead inside and I wish I had it back because I know it's in there. And they never let me have it. I would go to the closest to get angry and my mother would hear it and say, "You're talking to yourself? You're talking to the devil!" (*sobbing heavily*) There is no safe place to be angry. And sometimes I don't like things and I have no safe place to say it.

Diana was now very sad and Dave was feeling very compassionate toward her sadness. He waited out the anger and got the "prize" underneath: he got to see the hurt that fuels the anger. Now he was in a position and mind set to nurture the hurt. Diana was asked if she would be willing to let Dave hold her as she was gently guided into the Holding Position. Diana sobbed in Dave's arms for about 5 minutes as he provided a safe and nurturing space for her to reexperience and heal her hurt. Diana's sobs became very deep and she said several times, "Please don't let me be hurt anymore" and Dave gently held her. The rage had turned into passion.

This Container Process was a very intense and emotional experience for Dave and Diana. After Diana felt she had been held long enough, they took a minute to sit up and compose themselves. The emotional part was only part of the healing. Now Diana had to make several Behavior Change Requests of Dave. As might be expected, her request focused on being heard and for Dave to make it safe for her to disagree and express anger. She also requested that he stay present with her when she is mad no matter how much he wants to run. Dave was able to mirror these requests back and thought he would like to take a try at all of them because now he could really see why Diana needed him to be there and to listen to her anger and hurt. They ended this process with a belly laugh by playing "I Can Do That!" as they did in a previous session.

It is often interesting to view a couple at the end of a Container Process. This process uses all of the skills they have learned over the six sessions and the therapist hopes that the compassion that has been developed during that time is fully available during the process. It was there for Dave and Diana. Dave was now fully tuned to Diana and understands her hurt. Diana somehow looked different following her experience. Her faced seemed less tense and she had a younger appearance. They sat close and held hands. They were now in a committed and conscious relationship.

Since this was the last session for Dave and Diana, they were given the Follow-up Plan (see Chapter 9). The therapist warned them that if they did not use the processes every day, the warm moment they were experiencing would be a distant memory in a short amount of time. He also told them that they would have up and down days and the only way to get back on track would be through what they learned in therapy—to create safety, to use Couple Dialogue and to use all of the processes. Their work and their journey had really just begun. The therapy had given them a good start, but they would have to continue the process of growth that can be found in committed and conscious relationships. Except for some possible future brief follow-up visits, the work of the therapist with this couple was done.

OUTCOME MEASURES

Dave and Diana returned a week after their last session to repeat the outcome measures given in Session One (COMPASS and the Marital Satisfaction Inventory). COMPASS results are compared in Table 8.1. Both partners showed considerable improvement and their results indicated that further therapy was not warranted.

The Marital Satisfaction Inventory also showed a large reduction in several of the scales. Global Distress for Dave and Diana dropped significantly (T = 49 and T = 51, respectively). There was also a noticeable drop in Disagreement about Finances (T = 57 and T = 57, respectively) and Sex-

TABLE 8.1
COMPASS Score Comparison

	Diana		Dave	
	Session One	Session Six	Session One	Session Six
Well-being (Normal Range: Above 83) (Severe Range: Below 17)	43	95	46	98
Symptoms (Normal Range: Below 17) (Severe Range: Above 83)	27	12	68	14
Life Functioning (Normal Range: Above 83) (Severe Range: Below 17)	13	90	10	69
Mental Health Index (Normal Range: Above 83) (Severe Range: Below 17)	41	94	25	92

ual Dissatisfaction (T = 57 and T = 48, respectively). Diana also indicated that she was feeling more understood in the relationship as her Affective Communication score dropped significantly (T = 48). Overall, through anecdotal information and through valid and reliable outcome measures, we can see that Dave and Diana's marriage improved and they were feeling better.

Six Months Later

Dave and Diana returned to the therapist six months later to give the therapist permission to use their story in this book and to discuss how they had been doing for the past six months since therapy ended. They both reported that things had been going well for them and they continued to feel safe with each other. They admitted that there was a brief period in which they regressed to their old ways, but they began to talk and to use dialogue and their relationship stabilized again. They also said that they used dialogue as much as they could, but confessed they often returned to their "old way of talking."

Mostly they were impressed with their ability to keep the relationship safe and to appreciate differences in each other. They were adamant that they had not given in to the differences in each other, but rather had come to realize that these differences are what makes them unique and are traits that deserve validation. Since there was less conflict in their relationship, they also noticed that their son was more relaxed and seemed to enjoy his time at home more. They were very happy that the work they did on their marriage has had a positive impact on their child.

HANDOUT INSTRUCTIONS FOR THE THERAPIST

Examples of handouts are shown on p. 145.

SESSION SIX

If you have chosen to conduct a second session on Behavior Change Requests in Session Six, the homework will be for the couple to write up more BCRs and correct any discrepancy you may have found on their BCR forms in this session. If you find they are not in positive, doable terms, have them rewrite them so that the partners have clear behaviors to strive for.

If you have chosen the Container Process for this session, there are several forms you can hand to the couple at the end of the session to help them in their efforts to do this at home.

1. The Container Process

This sheet describes the seven-step process that the couple just experienced in the session. You might suggest to the couple that after they have made an appointment to express anger using the Container, they use this sheet to guide them through the steps until the process becomes natural. It is best if each partner learns the process so it becomes fluid, rather than depending on the sheet for each step and disrupting the flow.

2. The Container Record

This is essentially the same as the Container Process sheet except that it gives the receiving partner a place to write down the Behavior Change Requests made in the sixth step. Suggest to the couple that they make several copies of this sheet and use it to keep a record of their Container Process. It is easy to forget what the Behavior Change Requests are, especially in emotional exchanges, so this form makes it possible to keep track of requests.

3. Using the Container

This form gives the couple some suggested ways to use the Container Process. It explains the entire seven-step Container Process, the Container Transaction for mild annoyances, and Container Days.

As described in the chapter, to help the couple get started using containers, suggest that they practice Container Days for the next 90 days. This allows the partners to know that they will be heard on a particular day by the partner who has promised to make it safe for them to express anger, or allows them a day to know that anger will not be expressed by the partner who has promised to wait until the next day when the process switches.

4. Homework Instructions for Session Six

This sheet guides the couple through the initial stages of using the Container. It is meant as a guide for using the other sheets described. It also reminds the couple of the importance of a belly laugh at the end of doing any Container. It is crucial that the couple learn to spend time in a laugh or high-energy fun at the end of a Container so that they can retrieve some of the energy expended and also have a positive association with this emotional experience.

5. After the Therapy (Chapter 9)

Again, if this is your last session with the couple, you will also be handing them the Follow-up Plan, which is described in the next chapter.

The Container Process

Before you use this exercise, you should make three protective agreements:

- NO Hitting or Name Calling
- NO Physical or Verbal Attacks
- NO Property Damage
- NO Leaving Until All Seven Steps Are Completed

Partner A = Sender	Partner B = Receiver
1. Ask for an appointment.	1. Agree to a time ASAP.
2. Identify the "trigger" to your frustration; state the frustration in one sentence.	2. Paraphrase your partner's frustration; put on your "psychic armor."
3. Explode feelings.	3. Listen with empathy.
4. Implosion (anger turns to sadness and tears).	4. Provide physical holding, care, and empathy.
5. Separation and rest (optional).	
6. Ask for three behavior changes related to the trigger.	6. Mirror request. Commit to at least one change or offer an alternative.
7. Initiate high-energy play.	7. Participate actively in play.

The Container Record

Date: _____ Sender: _____ Receiver: _____

1. Sender requests an appointment. Receiver agrees ASAP. To begin the Container Process, the receiver prepares his/her armor—gets safe.

2. Sender states the trigger of the frustrating event in one sentence. Receiver mirrors and fine-tunes his or her armor—level of safety.

3. *Explosion Phase.* Senders share anger. Receiver listens and encourages anger. Tell me more about that! Say that louder! Maximum time: 10 minutes.

4. *Implosion.* Anger turns to sadness. Sender shares early wounds. Receiver holds and listens with mirroring and empathy.

5. Separation and rest if necessary.

6. Sender makes three Behavior Change Requests. Receiver writes them down, mirrors, and selects one to which he or she will commit.*

Behavior Change Request	Behavior Change Request	Behavior Change Request
_____	_____	_____
_____	_____	_____
_____	_____	_____
_____	_____	_____

7. Sender initiates high-energy fun or play. Receiver participates with energy.

8. Later, receiver practices at least one Behavior Change Request. The sender recognizes and appreciates when this happens.

*The Sender should add all three requests to his or her list of Behavior Change Requests so that he or she can review them regularly to fine-tune them and to be able to recognize them when they occur. The receiver should write all three Behavior Change Requests in his or her list of stretching behaviors. These should be reviewed at least weekly.

Using the Container

There are three ways to use the Container Process and I recommend learning and using all three as a way of developing tools to use in expressing anger.

☐ **The Container Process**

This is the seven-step process that was taught to you in the session. This process allow safe expression of resentment and rage. It also allows childhood anger or hurt to surface and be heard by your partner. This process replaces all spontaneous fights and is used for intense frustrations. It requires an appointment as well as a commitment to all seven steps, to safety, and to allow adequate time (usually 30 to 45 minutes) with little or no distractions.

☐ **The Container Transaction**

The Container Transaction is the process used when the anger is mild or for annoyances. For example, leaving a dish out may not require a 45-minute process to express intense anger such as in the Container Process. This can be handled using the Container Transaction, which utilizes the first three steps of the Container Process and a Behavior Change Request. Transactions should last no more than 5 minutes.

Sender	Receiver
1. Make appointment	1. Give appointment.
2. State trigger in one sentence.	2. Get safe and mirror back.
3. Explode anger for 3 minutes.	3. Listen with empathy and mirror back.
4. Behavior Change Request.	4. Mirror request.
5. Optional belly laugh.	5. Participate in belly laugh.

☐ **Container Days**

As a way of getting started in using Containers, I recommend the following structure: couples should alternate days, each being the Container for a 24-hour period. On the day he is the Container, he will listen to her anger and frustrations all day using only the Container process or the Container Transaction or he can respond with Couples Dialogue. On the following day, you switch and she listens to his anger and frustrations using either the Process or the Transaction. If you get angry or frustrated on the day that is not yours, you must wait until the next day as a promise of safety to the partner whose day it is to express himself or herself. Continue this for three months with both partners being available to each other on Sundays. However, high-energy fun is another option for Sunday.

HOMEWORK INSTRUCTIONS FOR SESSION SIX

1. This is very difficult homework to do. You may want to have some assistance in doing a Container and I, your therapist, will let you know how to get the help you need. I recommend that, for the next three months, you do Container Days, which are described to you in detail on the sheet labeled "Using the Container." Remember, even attempting a Container is probably safer, more structured, and more productive than what you are doing now. Use it as one of the tools in your toolbox that you have learned over the last six sessions.

   Remember to let your partner go through the anger and into the hurt that lies underneath. This is where the real healing takes place. Containers should last no more than 45 minutes and you should do only one er day. The receiving partner must wait until the next day to respond. You want to give your partner the sense that he or she has been heard and understood—even if it means sitting on your own anxiety until the next day.

2. Leaving a dish on the counter or the lid up on the toilet may not need a full Container and probably has no connection to your childhood. For the everyday things, I recommend the Container Transaction, which is also fully described on the sheet labelled "Using the Container." A Container Transaction takes about 5 minutes to complete and gives the sending partner the feeling that he or she has been fully heard. On your day, use the Container Transaction for all the little annoying things.

3. Never forget the high-energy fun at the end of any of the variations of the Container Process. A belly laugh is important to give you back some of the energy you just expended in doing a Container.

HOME EXERCISE SESSION SIX	Day 1	Day 2	Day 3	Day 4	Day 5	Day 6	Day 7
1. Container Days (for the next 3 months)							
2. Container Transaction (use as needed for the next 3 months)							
3. High-Energy Fun (after every Container)							

Thought for the Week:

It is more important to hear than to win!

9

AFTER THE THERAPY

This chapter consists of a weekly follow-up plan. This entire chapter, with the exception of this page, should be considered a handout and given to the couple in the final session.

The plan is designed to help the couple incorporate their new skills into their daily lives. They are expected to be fluid in the processes by week eight if they keep up with the work as outlined.

Each weekly assignment is designed to keep the couple in the process by easing them into the work, not by overwhelming them. Caution the couple to complete only that week's assignment, or they may grow tired of the work. Since the processes are new to them, they need to learn to do a little over a long period of time. However, stress to the couple that the skills will only become permanent when they become habit, and habit only comes through repetition.

Review several weeks' work with the couple to give them an idea of the process. For skills that may not have been taught in the sessions, such as the Container, tell the couple to skip the assigned task and repeat one from a previous week that they may have found helpful.

You must emphasize the importance of the follow-up plan. This will be the single determinant on whether the couple continue the Imago Relationship Therapy process for the improvement of their relationship. They will also gain the added benefit of using their relationship for individual growth and healing.

Follow-Up Plan

It is important to know that the work you completed is not the end, but only the beginning. To get the full benefit, you must continue the work you have done on a ***daily*** basis. In other words, it must become a way of life for you, for your partner, and for your relationship.

This eight-week follow-up program will set you on your way. Try not to think of it in terms of *eight weeks* but as a way to get you started on a lifetime of change and growth. Do not attempt to do any more than is listed in a week, because should you overdo it, you will tire of the work quickly. Remember, your goal is to change a little bit over a long period of time.

Week One

1. Complete any written exercises you started and were unable to finish.

2. Begin a three-month practice of Container Days.

3. Practice Couples Dialogue three times this week for 30 minutes at a planned time.

4. Practice Couples Dialogue in all conflict situations.

5. Reimage your partner as a "wounded child." See yourself healing your partner's wounds. Do this daily.

6. Agree to give each other a gift or appreciation every day.

Week Two

1. Practice Couples Dialogue three times this week for 30 minutes at a planned time.

2. Use Couples Dialogue in all conflict situations.

3. Repeat the Parent-Child Dialogue Exercise (I am your mother/father. What was it like to live with me?) Allow yourself to go deeper with this exercise. Use it to continue the process of reimaging your partner as wounded. Each partner should have at least 30 minutes to talk.

4. Review your Relationship Vision.

5. Have a very intellectual 30-minute talk, with both partners participating equally.

6. Remember to give each other a gift every day.

Week Three

1. Ask your partner for his or her Behavior Change Request list:
   - Rank the list in order of difficulty for you.
   - Memorize this list.
   - Starting with the easiest request, gift your partner with a request daily or weekly, as appropriate, until you have completed the list.
   - Do it, no matter how you feel.
   - When your partner gifts you, acknowledge verbally and also by recording the date on your list so your partner can see it.

2. Say to your partner every day this week, "I understand stretching is difficult, and I will make it safe for you."

3. Review your Relationship Vision and visualize yourself reaching your goals.

4. Use Couples Dialogue to express how you feel about giving and receiving the gifts from your partner this week. Make it safe.

Week Four

1. Use Couples Dialogue in all conflict situations.

2. Have high-energy fun or a belly laugh at least twice this week.

3. Continue gifting your partner with his or her Behavior Change Requests.

4. Do the Holding Exercise about a particularly sad moment in your childhood. Spend 30 minutes each being held. Continue to reimage your partner as wounded.

Week Five

1. Using the Couples Dialogue, share your thoughts about the Container Exercise. Discuss it until you both understand it.
   - Share your thoughts about practicing the steps.
   - Do a Container Transaction on a minor frustrating behavior your partner does. Make it specific.
   - Do a minor Container Process once this week to learn the steps.
   - Discuss your experience of doing the Container Process using the Couples Dialogue.

2. Have a 30-minute conversation about something totally silly (for example, the social implications of the Flintstones).

3. Give each other a gift every day.

Week Six

1. Do Caring Behaviors.

2. Do Behavior Change Requests.

3. Do a Container on a more serious subject.

4. Give each other a gift every day.

Week Seven

1. Use Couples Dialogue at least three times this week.

2. Do a Container.

3. Continue doing Behavior Change Requests.

4. Have at least one belly laugh, separate from the Container.

5. Give each other a gift every day.

Week Eight and Every Week Thereafter

These skills must become a part of everyday life. So for *the rest of your life* do the following:

1. Use the Couples Dialogue in all conflict situations.

2. Reimage your partner as wounded, and see yourself as healing those wounds. Do this until your partner tells you his or her wounds are healing or are healed. (This could take years.)

3. Once a month, do a Holding Exercise. Let your partner deal with a deep hurt in a safe environment with you. Visualize yourself healing his or her wounds.

4. Do Caring Behaviors daily. When the Caring Behavior becomes routine, come up with new ones. Keep the relationship safe and fresh. Surprise your partner once a month. Have a belly laugh once a day. Give a gift or appreciation every day.

5. Continue to stretch into the behaviors on your partner's Behavior Change Request list. When you have fully stretched into these be-

haviors and they are a part of you, ask your partner for a new list. Remember, your part has the blueprint for your growth. See your partner's request as an opportunity to grow in the exact ways that will lead to the recovery of your original wholeness.

6. Do Containers regularly. If these are difficult for you to do alone, commit to each other to find a therapist to help you do a Container.

Every Six Weeks

1. Review your Relationship Vision. Revise it as necessary.

2. Visualize your goals daily and see yourself reaching them.

10

BEING CREATIVE WITH THE BASIC FORMAT AND WORKING WITH SPECIAL POPULATIONS

As you know, this book was developed with the assumption that the therapist has six sessions in which to work with a couple. This chapter will give you some ideas on how to tailor the basic six-session format to meet the couple's needs as well as what to do if you have more than six sessions with the couple. It will also address special situations that may require a different rate of treatment than what was offered in the six basic sessions. Before you make any creative changes to the basic format, I recommend that you try it "as is" a few times to get the hang of the process. After a few tries, you will want to adapt the work to fit your personality and therapy style.

If you change the basic format, the main thing to remember is to keep the couple in the "process" as much as possible. That is, the couple should be using the Couples Dialogue process for at least half of any session because this will be their main tool once they leave the session. Using dialogue must become a habit and habits form only through repetition. The best skill you can teach any couple and the best experience you can give to them is Couples Dialogue. If you find yourself working too hard in a session, chances are the couple are not truly engaged in the dialogue process. Although you cannot "fix" this couple, they can come to understand each other through dialogue. That's why it's important for you to keep them in the dialogue process as much as possible.

Your creativity should be accessed when you see that the couple are not understanding the material in the time allotted. As you want to make as great an impact as possible on their relationship, you should see to it that when they finally leave the therapy, they will at least have grasped the information from the first three sessions, where they will learn dialogue and develop empathy. Try spending an extra week on the problematic sessions until they get the ideas. In doing so, you will have to decide which session to leave out if you are limited to six. Couples who get a clear picture of the purpose of a relationship, learn a dialogue process, and begin the process of developing empathy for each other are able to change their relationship significantly enough to desire more information about this process. Recommend that they read and complete the exercises in *Getting the Love You Want* by Harville Hendrix, Ph.D. You may also refer them to a weekend couples workshop.

Of course, if you have more than six weeks to complete the therapy, you will have the opportunity to call on your creativity. I would suggest that you alternate therapy sessions with practice sessions to review material the couple may not have understood from the previous session. For example, the week after you teach the dialogue process, have the couple spend the whole session using only the dialogue process as they discuss problem areas or their childhoods. Imagine yourself as the foreign language teacher who only lets the class speak in French during the class. Doing likewise will reinforce the dialogue process.

Here are some ideas on how to structure sessions according to how many more you have:

AN EIGHT-SESSION FORMAT

Session One

Present the session as written, but only teach the mirroring portion of the Couples Dialogue. Spend the extra time in this session emphasizing safety and having the couple accurately mirror each other. For homework, give the couple the assignment of mirroring each other for 30 minutes each night.

Session Two

Watch the couple mirror each other to check their homework. Add the validation and empathy portion of Couples Dialogue and have them practice for the rest of the session. Assign for homework the various exercises outlined for Session One.

Session Three

Spend half the session listening to the couple using dialogue on a serious issue in their relationship. Make sure their accuracy in the dialogue is improving and work with them on making the validation portion easier for them. Make sure they understand that they are not necessarily supposed to agree, but rather they are supposed to understand that they each see the situation in a particular way. Spend the second half of the session presenting the Development Lecture. For homework, have the couple dialogue about their childhoods and figure out where they may have been wounded in their development.

Session Four

Spend the first half of the session listening to the couple dialogue about their childhoods or on an issue they want to deal with. Remember that you are creating a safe environment and listening to the process of dialogue. The content is more important to the couple. Creating empathy in the receiving partner is most important to you. Spend the second 30 minutes presenting the guided imagery as described in Session Two.

Sessions Five Through Eight

Conduct these sessions as you would sessions three through six from the six-session model.

A TEN-SESSION FORMAT

In a ten-session format, conduct Sessions One through Four as stated above.

Session Five

Conduct this session as you would Session Three in the six-session format. Fill out the Finding Your Imago form and discuss this with the couple briefly. Do the Parent-Child Dialogue and Holding Exercise with one of the partners in the couple. For homework, the person who was the receiving partner should now be the sending partner in Parent-Child Dialogue and in the Holding Exercise with one of his or her parents. Thirty minutes of dialogue four times this week should also be assigned to the couple.

Session Six

In this session, have the receiving partner from last session be the sending partner in Parent-Child Dialogue and in the Holding Exercise on the parent that he or she did not do for homework. For homework, assign this session's receiving partner the Parent-Child Dialogue and the Holding Exercise for the parent he or she did not do yet.

Session Seven

Conduct the reromanticizing session as explained in Session Four of the six-session format.

Session Eight

This session involves a choice. If you notice that the couple lead very busy lives and seem to avoid each other in their home life, spend this session working on *Exits* as described in the additional exercise section of this chapter. If they seem fairly connected, have them work on the Relationship Vision as described in Session Four of the six-session format. Help the couple shape and write down what their dream relationship would look like.

Session Nine

Conduct the Restructuring Frustrations session as explained in Session Five of the six-session format.

Session Ten

Conduct this session as explained in Session Six of the six-session format with the option of continuing Restructuring Frustrations or Resolving Rage. Finish with the Follow-up Plan.

A TWELVE-SESSION FORMAT

Twelve sessions certainly give you a lot of room to help the couple grasp this material and is preferable if the time is available. A twelve-session format can be conducted in a manner similar to the ten-session format. You have the luxury of a floating session to use in areas that you perceive the couple to need more work or they may need more practice of a particular process. It is recommended that Session Twelve be used to review and emphasize the Follow-up Plan. The continuation of this work following therapy is very important to its success, so it seems essential to stress this and possibly help the couple design a way to institute the processes into their lives.

If the couple have completed all sessions and you still have a few weeks to go, have them begin to use their newly learned skills to work on particular childhood wounds. For example, if one partner had an event in childhood that made him sad, have him talk about it in a Holding Exercise. Many couples appreciate having the therapist available during their Container Process because often in the beginning it can be a bit scary to do these exercises at home. Encourage the couple to think of the skills and processes you have taught them as a box of tools and that there's a right tool to use for a particular situation. Use any additional time to teach the couple how to know which tool to select to get a specific job done. Since you will not be with the couple forever, they should learn how to use the tools for themselves.

ADDITIONAL EXERCISES

Most of the information you need will be in the six-session format. However, there will be days that you will know intuitively that the couple are not ready for what you have to offer them. In such cases, the following exercises may offer you some additional options to work with a couple on specific problems.

Exits

Some couples are pulled apart in so many different directions by family, work, hobbies, and responsibilities that they have little energy to devote to the relationship. In these cases, you might present the following lecture:

Commitment to the process and to the relationship is essential to the success of this work. To do that, you must focus your energy on the relationship and it seems as though your busy lifestyles may be hampering the process. Remember when you first met and your focus seemed to be on your relationship? Maybe you stayed up long hours talking and when you were apart you probably thought about each other often. There was fun, happiness, and connection. Some couples even run the risk of losing their friends when they start relationships because they spend so much time together that they exclude others.

Think of the relationship as two people in a box:
In the early or romantic stage of the relationship, all of the energy is in the

box and stays there. The energy makes the relationship feel alive. As problems arise, the box forms holes and the energy leaks out. We call these leaks *exits*, the most serious of which are *terminal exits*. If a relationship experiences a terminal exit, the relationship is over as all the energy has leaked out. Murder, suicide, and divorce are all terminal exits. Consider this: *20 percent of all murders are spousal murders*. Furthermore, although statistics have shown a marked increase in the divorce rate over the years, there's no telling how many suicides were as a result of a problem relationship.

A second type of exit is known as a *catastrophic exit*. Although it may not end the relationship, a catastrophic exit does drain it of energy and the relationship may require major reparation in order to mend. Catastrophic exits include drug and alcohol abuse, affairs, and insanity. When people are abusing drugs and alcohol, their focus is on the substance rather than on the partner. The same holds true in the case of an affair. Although the person having the affair may think he or she is successfully hiding the fact, the energy drain is evident in the relationship. These exits must be closed off before your relationship can mend and you can experience passion again. As far as insanity or having a "nervous breakdown" is concerned, it may not be of our choice as it may be how our body copes with stress. It does, however, require professional help at least to stabilize the situation before therapy can be done.

The most common types of exits are *deenergizing exits*. Deenergizing exits are energy-zappers that creep into a marriage and may include kids, in-laws, work, school, sports, TV, and any number of things that pull couples away from each other. What are some of your deenergizing exits?

At this point, have the couple begin to identify some of their deenergizing exits. Most couples can come up with a list of ten or more that have crept into the relationship over the years. The only firm decision they will have to make is whether to close the terminal and catastrophic exits. Their simply thinking about these exits will drain energy out of the relationship. If they are committed to both the process and the relationship, they will have to quit using these exits as a means of escape.

Next, have the couple dialogue about their deenergizing exits. This is sometimes difficult because what one partner may see as an exit, the other may see as a hobby or interest. Have them dialogue until they can validate the other's position. They should be committed to begin closing these activities as exits. If, for example, he has been spending four hours a week down at the firehouse or on the golf course, his commitment will be to find ways to cut back and spend more time at home. If she is working overtime or spending long hours at a friend's house, her commitment will be to close the exit to spend more time with the relationship.

Make sure you give a word of warning to the couple. When you first close the exits, things will worsen. Keep in mind that exits are created as ways to avoid what is turning into a painful relationship. Therefore, when couples close their exits they are now face to face with what they were try-ing to escape. This is where Couples Dialogue will help them over the rough spots. Help the couple recognize that the difference between now and when they created the exits is that now they have at least one tool to enable them to deal with each other. Closing the exits will put energy back into the mar-riage, and Couples Dialogue will make it safe to work with that energy.

Sentence Stems

Quite often, the Minimizer in the couple will have a difficult time express-ing himself or herself. It is the nature of the Minimizer to keep his or her energy bound. One way to help couples express themselves is through the use of sentence stems—a technique developed by Dr. Nathaniel Branden and explained in his book, *If You Could Hear What I Cannot Say* (1983). I highly recommend sentence stems as a gentle, yet effective method to guide couples in expressing themselves.

For partners who are having trouble expressing themselves, have the couple use the dialogue process in the session. Then, out loud, say sen-tence stems that may help them organize their thoughts and express them-selves. Sentence stems may include, but are not limited to:

- Sometimes I get upset when . . .
- I feel hurt when . . .
- When I get angry I . . .
- What I always wanted and needed as a child was . . .
- One of the messages I got about me from my father/mother was . . .
- One of the things I had to do to survive was . . .
- I would describe my childhood as . . .
- And that makes me feel . . .
- And that makes me think . . .
- My wish is . . .
- When I get frightened I . . .
- What I want you to understand is . . .

This technique is also useful for persons who are maximizers and may have trouble gathering their thoughts. Sentence stems help them answer specific questions and discourage rambling.

Family Sculpting

Family Sculpting is based on the work of Virginia Satir (1988) and can be used to help couples understand their partner's wounds from childhood. Sculpting enables couples to create a visual picture of relationships. In sculpting with a couple, the therapist will become a participant in the pic-ture. Have one of the partners use you and his or her partner as representatives of his or her parents. Have this partner think of you as being made of clay—that is, you are bendable and shapeable. Have the partner move the two of you into positions and shapes that best represent his or her views of caretakers. In addition, have the partner put himself or herself into the sculpture to represent his or her role in the relationship. Give the couple time to process this sculpture using Couples Dialogue. Then, have the other partner sculpt his or her parents along with his or her role in the family.

This exercise should be used as an information-gathering and empathy-developing tool. When couples see the relationships their partners had with their parents and their role in their family in a physical depiction, they are often able to feel a new empathy. I can recall when I first did this with my wife, our sculptures were very similar, which, in effect, told us that we had similar wounds. Sculpting is a very useful technique, especially with visual learners.

These are just a few additional exercises that may be substituted for the basic six-session package. Bearing in mind that the most important learning occurs in the first three sessions, you can make changes to the package to fit your needs and style of therapy. Several books are available that can offer you ideas on other structured techniques, including the *Handbook of Structured Techniques in Marriage and Family Therapy*, by Robert Sherman and Norman Fredman (1986) and *Passage to Intimacy*, by Lori Gordon (1993). It's always beneficial to have a few extra tools in the box!

SPECIAL TREATMENT POPULATIONS

Obviously, this six-session program has been designed to work with those marriages that have your everyday "things are not the same, we don't love each other as we used to" types of problems. For most therapists, this takes into account about 90 percent of the couples who walk into your office. Occasionally, couples with more serious problems—beyond the scope of this short-term work—will come to you, and you may not know how to handle them. Here are some ideas on what to do in such situations.

Drug and Alcohol Abusers

I've never been able to work with couples who present with an active addiction. It is difficult, if not impossible, for persons abusing drugs, alcohol, or both to work on their relationship. I used to hope that the addiction was being caused or aggravated by stress in the relationship. Instead, I find that the addiction takes on a life of its own. Therefore, I do not recommend that this work be done with a couple when drugs or alcohol are a present and active factor.

I do, however, recommend that the therapist work actively to get the addicted person into an Alcoholics Anonymous or 12-step program as soon as possible. You should also have a substance abuse specialist and a drug and alcohol partial hospital program available for consultation or referral for these couples. Be sure to adamantly stress to the couple that their marriage is headed straight downhill should the addiction continue. If the addicted person is able to maintain sobriety for three months, you may try to begin the six-session program. In doing so, be aware that the work on the marriage is stressful and could very well trigger a relapse. With this in mind, you should work directly with the recovering person on the importance of attending meetings regularly—especially during this period of therapy—and encourage him or her to speak out about his or her triggers and desires. We have seen great success with recovering people who are committed to the couples therapy sessions.

Codependent Couples

One question that will arise from those who are in codependency groups is, "Isn't giving your partner what they most need considered codependent?" The answer to that is "no" because in therapy we're dealing with a different type of need. Codependency groups stress that the spouse not do things for the partner that may foster his or her addiction (such as calling in sick for the partner or making excuses). These groups also guard against the act of taking care of others to the exclusion of oneself. In other words, codependency addresses the needs of daily living.

When we refer to *needs* in couples therapy, we are referring to needs that were not met in childhood—such as being held, being told you are special, feeling competent, having an identity in the family, and so on. These are needs that can be met only by our partners and should be given consciously and with the awareness that, by our giving them, we will heal our partners. "Codependent" partners should be made aware that such behaviors as calling in sick for partners or doing things for others to the exclusion of themselves will not help anyone and may even make matters worse. In contrast, by giving their partners what they need from childhood using the Behavior Change Request, they not only heal that partner, but they reclaim a part of themselves lost in their own childhood. Rather than giving up a part of themselves, they *find* a part of themselves on their path to wholeness.

Present Physical and Sexual Abuse

On occasion, you will have a couple who are experiencing physical or sexual abuse. Although these abuses are not uncommon in our society, it is rare that these couples will come into your office; most will guard their secret. If such a couple comes to you, their safety should be your first concern.

Keep in mind that there are still some underlying reasons for this couple to have chosen each other as partners. Still, no one asked to be hurt and you should neither condone nor be a party to any abuse. Help the couple with their behaviors first before working with them on the unconscious forces that bring about this behavior. Preventing couples from inflicting harm on one another is far more important than having them undergo the couples therapy sessions.

As I have stressed throughout this work, safety has to be number one and physical or sexual abuse precludes safety. When the couple can make safety a promise, only then can growth occur. If, however, the abuse is frequent or violent and they are not making a commitment to stop it, I strongly suggest that you consult an attorney and your County Victim Services Bureau.

Childhood Physical and Sexual Abuse

I have had very good experiences in working with couples in which one or both of the partners was a survivor of childhood physical or sexual abuse. With its emphasis on safety and communication, this work blends well with recovery from these traumas as it gives the survivor someone at home in whom he or she can confide and trust.

Again, teach the couple that Nature has put them together for a reason as you empower the nonabused partner to be the healer of the survivor. Many nonabused partners soon learn that they themselves have a wound that corresponds to the partner's and that they, too, can heal. Perhaps they had a parent who confided in them and they were "emotionally incested" (Love, 1990) or maybe their lost part is their feelings and, by helping in their partner's recovery, they will reclaim that part of themselves. Whatever the reason, help nonabused partners see their role in the recovery and empower them to work with their partner.

Furthermore, the nonabused partner may need your guidance in dealing with some of the scary things that can occur when a trauma survivor is recovering. When partners make the recovery safe, flashbacks occur and memories flood in. Help them see that flashbacks, dissociations, and reliving experiences are a normal reaction to an abnormal situation. Help them to see that this is part of the healing and is not "craziness." Suggest that they read *Allies in Healing* by Laura Davis (1991).

Affairs

Nothing I have seen brings about a stronger emotional reaction than the discovery of an affair in a relationship. Couples expect partners to be true and faithful to them and, when they are not, the reaction is typically rage.

If the couple still wants to make the relationship work, the rage must be dealt with first. If not, it will seep out through sarcasm, avoidance, or other behaviors that will make the relationship unsafe. As a consequence, the couple will not be able to do the work outlined in the sessions and growth will not occur.

Therefore, prepare yourself to have them deal with the rage by using Imago Therapy's Container Process. Let the couple know that dealing with the rage is your top priority and they will have to learn some skills to make it safe and effective for them. Spend the first session gathering information and teaching Couples Dialogue. Work extra hard on teaching safety and the "safe place" information, especially with the partner who had the affair. He or she is the one who will have to contain or listen with empathy to the partner's rage.

When the couple appears to have grasped the importance of safety as well as the dialogue process, walk them through the Container Process. Because they have not had the experience of using Behavior Change Requests or the Holding Exercise, you will have to take them through these exercises spontaneously. The important part is that the sending partner should be able to express rage safely and the partner who had the affair (the receiving partner) should be able to fully hear the partner's hurt and rage. The structure of the Container Process provides a way for the sending partner to express himself or herself fully. Make sure that the receiving partner "stays with" or fully listens to the sending partner. Sometimes these sessions get loud and the receiving partner may be observed "fleeing" or "playing dead."

There is a flip side to the sending partner's rage. We have found that affairs do not happen in a vacuum and usually occur when the couple are feeling distant from each other. Therefore, the person who had the affair most likely will have feelings about the marriage that prompted the affair. The partner who had the affair should also be given time in dialogue to talk about the marriage and the feelings of abandonment or loneliness they may have been experiencing at the time. It is probable that the marriage was full of exits which will have to be closed to return energy to the relationship. As a matter of fact, the affair is seen as a catastrophic exit, or an acting out of feelings. Have the person who had the affair get in touch with the feelings that prompted the behavior of the affair while in the dialogue process. If this person can discuss the feelings in a safe place, the likelihood of repeated affairs decreases unless there is some sort of an addictive quality to the affairs.

The Container Process may have to be repeated several times in various sessions to fully vent the rage. Couples report feeling rage at various times for months following the discovery of the affair. They also report "anniversary" rage a year after the discovery of the affair. It is important that they know the steps of the Container Process so that they use this tool outside of the office when the rage reappears. Affairs are very threatening to a relationship and some may never recover. The Container Process offers a way to get rid of the rage so the couple can then do the work needed to improve the relationship and avoid any future affairs. Some excellent books on affairs are *Adultery: The Forgivable Sin*, by Bonnie Eaker Weil (1994); *Private Lies*, by Frank Pittman (1989); and *Patterns of Infidelity and Their Treatment*, by Emily H. Brown (1991). It is important to become knowledgeable about affairs from various sources so that you are well prepared for these sometimes volatile sessions.

Undoubtedly, you will come across other special treatment populations. I have tried to cover some of the most common as a way of emphasizing the importance and benefits of making this work your own. Adapt it to fit your needs and your clients' situations. As I've mentioned, although 90 percent of your clients may be able to benefit from the six-session program, others will not. Ironically, it is the ones who present with special problems who will keep the work interesting for you.

WHAT IF THE THERAPY DOES NOT WORK?

I wish I could report otherwise, but the fact remains that we can't save all marriages. The reasons vary and all are disappointing in their own way. Sometimes couples will not "buy" what you are "selling" them. Sometimes the work is too scary for them to approach. Sometimes the relationship is too far gone to put back together. As hard as you try, the flame just cannot be rekindled. Having experienced them all, I thought it would be helpful to give you my thoughts on those cases we sometimes call "failures."

Most couples will come to your office with a preconceived idea of what marriage is about. Unless they have read books on the subject, everything you say will seem like a foreign idea to them. The reason the lectures and exercises presented in this book are so simple is to give you a greater chance to sell the idea to the couple. If they can have their own "theory" on marriage, they can understand their frustrations and use the marriage for growth. Sometimes you'll find that couples have a hard time giving up their theory in exchange for yours.

You've probably experienced going to a lecture only to find that the presenter is coming from a different theory base than the one you use. Perhaps you have been analytically trained and the lecturer is a behaviorist. Or you are trained in family therapy and the speaker's work is limited to individuals. Maybe you've had a similar experience in reading this book! You question everything, running it past what you know and will either absorb it or reject it. Couples doing this work will behave in a comparable way, so the more persuasive and safe you are, the more they will take in and accept.

There will always be those who stick to what they know, preferring their ideas to yours. They may question you along the way or keep their opinions and concerns to themselves. You may even get that dreaded phone call announcing, "We have decided not to come back"—an unsettling message that may make you question yourself. Just remember, these cases are to be expected—not everyone is ready for what you have to say! Keep in mind that even if they walk out of your office with the Couples Dialogue, you will have done them a great service. The dialogue is the main communication tool, and if they use only that, their relationship will improve. This is also a couple who may be back to see you at a later date when things get worse or they are now ready for what you have to say.

Other couples become scared of this work as it gets closer to their pain. This is more than fixing a marriage. This work involves doing some painful healing work. Some people may say that this is not why they came to see you. If that is the case, you may want to keep them talking about everything using Couples Dialogue for the duration of the treatment giving them the experience of communicating. They may also be a couple who will just quit only to return when they are ready to deal with their pain. If it does not feel safe, they will use their flight response and leave the therapy. Sometimes, no matter how safe you make it, the couple get too scared to do this work.

There will also be cases in which both you and the couple will know that there is little hope of saving the relationship and the best thing is for it to end. I never wanted to believe that, but sometimes there is no energy between the partners—there's "too much water under the bridge."

Divorce law in the Commonwealth of Pennsylvania states that if one partner in the couple does not want the divorce, the couple have to attend three sessions of couples therapy. I have had several of these cases and I must confess that I have had little luck in turning the relationship around. Usually when the relationship gets to this point, the partner seeking the divorce is mentally out of the marriage. He or she may have been pleading with the partner for years to get the counseling and were met with, "We can work it out on our own." Finally, after growing tired of this way of living, he or she files for divorce, and the other partner will say, "This caught me totally by surprise." When the partner who wants the divorce has made up his or her mind, the decision seems to be set in stone.

You will also come across couples who are trying to make one last go of it. If it works, it's great and they will usually take this work to heart. If you can see that it is not going to work, there is one wonderful gift you can give to the couple and that is giving them the chance to say good-bye and grieve over the relationship. So many divorced couples do not have this opportunity and they spend many years wondering or feeling bitter. You can give them the chance to prevent this by using the Goodbye Process.

The Goodbye Process

This process is designed to help the couple say goodbye and grieve for the end of the relationship. Paradoxically, sometimes in saying goodbye, the couple comes to realize the value of the relationship and may choose to stay in the marriage and do the work necessary to heal the relationship. Be prepared for anything, especially deep emotions and crying. Keep a full box of tissues on hand.

This work usually takes at least two sessions, with each partner having a week to say goodbye. At this point, they will have had at least one session on Couples Dialogue and know the value of listening and hearing each other. The receiving partner will be listening intensely only without replying or mirroring. The sending partner will be saying goodbye. You will want to encourage a bit of drama in this session because you want some deep emotion. Have the sending partner begin by slowly saying goodbye to the bad things in the marriage by starting each sentence with "I want to say goodbye to . . ." and then talking about what he or she hated about it. Have the sending partner end talking about each item by saying "Goodbye." For example:

> I want to say goodbye to your coming home late. I would sit and worry that you might be somewhere dead on the road. I would feel my stomach turn with every minute on the clock and wonder where you were. I hated that you did not even have the courtesy to call me to let me know you were okay. And now I will not have to worry about that anymore. Goodbye.

Have the sending partner do this for each of the negative things in the marriage until he or she feels that his or her list is exhausted. Then have the sending partner switch to the positive things he or she is going to say goodbye to in the marriage. This is done in the same way. For example:

> I want to say goodbye to the ways you smell. I always liked the perfume that you wore and it always reminded me of you when I smelled it. I could be on a busy street and if someone walked by with that fragrance on, you would come to mind. I will miss that smell. Goodbye.

> I want to say goodbye to making love to you on a Sunday afternoon. I used to love the way the light would come into the window and how we held each other for hours. I cannot do that anymore. Goodbye.

Again, have the sending partner do this until the list is exhausted, while the receiving partner listens with feeling, but without replying. The emotionally tearful part usually happens with the positive parts of the relationship. It is very hard for the couple to leave the good parts of the marriage, but it is best that they get the chance to say goodbye to these rather than carry the feelings around forever.

The final part of this process is for the couple to say goodbye to the dream. Every couple goes into a marriage with a dream of how it will be and what they will accomplish. One of the hardest parts of ending a relationship is knowing that things have not turned out as planned with the person you planned them with. This is where the bitterness of divorce usually lies and it is best that couples get to grieve the loss of the dream rather than live with the bitterness. Again, the sending partner says goodbye to the dream in the same way. For example:

> I want to say goodbye to the dream of growing old with you. I pictured us together to the end going to movies and on vacations. I really thought we would have raised our kids well, sat next to each other at their weddings, and then have the chance of being with our grandchildren together. Now that dream cannot be. Goodbye.

This work is so intense that it is best to do one partner each session. The sending partner is usually so emotionally drained, that he or she could not possibly listen to the other saying goodbye. I once had a man call me after he did this that summed up the process pretty well. He said, "I feel as though I got hit by a truck!" What he was experiencing was his own grief. Remember that we pick partners based on the positive and negative aspects of our early childhood caretakers so, to the brain, leaving your partner is akin to having a parent die. It's sad and you have to grieve.

When the couple come back for the next session, have them reverse the process—the receiver is now the sender. Do not be surprised if the couple change their minds about splitting up. Sometimes, this exercise makes things so real that the thought of leaving outweighs the problems. Proceed with the therapy if they change their mind.

11

CASE STUDIES

Most couples whom you will see in your office will be able to use this material without a problem—if they are really committed to growing in their relationship. Some, like Dave and Diana, the main case study in this book, will be psychologically minded and be able to do some very deep emotional work. Others may be more interested in the skills, just hoping to get their marriage back on track. Some couples may think that you're are out of your mind and will resent your meddling in their relationship. And then there are those who, while giving it a try, are so wounded, that they will fall back to their familiar albeit hurtful style of relating.

This chapter of case studies should give you an idea of some types of couples you may encounter or are indeed already encountering. It will also demonstrate how keeping them in the dialogue process may be their best hope in overcoming problems.

"JUST FIX IT!"

For many, this work opens a door they thought they'd shut years ago. They are amazed to learn how their childhoods contributed to their choice of mates as well as to their present power-struggle issues. Through the therapy, they become willing to look at behavior patterns and their origins. They begin to do the emotional work they thought they could avoid and, in turn, become firm believers in the psychological process. They come to understand that their many years of denial only served to contribute to the problems in their marriage as they'd unconsciously "take it out" on each other.

However, you will find that there are many couples who are interested in improving their marriage without having to do all of the "childhood" work. They lead very practical lives and simply want the skills. You will recognize them immediately; although they'll be interested in what you have to say, they will do the work merely by rote, without showing any real emotional response. They'll still leave knowing the skills and feeling better about the relationship, but you won't see them doing any real emotional work in the sessions. They may save that for home, or they may choose to use the skills to get through their daily routine and to lessen tension.

By no means are these cases failures. Being therapists, we want to see our clients work on their deep psychological issues. In fact, it's great fun when they do, and typically they'll become our favorite clients. However, these are the exceptions, not the rule. What you'll more commonly find are those who are interested in living their everyday lives, paying their bills, going to ball games, and taking vacations. These are the folks who want life to be as tension free as possible. They haven't a clue, and couldn't care less, that their childhoods may have contributed to the stressful situation in their marriage.

You can't help but recognize them. They'll often giggle or be at a loss for words while doing exercises such as Parent-Child Dialogue or the Container Process. They may stiffen and appear visibly uncomfortable in the Holding Exercise. They'll probably have very little to write in the Finding your Imago form and explain they don't remember much about their childhoods. For this couple, two options present themselves. You can spend every session in dialogue, having them talk about their everyday issues and giving them the experience of talking safely and efficiently. Or you can proceed with the six-session format as written and hope that one of the skills will be important to them.

Often, you'll be surprised by which processes become important to a couple. There will be times when you will think they've learned nothing; they may have spent the time laughing at processes many people consider important. Only later will you find out how important a process really is to them.

Jim and Susan

Jim and Susan were just the kind of couple I would describe under the "Just Fix It" category. Jim is a mechanic and Susan is a veterinary assistant. They live in a rural town. They sought therapy because Susan was feeling alone and neglected. An avid hunter, Jim would spend many autumn weekends in the mountains and a considerable amount of time tracking when the season was over. This left Susan at home with the children on many weekends. The most recent source of stress was the hunting dog Jim bought, an animal that requires constant attention and training.

The therapist observed Susan to be a tolerant person. Raised in a traditional religious family, she feels confident in her role as wife and mother. She works while the children are in school and greets them when they get home. She enjoys preparing meals every day for Jim and the kids, and she's proud of her meticulous housekeeping. Her complaint is not about the amount of work she does, nor is it about Jim's hunting activity. As she explains it, her father was also an avid hunter. Her gripe is the dog. The dog demands too much time and attention, she says, and much of the work falls on her while Jim is at work. During the sixth-session Container Process, Susan chose to vent her anger over the dog.

Susan: This dog is ruining our family. She's messy and I don't have time to take care of her—and you—and the house. I hate the mess. She use to crap all over the place (*laughs*). I just hate everything about her.

Jim: (*laughing to therapist*) You want me to encourage this?

Therapist: Yes, I do.

Jim: Tell me more about that.

Susan: I simply do not like this dog. She's a lot of work for me and has thrown me off of my routine. I hated last winter because she was in the house so much more and really got in my way. And I'm dreading this winter with her. I get mad just thinking about it. She's a pain and takes you away from us. You have to realize that your family is important to you. We are more important than the dog. Your kids need time to play with you, and I look out, and there you are—playing with the dog. We are important! We are more important than the dog!

Therapist: And when I don't feel important, it reminds me of when I was a kid.

Susan: (*pause*) Oh, I don't know. I guess it could. When I think of my mom. . . . Well, to my mom, a clean house was more important than we were. We all seemed to come second to the house, but I am very angry about this dog and how we come second to it. Something has to be done.

Susan appeared uninterested in going into any depth with her childhood wound. Although it may have been significant that she felt her mother was more concerned about the house than her, Susan was more concerned with the here-and-now and the dog in her house. Jim, in contrast, was able to listen to his wife by using the process. He was able to come to understand that she felt upset about the dog and how it pulls him away from the family. It seemed to the therapist that this process carried minimal emotional impact and instead was more of a venting and problem-solving session. Susan's Behavior Change Request, however, revealed the importance of the session to her.

Therapist: Can you ask Jim for three Behavior Change Requests that will help this situation?

Susan: Yes. When we talk about the dog, I would like to talk about her using this dialogue process. This was the first time that I felt as though you heard me, since you are usually defending her. If you had defended her, I would have felt invisible. Instead, I feel like you heard me, which will make it easier for me to deal with the dog. I would like you to do this for 15 minutes, two times this week.

Jim: So when we talk about the dog, you would like me to mirror, validate, and empathize with you or listen to your anger using the Container Process, because that will let you know that you were heard and you will not feel invisible. You would like for me to do that twice this week for 15 minutes.

Susan: That is correct.

Although the process was not deeply emotional and did not address childhood wounds, Susan felt as though the process had helped her feel heard by Jim. She wanted more of this so that she would not feel invisible. Of course, the therapist could interpret that Susan's wound was in the identity stage and that she feels as invisible with Jim as she felt with her mother. The therapist could also interpret that Jim had developed a rigid, masculine personality in which he likes to assert his authority and cut her off so that she remains Diffuse and unable to assert her power. But they may not have been ready or willing to hear that. At this point in their marriage, they were not discontent with the structure of their marriage. Instead, the dialogue process provided the means for Susan to have her needs met.

For couples who only want to have their marriage fixed and work more smoothly, dialogue provides the listening and understanding while Behavior Change Requests provide the change needed for the couple to get what they need. Susan's other Behavior Change Requests about the dog were practical requests that would make her feel as though Jim were more a part of the family and that he had her needs in mind. These included, "By the end of September, I would like for you to finish the work on the heated dog house so the dog can spend three hours a day outside in the winter" and "I would like for you to spend 30 minutes four times a week playing with the kids with your attention focused only on them." For Jim, who tends to isolate himself and avoid relationships, this third request will help him stretch into his compassion, even though he may not be aware that he is in need of this area of growth. For Susan, these requests will help her begin to be taken seriously, make her visible, and help her claim some power in the relationship.

EARLY WOUNDED COUPLES

Some couples will have early wounds in their childhoods that will make this work difficult; they may possibly need a longer amount of time in Imago

Therapy. Early wounded couples are those with developmental wounds in the Attachment or Exploration Stages. As children, these people did not receive or, for some reason, could not take from their early childhood caretakers the necessary holding and warmth or the encouragement to explore. Their marriages tend to be volatile, loud, and sometimes even violent.

Couples wounded in the Attachment Stage, Clingers and Isolators, did not receive holding or proper nurturing in the first year of their lives. Therefore, their needs in the marriage are basic. They need touch, and yet being touched frightens them.

Partners referred to as Clingers are aware that they need touch, and they ask for it constantly from their partners and from others, such as pastors or those in the health profession. They often have numerous nonspecific illnesses that require frequent visits to the doctor. Although they are very aware of their need for human contact, they fear it because they think they might lose the contact after having received it. This fear often comes true because, when they do receive attention or affection, they will overwhelm the person giving the attention with frequent phone calls, gifts, card, questions, or hugs. Such behavior smothers the Avoidant person they marry, who will retreat. This, in turn, feeds the Clinger's fear of making contact.

For the Avoidant person, any contact is overwhelming. Avoiders prefer jobs that are not people-oriented, relating better to computers and laboratory instruments than to people. They often have a difficult time with being touched and tend to be asexual in nature. They can be very bright, logical, and successful if they can find their niche. These people are typically stiff in posture and uncomfortable in groups. Again, this is due to early attachment and trust wounds.

Couples wounded in the Exploration Stage can have volatile marriages. Diagnostically, these couples, Fusers and Isolators, are referred to as Borderline and Narcissistic, a mix that can be explosive. Their wounds occurred at about 2 years of age when they were unable to explore their environment. They were also wounded when the excitement and awe of their new discoveries were not mirrored by their caretakers. When parents mirror children at this age, they learn through the connection that it is okay to explore, look around, and begin to separate—without losing the relationship with the parent. The growth occurs in the connection.

The Isolator learns that it is not okay to explore. Isolators may be children you would call spoiled or overprotected. They are told as toddlers that they must stay close and that, if they stray, they may lose the relationship. Yet the natural urge is to separate, and when they grow up, they tend to do just that. The unspoken message they live by is, "I'm going to do whatever I want, whenever I want, and I am going to be the best at it." For them to be in a relationship is to lose the ability to live by this motto, so they'll get involved in businesses and buy "toys" (cars, boats, clothes). They become narcissistic.

To heal the wound, Nature puts this person in a relationship with the person we call the Fuser. As children, Fusers were allowed to explore, but no one shared their excitement when they saw or did something new. They could explore, but doing so severed their relationship with the caretaker. In the present relationship, they scream to keep the partner in the relationship with them. The louder they get, the more someone has to pay attention to them. But when these people are truly mirrored, they quiet themselves and feel human. There is, after all, no need for them to scream if someone is in a true relationship with them and validates their thoughts. But mirroring them is the hardest thing for their partners. In fact, the narcissistic partner would rather believe that the Fuser is crazy and in need of help.

I mention these couples here because they are difficult to manage in short-term therapy. Progress can be made and seem to disappear quickly when one of the partners gets scared. It is important for the therapist to mirror these couples in all interactions with them. You want them to remain connected to themselves and to what is happening in the session, rather than resort to the typical yelling, withdrawing, or possible violence. If, over the six sessions, these couples learn the importance of dialogue, they may do well on their own in the long run. Couples wounded in the Attachment or Exploration Stages need much more coaching than usual and, with it, can have brief glimmers of a trusting, empathetic relationship. Often, however, they'll fall back into old patterns between sessions and feel despair. Bob and Glenda are a good illustration of a couple wounded at the Attachment Stage.

Bob and Glenda

Bob and Glenda began therapy due to the severe fighting in their marriage. They were known to get very loud and throw things, after which Bob would retreat to his lab where he had been a scientist for 15 years. Glenda is disabled with sundry nonspecific ailments. Over the years, she's explored alternative treatments for her physical and emotional health. "I have been to every doctor, and none of them can help me." Glenda is well-read and can often be found at her local New Age bookstore.

While Glenda often appears sad and teary-eyed, Bob is observed to be stiff and seemingly self-absorbed. This made their third session all the more remarkable. With a considerable amount of coaching from the therapist, Bob was able to loosen his stiff posture and listen to Glenda as she described her abusive childhood. He seemed interested when she began to describe tearfully how she had no memory of her mother ever holding her or telling her she was special. He seemed very touched when she actually fell asleep in his arms during the Holding Exercise. By all accounts, this was a wonderful, empathetic healing session.

The therapist had every reason to expect a good report for the fourth session, but as we will see, quite the opposite occurred:

Therapist: So how was your week?

Bob: I think we probably hit an all-time low.

Therapist: How so?

Bob: The concept of "safe place" is lost on me. I get really defensive. I can't make myself safe with Glenda. I cannot feel for her.

Therapist: You did in the last session. Did you do the homework?

Bob: I have trouble with the physical contact. I don't relate to her that way.

Glenda: The homework helped me understand what's going on.

Therapist: Can you see his pain?

Glenda: I can see it every minute of every day. It's so evident.

Therapist: (*to Bob*): Can you see her pain?

Bob: I just see it as an attack. She says it's pain, but since it's personal, I take it as an attack. This has brought out the worst in me. There was a time that I enjoyed that. I use to like when people brought out the worst in me. But I don't enjoy that anymore.

Therapist: So you want to be different?

Bob: No, I want to be the same, but I want to be it by myself. I'm one of those people who should be by themselves, because I'm one of those people who others would characterize as abnormal. I'm better off by myself.

Therapist: So you are saying that you are one of those people who should be by themselves because you are one of those people others would characterize as abnormal. How would others say you are abnormal?

Bob: They would probably say that I'm antisocial. I'm not a real people person. I see myself as an outsider. It's a role that I got into early, and I enjoy it.

As is often the case, early wounded couples have a difficult time maintaining the empathy and closeness. The wound they sustained was around attachment, so it is intimidating when they experience closeness. Glenda was, of course, devastated by this turn of events. The moment of closeness she experienced the week before was exactly what she wanted. However, just as she feared, it did not last. The intimacy in Session Three probably occurred too quickly for them. Couples wounded at this stage need change to come slowly. One possible way is to have Glenda begin by touching Bob's hand and have Bob talk about his experience of being touched, with Glenda mirroring. This may seem a small step, but intimacy is scary for the early wounded couple. And although it seems to most observers that these marriages will not last, these couples often remain together, albeit sleeping in separate rooms and living parallel lives.

It is important for the therapist to recognize the fear these couples have of intimacy. The tendency for most of us trained in the pathology model is to diagnose and pathologize the relationship. But these couples are scared and terribly wounded. The best help you can give to them is to create a safe place in which they can slowly explore, and mirror them so they feel they are in a safe and empathetic environment.

For the attachment-wounded couple, provide a safe holding environment. When they begin to feel safe with you, they will allow you to take them into the harder terrain that is necessary for their growth. For the exploration-wounded couple, mirror constantly so they can learn that it is okay for each of them to have their own ideas and, at the same time, stay in relationship. Be aware that this couple will resort to using the defense mechanism of splitting. They'll vacillate between your being the best therapist in the world and your not knowing what you are talking about. Be sure to mirror that back, too.

THE RIGID-DIFFUSE COUPLE

The Rigid-Diffuse couple have, for the most part, looked rather good to those around them. They are often hard-working, neat, thrifty, and strict with their children, who respect them. They are a model family by all outward appearances. They have a familiar groove that keeps all involved on course. Should anyone get off course, they are pressured back into the groove through stares, manipulation, or threats of abandonment from the family. And then the children grow up.

This is the couple who are usually 17 to 18 years into their marriage. Often they come to you because of the desire for change from the Diffuse partner. There seems to be an awakening that occurs in which the Diffuse partner wants to begin a career, go back to school, or to be recognized as an equal. The Rigid-Diffuse couple spends many years in a state of inequality which is condoned in the patriarchal society. The Rigid person has a need to maintain control and seems to maintain *his* identity through controlling *his* environment and family and by looking and acting a certain way. This makes sense, when you consider that this couple have been wounded in the Identity Stage.

Diffuse partners have long given up their identity to the Rigid partners who seem so sure of themselves. The power struggle heats up when the Diffuse partner decides that it is now time to find an identity. We therapists may never know how many of these couples exist. I suspect that Rigid persons work hard to convince their partners that they are making a mistake—that they shouldn't rock the boat. Still others may use threats and violence to maintain the equilibrium. It is the strong person who decides when "enough is enough"—to shake the marriage in an effort to get help.

There are several ways the Rigid-Diffuse couple may present themselves for therapy. They may come in with the Rigid partner only wishing for you to fix the Diffuse partner and talk some sense into *her*. The Diffuse partner may say, "I need some space to find myself and develop new skills and friends." The Rigid partner will counter rather self-righteously by saying, "I'm all for that," knowing all the while that the rope will only be let out so far. In other cases, this couple may come in with a Diffuse partner filled with confidence as she's been working hard and is ready to enter the world. The Rigid partner, in turn, is gripped with fear. He's in tears, because the world he created seems to be falling down around him.

Don and Jean

If you're lucky, Rigid-Diffuse couples will come in early in their marriage to work on these power struggles, before it gets to that point. If they do, the Couples Dialogue is a wonderful skill to change the pattern and break the symbiosis that is prevalent in these couples.

Don and Jean are in their early 50s and have been married for three years—a second marriage for both. They have grown children and enjoy each other's company immensely. They feel fortunate to have found each other and are committed to staying together to the end, but they've run into some significant communication difficulties, which have prompted them to enter therapy.

In the first session, the therapist asked them to produce a 3-minute frustration. It went something like this:

Jean: I get upset with you because you just don't let me express myself with you. When I do, you tell me that my ideas are stupid or off the wall. You say that there is no reason for me to feel that way.

Don: When I ask you for specific examples of what you mean, you can never give me any.

Jean: Because you get me so worked up, I can't think. I really can't think.

Don: How can you be upset about something if you can't express what it is you're upset about? You speak in nebulous terms.

Jean: Because I'm afraid to express it to you, because you get angry.

Don: I get angry because you can't communicate what it is that's bothering you. You use terms that don't have any real meaning. They can mean anything. You don't give me specific instances of what it is that I did or what I did that bothered you.

Jean: Because it could encompass a whole thing. It could be a general area.

Don: Well, put a name on it.

Jean: You have to have one specific general thing . . .

Don: Put a name on it.

Jean: . . . at that particular time, and sometimes I can't think of it. It's so frustrating.

Don: With your way of thinking, it can be anything. Anything could fit your package. Sometimes you go on and on and on, and you cannot put a label on anything.

Jean: But if I do tell you, you say, "That's crazy. That is just crazy."

Don: This is what I would say now. "Give me an example."

Jean: Oh! But see, now I can't think of one. Okay. If you raise your voice to me, that's okay, but if I raise my voice to you, you say, "I'm not going to stand for this," and you walk out of the room. A lot of things are okay for you, but they're not okay for me.

Don: For example?

Jean: Ohhh!

Don and Jean are a clear example of a Rigid-Diffuse couple. Don obviously wants things presented to him in a certain way and would like nothing more than for Jean to think like him. He uses coercive and sometimes verbally abusive techniques to throw Jean off and make her feel that she is wrong. Because of her wounding, Jean is not able to gather her thoughts and presents heavily from her feelings. She'll need a sense of safety and understanding from Don to express these feelings accurately. Don and Jean were smart to have come in early in their marriage, because they can easily work on their problems with the dialogue process. They were taught the dialogue in the first session, which proved difficult for Don to do because he wanted to control Jean's thinking. So they were asked to practice this skill for homework. They produced the following dialogue in the second session.

Jean: I feel you treat me like a child sometimes and that you don't respect the way I feel. It seems that you want me to behave the way you want me to behave, and sometimes I can't do that.

Therapist: Mirror.

Don: If I am hearing you correctly, you said it feels to you that I treat you like a child and I do not respect the way you feel. You feel like I want you to behave the way I want you to behave, and sometimes you cannot do that. Did I get that?

Jean: You did.

Don: Is there more?

Jean: I feel angry and frustrated when I can't talk to you and tell you how I feel, but you can come to me very upset.

Therapist: (*softly to Don*) Stay safe and mirror back just what you heard.

Don: If I got that, you resent that I can come to you with how I feel, but you can't talk to me about how you feel. That makes you angry and frustrated. Did I get that?

Jean: (*smiling*) You got it.

Don: Is there more?

Jean: You treat me like a little girl sometimes.

Don: So you are saying that I treat you like a little girl sometimes. Did I get that?

Jean: (*giggling*) Those were my exact words, yes.

Don: Is there more?

Jean: You make me very angry when you treat me like a little girl.

Don: So it makes you angry when I treat you like a little girl.

Jean: Yes. But in some ways I love it because you protect me, and I love that you take care of me. But I want to have feelings that you respect.

Don: So you love it sometimes because you do like being taken care of, but you also want to have feelings that I respect. Did I get that?

Jean: (*laughing now because she is being mirrored and heard*) Yes, you're getting it! I like that you take care of me, but there are times when we argue that I want to be able to tell you how I feel without you judging me—without your yelling at me, just listening to me.

Don: So when we disagree, you would like to be able to tell me how you feel without feeling judged and without my yelling at you. You just want to be listened to. Did I get that?

Jean: Yes. I want you to think of me as grown up and with feelings. I need you to listen to me and try to understand my feelings.

Don: So if I am getting that, you want me to think of you as a grown-up with feelings. You want me to listen to you and try to understand your feelings. I can understand that. You make sense to me, because anyone would want to feel like a grown-up and have their feelings understood. I imagine when I do not, you feel childish, unheard, and invisible.

Jean: You got it! Thanks.

The therapist saw Jean laugh and have a look of joy on her face several times during this interaction. She had come from a family in which she was not heard as a young girl and was left to deal with her own feelings. Her first marriage was to an abusive man who tried to control her every move. Although Don is also controlling, he is open to change and to making the relationship work. If Don and Jean are able to keep up the dialogue process and stay attuned to each other's feelings during their disagreements (Jean will also need to mirror Don's discomfort when he feels he is not in control), they will be able to let each other develop in their personal lives. There will also be less of the hierarchical relationship often seen in Rigid-Diffuse marriages and, instead, more of a partnership marriage. Couples

Dialogue will also give them the opportunity to discuss on a deep level where their patterns started in childhood. This will increase empathy from the receiving partner.

Unfortunately, however, this is not always the case. Sometimes these marriages go on for many years before they reach a crisis point. As stated previously, the crisis usually comes when the Diffuse partner decides it's time to find an identity and stretch out from under the rigid structure endured for many years. The crisis can be dramatic: what seems like a strong family suddenly splits apart. The call typically comes from a distraught Rigid partner who says he never say it coming. John and Sandra best illustrate this.

John and Sandra

John and Sandra were married for 17 years and had a son, 16, and a daughter, 14. John started a manufacturing business soon after they were married that has now made them financially secure. They have all of the trappings of wealth: a nice house, luxury cars, a mountain home, and beautiful furnishings. But all of this came at a price.

Their first child arrived a year after they were married, and they quickly assumed their roles. Sandra devoted her time to home and family, while John immersed himself in his work. John would work at least six days a week—often until late in the evening. When he would come home, he would complain to Sandra about her housekeeping. "What are all of these toys doing all over the place. You're home all day and you don't have time to clean? Do you just sit on your ass all day?" Sandra would try to explain to John that taking care of small children was much harder than he thought, but he would have no part of that. "It can't be harder than what I do in a day. I expect this place to be clean. Stay off the phone with your friends, and maybe you'll get some things done around here."

Sandra decided early in the marriage to tolerate this for the children's sake. Every day she would clean, run the children here and there, and be the perfect "businessman's wife." Having quit college after two semesters, she figured this was the best job for her, so she became dutiful and learned to let the insults roll off her back.

When her youngest turned 12 two years ago, Sandra decided to take a college course. John thought the idea was "cute" and figured it was better than her sitting around all day. Sandra enjoyed the class so much that she decided to pursue her associates degree, with the possibility of going further in her education. She began spending more time at school as well as socializing with a group of younger students.

John was now becoming concerned. He began to question why she needed to be out so much and whether she should be out with her fellow students. Sandra would tell him, "I am trying to start a life of my own. I have given up everything for this family. It is time to do something for myself." This began to make John upset, and he started to feel suspicious. He'd call her names like "tramp" and "whore." "What will others think?" he would yell at her.

Then Sandra announced that she would be getting an apartment. John called her a "fool." "You'd give everything up just so you can find yourself? You're dumber than I thought!" But Sandra was not shaken by this. She knew what she wanted to do. And John sat in disbelief and anger as she packed.

John called for the appointment two weeks later when he realized that this was not a phase his wife was going through. During the session, he admitted to being distraught that the world that he created was falling apart. He could not believe that he didn't see it coming, although Sandra assured him that this had been building for years. She reminded him that she asked him several times to go to therapy with her, but he would blow it off, telling her that they could work it out. He would be nice to her for a few weeks and then he'd return to his old ways. All the while, Sandra appeared confident in her decision to leave.

This is a real "iffy" time for many relationships. Sandra had been through a lot in the past 17 years. There was a lot of hurt and little recognition for what she had done to support her family and support John in his success. She had been invisible in the relationship. The material things have done nothing to make her feel important, but school has. She was now beginning to feel a sense of accomplishment as her years of life experience were paying off in good grades. She was being recognized by her professors as a student with real potential, and she liked the feeling. A break up at this point could be permanent if Sandra feels that going back to John is a step backwards. She found what she was looking for, and she was not about to give it up. She wanted to pursue it.

One curious aspect is that Sandra seems happy that John is feeling distraught. Not so much in a "now you know how it feels" demeanor, but rather that she feels that it is good for him. "I like that he is having feelings about this. It lets me know that he is human. I think it will be good for him in the long run." And although Sandra was not willing to go back to John yet, she stated that she was willing to learn the processes with him so that they can learn to communicate. The second session produced this dialogue.

John: This feels so sad to me. The house feels so empty. I've been crying myself to sleep every night.

Sandra: I hear you saying that it feels sad and the house feels empty. You have been crying yourself to sleep every night. Did I get that?

John: Yeah. (*crying*) I don't think I have ever felt hurt like this before. My guts feel like they are ripping out. I have really messed up.

Sandra: If I hear you right, you are saying that in your life you have never felt hurt like this before. It feels like your guts are ripping out. It really feels like you messed up.

John: I left you alone so much. I blamed you for your unhappiness, and it was me. I thought the business would make me happy—and to some extent it did. People told me how great I was all the time and I loved that, but I missed my family, my kids growing up.

Sandra: You realized that you left me alone a lot and blamed me for my unhappiness. You now know that you may be to blame. You said that you thought that the business would make you happy, and it did to some extent because of all the praise you got. In the process of being at the business so much, you missed your family. Did I get that?

John: (*sobbing*) It's all falling apart. Everything I tried to create is falling apart. I thought the material things would make you happy. I thought my success would make you happy. I did not see, I did not ask you what would make you happy. I messed up.

Sandra: So it feels like your world and everything you tried to create is falling apart. You thought that your success and the material things would make me happy, and they did not. You said that you did not ask me what would make me happy and you feel you messed up.

Therapist: Can you validate that?

Sandra: Yeah, I can see that you feel that you messed up and it feels like your world is falling down around you. Everything you tried to create is up in the air. It makes sense, and I imagine that you might feel sad, overwhelmed, and hopeless.

John: Yeah, that's it.

Therapist: And that reminds me of when I was a kid.

John: You know how my family was. Dad was so mean, especially when he was drinking. Mom was so busy with the others, and he would abuse her so much. He was always yelling at her. It was horrible.

Sandra: So in your family, your dad was so mean when he was drinking. He was always yelling at your mom, and she was so busy with the other kids. Did I get that?

John: Yeah. The house was so filthy and disorganized. I couldn't bring anyone home. I promised myself that I would not live that way, and I kept that promise. But I messed up. I tried to control everything. I was scared. Scared that I would end up like them. (*sobbing*) That's so scary to me. I messed up.

Sandra: So you promised yourself you would not live like your family who were disorganized and filthy. To do that, you had to control everything. You felt scared, and it feels like you messed up. That makes sense to me. I can see how you would think that you would need to control things so it would not end up like your family. I imagine you feel very scared and down and disorganized.

John: Yes.

John is touching the core of his wounds—a place he was trying to avoid since he left his family for college. Unfortunately, he has avoided it on the back of Sandra. And while her compassion is available for him, it is probably too soon for her to totally recommit to the relationship. John needs to feel his pain, and the best place to feel it is in dialogue with Sandra. She does need to see his humanness show itself through his pain. And he needs to touch it so he can deal with his verbally abusive childhood as well as discover again that life has successes and pain. Those in Rigid-Diffuse relationships often cause pain in order not to feel their own. It was now time for John to drop his guard.

With Rigid-Diffuse couples it is important to be watchful for the Rigid partner using the dialogue to manipulate and control the Diffuse one. I have observed Rigid partners using Couples Dialogue to coerce the Diffuse partners back home and into the same pattern they were living in before the breakup. Although this may work for a while, it usually results in a future breakup and a dissatisfied couple. What seems to work is helping the Rigid partner to sincerely encourage the Diffuse partner's growth through mirroring and validating. At the same time, the therapist should help the Rigid partner experience and reveal his pain in a safe, compassionate place with his partners by using the dialogue process.

Sandra will also need time to dialogue, with John hearing her clearly. There have been many years of hurt in this marriage, mainly caused by John not hearing Sandra and understanding her needs. If John wants this marriage to work at all, he will have to learn to fully hear Sandra and understand her needs in the relationship. He also has to become more flexible in his dreams for the family to make room for Sandra's dreams and her growth. She cannot become what he wants her to become; she is in a growth path that will need to be encouraged using Couples Dialogue in the relationship.

CONCLUSION

These couples cases are a few of many that we encounter in our offices. Keep in mind, that although couples will present themselves in many ways and deserve to be treated as individual cases, they are basically wounded on a developmental level. This means that as you begin to use this work regularly, you will begin to notice patterns. These patterns will give you the guidance you need to apply your basic tool: Couples Dialogue. I am continually amazed that whenever couples seem to be getting out of control, if I can get them to use the dialogue process, they become centered and they listen to each other. To be heard and understood is a basic need we all have. To provide a structure for couples to learn to hear each other is a service that we should strive for in our work.

12

EPILOGUE

To What End—Couples Therapy?

Your work with the couple is almost over, and you are about to send them on their way—but on their way to what? Why do we spend the time we do on saving marriages and relationships? To stop pain and to rebuild productive lives? Most certainly. To protect children if they are involved? Absolutely. But there's even more to it than that, and to find out what that is, we have to look at a much larger picture.

We have to begin by asking ourselves a few age-old questions: "Why are we here?" "Why did we evolve?" "What is the purpose of love relationships in this evolutionary process?" If relationships serve a purpose other than the continuation of the species—perhaps a spiritual one—then a big question for therapists could be, "What is the therapist's purpose in all of this, and how does the work we do contribute to a healing and conscious universe?" If, as therapists, we can recognize our society, with its poor and oppressed people, as wounded and suffering from a lack of community, we may come to view our work with couples as a vehicle of hope for healing these wounds and for taking care of its people.

As you know by now, the basic philosophy behind Imago Relationship Therapy is that relationships are Nature's way of bringing two people together who have been wounded at the same place developmentally, so that they can heal the wounds of their childhoods. Healing childhood wounds is certainly not a new concept in the fields of psychology and marital therapy. Since the study of psychology began, we have been blaming our childhoods, our mothers, and our fathers for most of our ills. But I can't help but wonder: if my parents wounded me, what happened to them, and their parents before them, and their parents before them, and so on? If this wounding has an origin, how far back does it go? And is there something about our relationships that can serve as a clue to the source of our pain as well as a remedy?

PROBING THE PREHISTORIC

To research this answer, we have to go back as far as we can to the earliest civilizations. Our understanding of these civilizations is changing rapidly as archaeologists are uncovering more artifacts and sites. Once a male point of view dominated such studies, mainly because archaeologists were men. But now scientists and historians are looking at these prehistoric discoveries more objectively than ever before. Keeping in mind that the term "prehistoric" is applied to anything predating actual written accounts of history—and not to cavemen and cavewomen—we can appreciate the relatively new evidence of very sophisticated societies existing in what is considered Old Europe *as early as 30,000 B.C.E!*

According to archaeologist Marija Gimbutas (1982), groups began to settle in the warmer and more fertile regions of Old Europe soon after the Ice Age. The societies they formed were considered goddess cultures because, as archaeological evidence indicates, they worshipped the goddess as Creator. Possibly the most recognized of these goddesses is the Earth Mother of Willendorf (c. 25,000 B.C.E.). This representation of the Earth Mother was uncovered in the form of a four-inch limestone statue depicting a round, large-breasted female figure, which was used as a sacred symbol for the abundant, nurturing, and life-giving qualities of the earth. And it makes sense that these early cultures would worship the feminine, because whenever they would gaze around, they would witness the earth as being creative—always giving birth. With each new spring season, the earth would push new life out of its ground, and the birth, life, death, and regeneration cycle would begin anew.

They were also able to associate the women as having a part in this creation process. Women, like the earth, were also able to give birth each year. What they probably were not aware of at the time was the men's role in this birth process; and so it must have seemed quite miraculous and awe-inspiring to them that women were able to give birth. It is also likely that a connection was made between the women's 28-day menstrual cycle and the phases of the moon. Since these were small communities, the women most likely all began their periods on or around the same day (as women today who live in dormitories or work together commonly report), which must have been quite impressive and scary to the men of that time.

Such groups were not matriarchal societies, however. Rather, they were partnership societies, according to Riane Eisler (1990), in her book *The Chalice and the Blade*. Archaeologists speculate that men were in awe of women and showed a deep respect for their connection with nature. Men and women shared a respect for each other, an equality, a love for the earth and a reverence for creation. Men hunted in service to and respect for the women in the group. In line with this, it is interesting to note that archaeologists have been unable to find any evidence of war, fortifications, or violent deaths during this era.

But this account is true for only a part of civilization, for there were other areas of the world that were not as friendly or fertile. Nomadic groups called the Indo-Europeans were roaming both the deserts and colder climates in search of better areas in which to live. Their biggest concern was survival, and they found an easy target in Old Europe. Beginning about 7000 B.C.E., the Indo-Europeans were able to settle in these heretofore peaceful areas and take over with very little resistance from the unarmed Neolithic goddess societies. Taking over a land is one thing; taking over a culture is quite another—and a long, drawn-out process at that.

People are traditionally steadfast in holding on to their cultural traditions, as we see even today in modern America. So it goes that in order to make the changes toward patriarchy, civilizations found it necessary to attack the symbol systems established by the goddess cultures they were attempting to overpower. For example, the color black was once considered a positive color because it was the color of the soil; therefore, black became the color of the goddess. Conversely, the color white once symbolized death because it was the color of bones and carried a negative connotation. Over the thousands of years of the patriarchal takeover, this concept of color became reversed—with black symbolizing evil and white symbolizing goodness. The goddess symbol of the bull, whose head and horns resemble the uterus, was later transformed into the horned devil. In addition, the idea of the goddess, who really symbolized the earth in all of its abundance, began to change significantly, and—at some point during a 7000-year period—the goddess evolved into a god.

Ending the worship of the goddess was no easy process. For the ancient Greeks, this process began to be manifested in their mythology when they removed the goddess from the earth and placed her in the sky. New gods were also added who were often in conflict with the goddesses. In the story of *Oresteia*, for instance, Athena is left to cast the deciding vote in the trial of Orestes. Orestes was accused of killing his mother—an act that the god Apollo, contending that children are not blood-related to their mothers, stated in Orestes's defense, "The mother is no parent of that which is called her child. . . . [She is] only nurse of the new planted seed that grows"

(Aeschylus, 1953 translation, p. 158). When the 12-member jury arrived at a split decision on Orestes's guilt, Athena was left the task of casting the deciding vote. She voted to acquit Orestes on the grounds that he was not related to his mother, and explained, "There is no mother anywhere who gave me birth and, but for marriage, I am always for the male with all my heart, and strongly on my father's side" (Aeschylus, 1953 translation, p. 161).

Unlike today, plays back then were not written for entertainment purposes. The Greeks used their plays and mythologies to influence people. Imagine, if you will, all of Athens watching this play at a Greek ceremony and picture how it could affect them emotionally as well as change their thoughts about the role of women and the power of men. Envision the shift over a 7000-year period from the goddess-woman being the creator of all to women as mere vessels for man's seed. Still, the shift was not complete, because there still remained a goddess.

THE BIBLE AND THE BATTLE OF THE SEXES

The Hebrew Bible contains many stories—and warnings—about the power of women, beginning with the Book of Genesis. In the story of Adam and Eve, the couple were warned about eating fruit from the Tree of Knowledge—held to be a symbol of the goddess. Eve was persuaded by the serpent—another important goddess symbol—to eat from this tree and to persuade Adam to partake as well. This, according to Genesis, was the fall that drove Adam and Eve out of the garden. Thereafter, they would suffer from their sin, and women would forever bear children in pain. The message was clear: stay away from the goddess and the temptation of the woman. Even to this day, a Hebrew daily prayer is recited by observant men: "Blessed Art Thou O Lord Our God, King of the Universe, who has not made me a woman" (Stone, 1976, p. 224).

Later in Genesis, the Israelites were to receive the Ten Commandments as brought down the mountain by Moses. The First Commandment stated, "Thou shalt have no other God before me." This was a most unusual order considering the times, because polytheism was the rule, and now the people were being asked to give up their gods and goddesses.

By the time of Jesus, monotheism and the patriarchy had been firmly entrenched. Men and women rarely talked about serious matters. In fact, men "owned" their wives. And so naturally Jesus—who liked women and believed in peaceable solutions—posed a problem for the society. Instead of preaching the popular values of his times—those of toughness, aggressiveness, and male dominance—he advocated ideas such as the meek inheriting the earth and loving one's neighbors *and* enemies. Do unto others as you would have them do unto you, he preached. Or, when someone slaps you, turn the other cheek. Likewise, if we were to read all of Jesus's words as presented in the Gospels, we would find that this man was a very well-rounded person who upheld many feminine values.

The relationship Jesus maintained with women was unheard of among his contemporaries and was even considered to be heretical. Contending that we should all be spiritual equals, Jesus was often seen in the presence of women, the most notorious being Mary Magdalene. Mary Magdalene had been accused of prostitution, which at the time could have meant that she was with a man who was neither her husband nor her owner. Jesus stopped an angry mob from stoning her to death with his statement, "Let him who is without sin cast the first stone." Following this incident, many began to view Jesus as a dangerous heretic for his teachings and actions, and his death was actively sought by the priests and noblemen of his time. That he would first appear to Mary Magdalene upon his resurrection can be interpreted as another illustration of his genuine fondness for women.

After his death, the disciples of Jesus split up into two factions: one based on a hierarchy and one based on a membership of equality. Such a division was inevitable. Some of the disciples took very seriously Jesus's teachings that segregation and subordination of women and slaves were to be rejected, while others adapted his teachings and formed an organization based on the hierarchal structure they already knew.

Those who believed in equality became known as the Gnostics (from the Greek *gnosis*, meaning knowledge), whose most well-known member was Mary Magdalene. Instead of meeting in a church or a temple with a priest, the Gnostics would meet at the various homes of its members—including the homes of women. Instead of a permanent priest, the members would draw lots to determine the priest and prophet for that meeting, and this designated person was quite often a woman. To the Gnostics, this seemed fair; moreover, it precluded a hierarchy.

To the other faction, however, this method posed a threat. This second group of Christians, with the disciple Peter as its first leader, was based on a hierarchy. They believed that, in order to attain spiritual knowledge and blessing, the people had to go through the Church and its priests for teaching, curing, and baptizing. To these people, the Gnostics posed a serious problem. Like the goddess culture before them, the Gnostics became vulnerable to the dominating patriarchal structure evolving in what would later be considered the only true or "Mother" Church.

The Gnostics meanwhile had written volumes of scripture about their beliefs and experiences with Jesus and with their faith. Beginning around 300 A.D., the orthodox church, proclaiming these scriptures as heretical, ordered the Gnostic texts to be destroyed. No traces of these writings were found—until 1945 in the form of the Dead Sea Scrolls. Elaine Pagels (1979), a biblical scholar who studied the new Gnostic Gospels, suspects that a monk in a nearby monastery hid the documents in a jar which was unearthed in a cave in Nag Hammadi, Egypt. After over 30 years of translation and interpretation, we are beginning to find out about the gentler and more cooperative side of the early Christians. And this lies in marked contrast to the overall impression that has been documented in history.

THE CHURCH AND FEMALE PHOBIA : THE MISOGYNISTIC MOTHER CHURCH

With the conversion of Constantine in the fourth century, the Church began to take hold of most European society. The Roman Empire soon became the Holy Roman Empire, and it became heresy to be anything other than a Christian. To not believe was a crime, punishable by torture and death. This societal metamorphosis, which evolved over a short 400-year period, is certainly a far cry from the messages professed by Jesus regarding peace and love. And women, again, were nowhere to be seen. Patriarchy ruled.

But perhaps the most telling time of misogyny—the fear and mistrust of women—and a declaration of patriarchy came from the year 1400 to the mid-1700s in the guise of the witch hunts. We often hear about the 20 or so women who were put to death in Salem, yet that tells only a fraction of the story. By the time these events occurred in America in the 1700s, Europe had already experienced 300 years of these hunts. What happened in Massachusetts may have been a warning to women in the New World to stay in line or else face a massacre such as had transpired in their homelands, for it is estimated that over nine million women were burned, drowned, or died in prison for being suspected as witches.

In actuality, these women were not witches at all but were murdered for doing what they knew how to do best: to feel and to be intuitive. Women who would gather to be supportive of one another were suspected of plotting to do the Devil's work. Herbal medicines were suspected of being potions, and the women who practiced folk medicine were killed. This effectively spelled the end of folk medicine and allowed for the rise of our male-dominated allopathic medicine, which is currently the type of medicine being practiced in the U.S. A disproportionate number of the women accused were older women, whom the male-dominant society had little use for. Older women had gone from being perceived as wise and able to impart their wisdom to younger women, to being seen as dangerous broom-riding witches who taught younger women how to cast spells and who sacrificed babies to the Devil.

The Church's role in this widespread holocaust is quite significant and centers around the 1484 publication of the *Malleus Maleficarum* (Hammer of the Witch), which was written by two Dominican priests—Heinrich Kramer and James Sprenger. The *Malleus Maleficarum*, in effect, served as the handbook for all witch inquisitors. Possibly every magistrate in Europe was armed with a copy of this fantastic propaganda, which covered in gruesome detail how to find, torture, and kill suspected witches. As one reads this most horrifying book, one realizes how precious few rights the accused persons had in defending themselves (I refer to "persons" because, although the overwhelming majority of victims were women, some men were tried and killed for witchcraft). Anyone could accuse another of being a witch. For the most part, the accused were guilty until proven innocent.

The *Malleus Maleficarum* was cleverly compiled and covered all the bases—even going so far as to warn magistrates that witches would deny everything, and thereby advising them to proceed with torture. They were warned that witches could make them feel sorry for them, that the magistrates would feel tempted to drop the charges, but they should resist this urge as they continued with the torture. They were told that the witch had a "mark" that she carried on the inside of her skin and were given instructions on how to find it. The *Malleus Maleficarum*—essentially a book of torture—became one of the most important volumes of its day.

Of course there were those who protested this treatment of women. But Kramer and Sprenger thought of this also and persuaded Pope Innocent VIII that they were doing important work for the Church. In response, the pope issued the Bull of Innocent VIII, which was included in each copy of the *Malleus Maleficarum.* This essentially made even the protest of witch hunts a heresy, punishable by excommunication—or even torture and death if so deemed. In their book *Riding the Nightmare,* Selma and Pamela Williams (1978) detail the torture that women were made to endure, including the reading of their own death sentences at the burnings. If the women refused, they were taken back and tortured until they agreed to read the sentences that proclaimed their guilt and their fate. Pyres were set up in the marketplace for all to see these atrocities and to warn others against "dealing with the devil."

But we should keep in mind that the victims of this era were not only the ones who died, but also those who lived through these times. Like the mythology and theater of the ancient Greeks, these trials and ritual burnings were also meant to influence the thoughts and actions of the people. And the effects of this history on our society resulted in a polarization between men and women that I believe exists even today. Women were burned for being intuitive and having feelings. The clear message to men of this time was to disregard their own feelings and intuition and to think logically and to accomplish things—the Renaissance gives way to the Age of Reason which gives way to the Industrial Revolution.

Once again, thinking and accomplishment became male domain, while women were relegated into expressing themselves through feeling, intuition, and nurturing, but quietly, lest they risk certain torture and death. Intuition became a learned survival mechanism in a world violent toward women. To quote a phrase often said today, women essentially had "lost their voice."

In the late 1800s, as medicine became specialized, the new field of psychiatry became popular. This new specialty gave society's view of women its seal of approval by coming up with the diagnosis of hysteria (*hyster* from the Greek meaning "womb") for women who were highly emotional. An overabundant display of emotion was thought to be a disorder of the womb, for which one of the most popular treatments of the time was called the "medical massage" (Blank 1989). In this procedure, a doctor was called to the bedside of a woman who had either lost control emotionally or had fainted. He inserted the two fingers of his right hand into the woman's vagina and with two fingers of his left hand, he rubbed the external genitalia, continuing this until the woman experienced what was called a Hysterical Paroxysm. Symptoms included rapid respiration, a reddening of the vagina, rapid heart beat, and abdominal contractions—essentially an orgasm!

However, this procedure was very labor intensive for the physician, who often had to spend 30 or more minutes working on his patient, so an alternative was sought. This resulted in the invention of the vibrator, which was initially sold in Sears catalogues and fashionable women's magazines for the treatment for hysteria. Amazingly, hysteria remained a valid diagnosis in psychiatry until 1952.

It should be noted here that modern Christian churches and Jewish synagogues are more interested than ever in promoting equality and understanding among the sexes. The early violent history was more a reflection of the times than the basic beliefs of religion. Many of the leaders who have moved us to nonviolence, such as Martin Luther King Jr. and Ghandi, have been religious leaders. Many others have been influenced by their religious upbringing. As Western culture has settled into a less violent period, religion has followed and most churches have become more attuned to human nature. With some extreme exceptions, modern religion seems to want to understand and appreciate human behavior, rather than control it. Nonetheless, Western civilization has been shaped by history—much of it violent. And to make changes, we must appreciate what effect this 30,000-year history has had on us.

TWO DIFFERENT TEMPLATES

This history has caused a collective wounding by essentially creating separate templates for raising children. A template is like a bill you might get from the doctor. There is standard preprinted information, and there is specific information handwritten by the physician about you. We are raising children who are more or less allowed to become individuals, as long as they fit into their male or female template. But there is a problem with the template.

As we have seen through doing Imago work, the template that has emerged for men generally involves the thinking and doing parts, while the one for women is commonly geared toward sensing and feeling. This is by no means simply a biological gender difference; rather, it is a majority difference. You see many combinations of expressions in males and females, yet those people who fall out of the traditional male Thinker/Doer and female Senser/Feeler roles seem to develop what might be termed a "reputation."

In other words, there is a feedback loop that keeps the genders divided in the traditional arrangement. A man whose ability for sensing and feeling are highly developed might be called a sissy or be judged as soft or passive. A woman who is a highly evolved thinker or doer is often judged as cold, domineering, or "bitchy." Yet reverse the gender on these comments, and you have exactly what the template desires in men and women. And although the name-calling may be designed to push people back into their traditional roles or templates, it might be better for us to look at what Nature intended in setting up relationships in this manner.

AN EMPHASIS ON EMPATHY

Female therapists, in my opinion, will usher in the next wave of psychological theory. My advice to male therapists is to read and to learn. One of my favorite books of late is a compilation of works entitled *Women's Growth in Connection: Writings From the Stone Center* by Judith Jordan, et al. (1991). In one of her own chapters, Dr. Jordan states that empathy involves two processes: affective surrender and cognitive structure. In other words, to feel empathy for the other, a person has to be able to say, "I can see you feel that way. It's not me, but I can see YOU feel that way." Empathy is a momentary surrender to and an experience of another's feelings. Following that momentary experience, the empathetic person must then have the cognitive ability to set a boundary so the other's feelings do not overwhelm him or her and, in turn, become his or her own feelings. Empathy, you see, is always a two-part process.

But empathy seems to be a lost art with couples. Couples will come into your office and complain, "He is so cold! He never tries to understand my feelings!" Or you might hear, "Every time I try to tell her something she gets so emotional, so now I just keep things to myself." Statements such as these give clues as to what is missing in couples' communication and why the templates that have evolved do not support empathy between couples. It is hard to be empathetic when you are missing half of the process—which is either the cognitive or affective—to do so.

The communication style that has evolved from the templates makes it easy to understand how men and women seem to be from two different planets. The partners who sense and feel see their partners' problems with their affect and say, "I can see you feel that way. I can see you feel that way. I can see you feel that way. Now I am feeling that way. Is it you or me who feels that way?" These partners do not have the cognitive structure to pull their emotions back and say, "But it is not me."

On the other hand, the partners who use thinking and actions view their partners' problems with their cognitive abilities and say rather coldly, "But it's not me. But it is not me. It is your problem, not mine." They are so cognitive that they are not able to surrender themselves for a brief moment to feel their partners' pain.

In a way, we are all victims—but not so much of our parents' abuse as has been thought for the past 100 years. More accurately, we are victims of a 10,000-year history of male-female violence which now dictates that we give up a part of ourselves to fit into society. But herein lies the hope, because Nature—in its wisdom—set up couples' relationships in such a way that partners fall in love with the parts of themselves that are lying dormant. A reclaiming of the dormant parts is what is necessary for a return to empathetic communication. As I have said throughout this work, the best place to do this is not in individual or group therapy but in working with the very person whom nature set you up with and who can show you the parts you need to reclaim—your partner!

I often tell couples that I am not the best therapist for them. This is a very difficult admission for a therapist, but I like the role I play better. For years, therapists were taught that the client had to form a transference onto them to deal with the unconscious problems that troubled them. What we did not see is that there is a ready-made transference in a couple that continuously brings up unconscious hurts. Relationships can be healing vehicles if, as therapists, we can show a couple how to be therapeutic with one another. If we continue to take the role of professional authority, we run the risk of perpetuating a one-up society.

PSYCHOTHERAPY AND THE PATRIARCHY

Modern psychotherapy grew out of the individualistic paradigm that proceeded the shift from the goddess culture to monotheism. The idea of community changed greatly as humans went from a "communion of subjects" to a "collection of objects" (Swimme & Berry, 1992). Since the turn of the century, psychotherapists have been given the task of making each object optimal. And we boldly took on the task, as we all believed that a collection of optimal people who could be productive and logical would make the world a better place. But has it?

We have witnessed more destruction of natural resources over the last 150 years than the earth has ever experienced. As development has sprawled into suburban areas, natural beauty is destroyed and becomes secondary to buildings and roads and telephone and electrical wires. The planet and nature have become something to own, control, and alter, rather than cooperate with and look at with respect and awe. I am reminded of a beautiful Pennsylvania waterfall that has been commercialized with boardwalks, shops, and an admission fee. Its long-time "owners" proudly placed a sign at the entrance announcing it was now 90 years old. I wondered how many people who came to the area actually stopped to think that it was only the commercialism that was 90 years old; the beauty of the waterfall had been there for hundreds of millions of years.

And as more and more of our natural settings become commercialized and developed, we begin to lose our soul. When we lose our soul, we become depressed and anxious because our relationship is not so much with the natural wonders of the earth, but rather with the owner of the land to whom we have to pay an admission to enjoy what he or she owns. We become separate and isolated from the very earth that gives birth to us all. And because we are all born into this rugged individualist, patriarchal paradigm, we cannot see that it is this loss of connection that makes us anxious and depressed. Indeed, we go into therapy with therapists born into the same paradigm who tell us we have to find happiness ourselves and not depend on others. Early in this century, insight became the cure, yet the observation of "penis envy" became a pathology of women rather than a recognition of women's awareness of an imbalance of power. The therapist's job in this society, although therapists may not be aware of it, has been to help people feel comfortable with the patriarchy and the way society has evolved to this point.

The past 150 years of psychotherapy has been costly in terms of dollars and outcomes. Traditional psychotherapy assumed that patients had to form a long-term relationship with the therapist in order to gain insight and relieve symptoms. These costs have been passed onto insurance companies who, until the mid-1980s, paid with little question. The advent of managed care has shortened therapy time considerably and threatens the livelihood of many therapists who practice long-term methods of treatment. And although managed care has possibly saved the field of psychotherapy from its own greed, it may present another ominous problem.

The treatment methods that seem to work best in a managed care environment are short-term, solution-focused cognitive-behavioral-based therapies. And although these methods have been proven to work on symptoms, they do little to promote a world view that sees connection and relationship as a longer term solution to the client's ills. Rather, these methods work with clients to change their thoughts or behaviors until they feel comfortable with their environment—the same environment shaped by the 30,000-year history presented earlier.

A NECESSARY PARADIGM SHIFT

Science has made extraordinary leaps in the last 70 years as it shifted from embracing Newtonian physics to the more holographic view presented in quantum physics. Basically, Newtonian physics view the universe as a collection of individual objects all subject to the same laws. Quantum physics says that every object affects every other object—what is done to one object has an effect on all others. Observing something affects the observer and the observed. Science has made a leap toward relationship.

We have had a difficult time shedding ourselves of outdated ideas. Most of the world still believed that the earth was only 5000 years old well into the mid-1700s, and for a long time after, the figure was only revised to 80,000 years. It is only within the last 70 years that we have learned that the earth is 4 billion years old, with the universe in the 15-billion-year-old range. Although this information seems to be common knowledge in science and anthropology, it has not trickled down and made a significant impact on psychology. Nor has our violent history made an impact on our treatment modalities.

The Universe Story, by Brian Swimme and Thomas Berry (1992), is an epic that traces the history of the universe from the Big Bang, the beginning of life, the development of culture, through to where we are today. It is a telling of physical and human history from the knowledge that has been accumulated from modern science, quantum physics, anthropology, and cultural history. As one reads this story, one begins to realize that the universe, the earth, and even one's own life has not always been there, but rather is an unfolding story in which everything exists in relation to something else. Our present lives were shaped by those before us, and lives after us will be shaped by how we live and how well we take care of the planet and one another.

Riane Eisler's latest work, *Sacred Pleasure* (1995), tells quite clearly how those who lived before us were influenced by an individualistic dominator model that has shaped our lives, especially the lives of women, through violence and threat of pain. The dominator model has allowed the few (mainly men) to govern the many and has done so through coercion, threat, and violence. And this history of fear is in each of our cells—on some level we all know the fear. To truly heal the earth and its inhabitants, it will not be enough to adjust to the culture or the home situation. That is akin to putting a finger in a leaky dike.

The work of Swimme and Berry tells us that everything is in connection and everything we do on this earth will affect everyone else. The work of Eisler tells us that the wounding that has occurred through gender violence can only be healed by a new consciousness that expresses itself through a re-thinking of our history, genuine equality, and a promise of safety. To be a part of the healing of the planet and its people, psychology must undergo a paradigm shift. That shift is the transition from individual healing to healing in connection. What is needed is a relational paradigm in which the welfare of the other is our primary concern, and our welfare is theirs. Only then will we all experience the safety that will allow us to relax our defenses and heal our woundedness. When we can do that, true love and creativity will emerge.

Psychotherapists are now being asked to help more people in less time. The only way to do that is to offer hope. And in a relational paradigm, that hope will not come from our own successes and claims of victory. Rather, it will come from a validation of our successes by the significant others in our lives, and from our validation and sense of joy for them. We must all come to the realization that we are all on the same lifeboat paddling in the same direction; in a true partnership, we will all arrive at the same time and experience equal glory for the effort.

At the time of this writing, managed care is in its infancy. It is having a great impact on the field of psychotherapy as therapists scramble for shorter term and more powerful models. In writing this book, my hope is that it offers more than just solutions. Solutions are fine in the short term, but humankind seems to be suffering more from a lack of connection and soul rather than from a lack of solutions. It is my hope that the shorter term models being developed as a response to the dictates of managed care carry with them more than just outcomes. New models must also consider the cultural and historical factors that have brought about depression and despair. To fully understand anxiety and stress, they must consider the culture of progress and greed that has contributed to it. And they must consider that many of the problems that clients bring into therapists' offices are not about a lack of solutions, but rather about the lack of connection that allows solutions to emerge and differentiation, through validation and pride, to occur.

IMAGO RELATIONSHIP THERAPY AND THE RELATIONAL PARADIGM

Imago Relationship Therapy, as presented in this book, is a shift toward the relational paradigm. Safety and Couples Dialogue, the main focus of the work, promote equality and allow for expression and validation of early childhood wounds and fears. It promotes empathic connection and an interest in the growth of the other. For partners to learn to transcend their own selves, for just a moment, to experience the pain and pleasures of the other is truly the highest form of being human. And when partners are released from their self-absorption through the true recognition of their pain by one another, the creative process can begin. Defensiveness is replaced by concern which allows solutions to reveal themselves. Partners discover that the true solutions to their problems are not found in the therapist; they lie buried, waiting to be discovered in the relationship.

I have no illusion that Imago Relationship Therapy itself will change or save the world. The work of psychotherapists will be only a part of the total paradigm shift within social, economic, and religious institutions all over the world—a shift that is desperately needed to make this world a better and a healthier place to live. As Swimme and Berry (1992) say:

> The well-being of the planet is a condition for the well-being of any of the component members of the planetary community. To preserve the economic viability of the planet must be the first law of economics. To preserve the health of the planet must be the first commitment of the medical profession. To preserve the natural world as the primary revelation of the divine must be the basic concern of religion. (p. 243)

I would like to add:

> To promote and preserve connection between people through dialogue so that humans can live consciously, safely, and equally, and thus become caretakers of the planet must be the primary goal of the psychotherapist.

Imago Relationship Therapy is a therapy for our time. It is a work that will preserve families, promote equality, decrease violence and coercion in marriages, and bring about a new consciousness regarding the purpose of marriage. If we can see ourselves as gently guiding a couple through a process that uses the relationship to heal and help them to recover their lost selves, we will see a return of empathy and concern for the other. And when couples' wounds are finally healed in relationship, we will then see people who will take notice of the needs of the planet and each of its components.

Which brings us to our original question: To What End—Couples Therapy?

A BIGGER PURPOSE

In his work, Creation Spirituality leader Mathew Fox (1988) explains that humans were given a large cerebral cortex because the world already had everything in it except someone to witness the creation and to be in awe of the world. In other words, we are here to say, "Wow!" This hit home with me one day as I was driving through the country with my two boys who are being raised by parents struggling to reclaim our lost selves. From their birth, we have validated their thoughts, deeds, feelings, and intuitions to the best of our abilities. As we were passing a farm, I saw an old tractor and, doing what most dads probably do when impressed by machinery, I said, "Hey, boys! Look!" To my surprise, they shouted back in a chorus, "Queen Anne's lace!"

They had seen the flowers in the field rather than the tractor. They were more impressed with what nature had created than with what man had built. And I thought, "This is why we do it!" Healthy couples will raise healthy children who have all four ways of expressing themselves. Children who are more impressed with beauty than machinery. Children who would rather pick up trash in the park than play army and fake their deaths as they are "shot." Children who are more concerned about their neighbors' well-being than their high score on video games. Children who are in awe of, have respect for, and see an equality in the sexes because they all express themselves in the same way, rather than seeing and dwelling on the differences.

This hopeful and gentle idea may start in the office of a couples therapist. Nature may have chosen us as one of its agents of change. Couples we have worked with, who have learned that their relationships may have a healing purpose, report not only differences in their relationships and how they express themselves, but also a difference in their children. Perhaps we are seeing human evolution take a trip back in time to 30,000 years ago when men and women showed respect and awe for creation and for the woman's role in it—when they all believed in an equality of the sexes. If human beings are able to reclaim their expressive parts through relationships, perhaps the last 10,000 years can be seen as a violent but unnecessary blip of time in what we hope will be millions more years of civilization on earth. And perhaps, if we do our jobs right, couples therapists will be seen as one of nature's agents who brought human evolution back on course.

Appendix I

Resources

PROFESSIONAL ASSOCIATIONS

The Institute for Imago Relationship Therapy (IIRT)

IIRT is the credentialing body for Certified Imago Relationship Therapists. The Institute distributes a resource catalogue listing Certified Imago Relationship Therapists throughout the country. This catalogue also lists weekend couples workshops conducted by certified workshop presenters internationally, as well as products you may find useful for your couples. Also available is a professional training resource directory listing courses for therapists wishing to become Certified Imago Relationship Therapists, as well as other courses available to increase your couples skills. Both of these catalogues are available by calling or writing:

The Institute for Imago Relationship Therapy
335 N. Knowles Avenue
Winter Park, FL 32789
1-800-729-1121

The following professional associations have established committees to respond to managed care. Information is available to members.

American Association for Marriage and Family Therapy
1133 15th Street, NW
Suite 300
Washington, DC 20005-2710

AAMFT also publishes an excellent newsletter entitled *Practice Strategies* that covers managed care issues and how therapists can survive in the new health-care marketplace. To subscribe call: 202-452-0109.

American Psychological Association
1200 17th Street NW
Washington, DC 20036
202-955-7600

American Psychiatric Association
1400 K Street NW
Washington, DC 20005
202-682-6000

National Association of Social Workers
750 1st Street, N.E.
Suite 200
Washington, DC 20002
202-408-8600

National Board for Certified Counselors
5999 Stevenson Ave
Alexandria, VA 22304
703-823-9800

Employee Assistance Professionals Association
4601 N. Fairfax Drive
Suite 1001
Arlington, VA 22203
703-522-6272

BOOKS AND NEWSLETTERS

The following books and newsletters are excellent resources for therapists interested in keeping up with the managed care environment.

Poynter, William (1994). *The Preferred Provider Handbook: Building and Maintaining a Successful Private Therapy Practice in the Managed Care Marketplace.* New York: Brunner/Mazel.

Psychotherapy Finances. Published by Ridgewood Financial Institute, Inc., 1016 Clemons Street, Ste. 407, Juniper, FL, 33477, 407-624-1155

Open Minds Newsletter. 44 South Franklin Street, Gettysburg, PA, 17325, 717-334-1329

ORGANIZATIONS TO RECOMMEND TO CLIENTS

Substance Abuse

For couples experiencing substance abuse in the marriage:

Al-Anon Family Group Headquarters
1372 Broadway
New York, NY 10018
212-302-7240

Alcoholics Anonymous World Services
Grand Central Station
P.O. Box 459
New York, NY 10164
212-686-1100

Narcotics Anonymous
P.O. Box 9999
Van Nuys, CA 91409
818-780-3951

Domestic Violence

For couples experiencing domestic violence:

National Domestic Violence Hotline
800-333-SAFE (7233)

National Child Abuse Hotline
800-422-4453

National Coalition Against Domestic Violence
P.O. Box 15127
Washington, DC 20003
202-293-8860

Professional Legal Services

For divorcing couples:

American Academy of Matrimonial Lawyers
20 North Michigan Ave
Suite 540
Chicago, IL 60602
312-263-6477

American Bar Association, Family Law Section, Mediation and Arbitration Committee
750 North Lake Shore Drive
Chicago, IL 60611
312-988-5584

Women's Legal Defense Fund
122 C Street, NW
Suite 400
Washington, DC 20001
202-887-0364

Appendix II

The Efficacy of Short-Term Imago Therapy— Preliminary Findings

Wade Luquet, A.C.S.W.
Mo Therese Hannah, Ph.D.*

The study presented here was designed to measure improvement in marital functioning following a structured six-week program of Imago Relationship Therapy (IRT). Because IRT is hypothesized to have a positive effect on couples' communication skills and to facilitate the development of empathy, intimacy, and conflict resolution, the Global Distress, Affective Communication, and Problem-Solving Communication scales of the Marital Satisfaction Inventory (MSI, Snyder, 1981) were selected as outcome measures. It was expected that scores on the MSI would decrease from pretreatment to posttreatment, indicating an improvement in marital functioning.

Subjects

Couples were recruited through agencies and therapists, who were sent a letter informing them of the study and asking them to prescreen couples prior to referring them to the study. Inclusion criteria were as follows: couples must have been referred from an outside source; must have been married at least one year; and must have no current substance abuse problem and were not experiencing domestic violence by either partner. The present study was limited to heterosexual couples. Once referred, couples were further screened to assess their interest in completing the brief therapy program. All subject couples were seeking couples therapy for current relationship distress.

Although the original sample was composed of 12 couples, three couples were dropped from the study prior to its completion. One was dis-

---

*M. Therese Hannah, Ph.D., is Assistant Professor of Psychology, Siena College, Loudonville, NY.

covered to be experiencing domestic violence; a second developed health problems that prevented them from completing the program, and the third couple was lost to follow up.

The ages of the 18 participants ranged from 26 to 58 (mean = 44.7, $SD = 9.7$), with an average age for females of 43.6 and for males, 44.8. These couples, all Caucasians, had been married for an average of 14 years (the range being 1 year to 29 years). Five of the couples were in first marriages; the other four were in their second or later marriages. Of the 18 subjects, two did not complete high school, two were high-school graduates, five had completed some college, and five were college graduates. Four participants had graduate or professional degrees.

Procedure

The six-session IRT intervention was based on the 20-hour *Getting the Love You Want* weekend workshop for couples and utilized shortened workshop lectures and a subset of the workshop processes.

During the first of the six sessions, couples completed the Marital Satisfaction Inventory (MSI, Snyder, 1981) as a pretest measure of marital adjustment. This was followed by a one-hour therapy session. During this and the five subsequent therapy sessions, which were spaced one week apart, couples were given a brief lecture on one of the following topics: the triunal brain and its effects on safety in the relationship; childhood development and mate selection; the importance of empathy; caring behaviors; restructuring negative behaviors; and resolving rage.

The couples were then taught an experiential process that enabled them to apply the lecture topic. For example, in the third session, a lecture on the importance of empathy was followed by a process called the Parent-Child Dialogue. This process typically produces an empathic experience within the receiving partner, thus affording him or her a deeper understanding of the sending partner's "woundedness." At the end of each session, couples were given several forms, including a homework sheet detailing the processes that the couple were to practice prior to the next session. After the sixth therapy session, the couples again completed the MSI.

Therapists

Five Certified Imago Relationship Therapists were selected to participate in the study. Selection was based on the therapists' interest in participating in the study as well as on their proximity to the senior author. Each had been certified for at least two years by the time of the study. Therapists were trained in the brief IRT model as follows: First, they read the author's manual, which describes the steps through which couples are led during each of the six therapy sessions. They also viewed a videotape of the senior author conducting each session with an actual couple. Therapists were instructed to adhere as closely as possible to the author's modeling of the sessions. They were also given telephone access to the author, who called them weekly to discuss problems or concerns.

Measures

The MSI (Snyder, 1981) is a 280-item self-report inventory. It yields scores on 11 scales: Conventionalization, Global Distress, Affective Communication, Problem-Solving Communication, Time Together, Disagreement About Finances, Sexual Dissatisfaction, Role Orientation, Family History of Distress, Dissatisfaction With Children, and Conflict Over Childrearing. The measure consists of a test booklet and answer sheet to which partners respond individually.

The MSI has demonstrated both internal consistency and test-retest reliability. Internal consistency coefficients derived from combined general population samples and clinical samples ranged, for individual scales, from .80 to .97 (Mean = .88). Test-retest coefficients showed a mean correlation of .89 for the scales.

Evidence for construct validity includes the ability of MSI scales to differentiate between distressed, mildly distressed, and contented couples (Scheer & Snyder, 1983, cited in Snyder, 1981). Snyder and Wrobel (1981, cited in Snyder, 1981) found that couples preparing to divorce and couples entering therapy showed similar MSI profiles, as would be expected for scales reflecting marital distress.

The three scales selected for focus in this study, for reasons discussed earlier, were Global Distress, Affective Communication, and Problem-Solving Communication.

The Global Distress Scale (GDS) consists of 43 questions about distress in the marriage. Affective Communication (AFC) is a 26-item scale designed to measure a partner's understanding of the other's moods, feelings, and thoughts. Problem-Solving Communication (PSC) consists of 38 questions that tap the couple's ability to solve their differences in a positive manner.

Raw scores on each of the three scales were converted to T-scores. As discussed by Snyder (1981), T-scores below 50 were indicative of low levels of distress; T-scores from 50 to 65 reflected moderate distress; and T-scores above 65 were viewed as indicative of severe marital discord.

RESULTS

Pretreatment scores on the three MSI scales all reflected moderate levels of distress: mean GDS = 59.9; mean AFC = 57.3; and mean PSC = 59.8 (see Table II.1). Statistically significant declines occurred on each scale

TABLE II.1
Pre- and Posttreatment Scores on MSI Scales

	Pretreatment		Posttreatment			
	X	SD	X	SD	Mean Difference	t
GDS	59.8	9.6	53.4	8.6	6.4	3.51**
AFC	57.3	9.9	48.4	8.9	8.8	5.11***
PSC	59.8	7.14	50.7	6.8	9.2	6.34***

**$p < .01$
***$p < .001$

from pre- to posttreatment. Global Distress scores dropped an average of 6.4 points ($t = 3.51$, $p < .01$, one-tailed). A mean drop of 8.8 points was noted on Affective Communication ($t = 5.11$, $p < .001$, one-tailed). Problem-Solving Communication showed a decline of 9.2 points ($t = 6.34$, $p < .001$, one-tailed).

When data for males and females were analyzed separately, interesting gender differences emerged. Whereas females showed statistically significant declines from pre- to posttreatment on all three MSI scales, for males only two scale scores dropped significantly—AFC and PSC. The amount of change, pre- to posttreatment, was greater for females than for males: on AFC, females dropped an average of 12 points, while males declined by 5.5; on PSC, female scores declined an average of 12 points, with males dropping an average of 7.4 points.

DISCUSSION

These data suggest that the use of Imago Relationship Therapy in a standardized, short-term, structured format is associated with improvements on three dimensions of marital functioning, as measured by the MSI. Whereas pretreatment MSI scores fell well within the moderate range of distress, posttreatment scores dropped to at or near a T-score of 50—the level of distress reported by couples who describe their relationship as close, committed, and feeling-oriented and who also report being able to resolve differences when they occur.

REFERENCES

Scheer, N. S., & Snyder, D. K. (1983). Empirical validation of the Marital Satisfaction Inventory in a nonclinical sample. *Journal of Consulting and Clinical Psychology, 52,* 155–164.

Snyder, D. K. (1981). *Marital Satisfaction Inventory manual.* Los Angeles: Western Psychological Services.

Snyder, D. K., & Wrobel, T. (1981). *Determinants of marital dissolution: An objective comparison of couples seeking divorce with couples entering marital therapy.* Unpublished manuscript, Wayne State University.

Bibliography

American heritage electronic dictionary. (1992). Houghton-Mifflin Co.

Aeschylus. (1953). *Oresteia*. Chicago: University of Chicago Press.

Asaad, G. (1995). *Understanding mental disorders due to medical conditions or substance abuse: What every therapist should know*. New York: Brunner/Mazel.

Blank, J. (1989). *Good vibrations*. Burlingame, CA: Down There Press.

Branden, N. (1983). *If you could hear what I cannot say*. New York: Bantam Books.

Brazelton, T. B. (1992). *Touchpoints*. New York: Addison-Wesley Publishing Co.

Brown, E. M. (1991). *Patterns of infidelity and their treatment*. New York: Brunner/Mazel.

Davis, L. (1991). *Allies in healing*. New York: Harper Perennial.

Eaker Weil, B. (1994). *Adultery: The forgivable sin*. Mamaroneck, NY: Hastings House.

Eisler, R. (1990). *The chalice and the blade*. San Francisco: HarperSanFrancisco.

Eisler, R. (1995). *Sacred pleasure*. New York: HarperSanFrancisco.

Erikson, E. H. (1959). Identity and the life cycle. *Psychological Issues*, *1*, 101–172.

Fisher, H. E. (1992). *The anatomy of love*. New York: Norton.

Fox, M. (1988). *The coming of the cosmic Christ*. San Francisco: Harper and Row.

Gadon, E. (1989). *The once and future goddess*. San Francisco: Harper and Row.

Gilligan, C. (1982). *In a different voice: Psychological theory and women's development*. Cambridge: Harvard University Press.

Gimbutas, M. (1982). *The goddesses and gods of Old Europe: Myths and cult images*. Berkley: University of California Press.

Gordon, L. (1993). *Passage to intimacy*. New York: Fireside Books.

Gottman, J. (1979). *Marital interaction: Experimental investigation*. New York: New York Academic Press.

Gray, J. (1992). *Men are from Mars, Women are from Venus*. New York: HarperCollins.

Hendrix, H. (1988). *Getting the love you want: A guide for couples*. New York: Holt and Company.

Hendrix, H. (1992). *Keeping the love you find: A guide for singles*. New York: Pocket Books.

Howard, K. I., Brill, P., Lueger, R. J., & O'Mahoney, M. T. (1992). *The COMPASS system*. Available from COMPASS Information Services, 1060 First Ave., Suite 410, King of Prussia, PA, 19406.

Jordan, J. V., (1991). *Women's growth in connection: Writings from the Stone Center*. New York: The Guilford Press.

Kohut, H. (1978). The psychoanalysis in the community of scholars. In P. Ornstein (Ed.), *The search for the self: Selected writings of Heinz Kohut*, Vol. 2 (pp. 685–724). New York: International Universities Press.

Kramer, H., & Sprenger, J. (1948). *The Malleus Maleficarum.* (Montague Sumners, Trans., 1928) New York: Dover Publications, Inc. (Original work published 1484)

Lambert, M. J. (1992). Implications of outcome research for psychotherapy integration. In J. C. Norcross, & M. R. Goldfried (Eds.), *Handbook of psychotherapy integration.* New York: Basic Books.

Love, P. (1990). *The emotional incest syndrome: What to do when a parent's love rules your life.* New York: Bantam Books.

Mahler, M., Pine, F., & Bergman, A. (1975). *The psychological birth of the human infant: Symbiosis and individuation.* New York: Basic Books.

MacLean, P. (1964). Man and his animal brains. *Modern Medicine*, February 3.

Miller, J. B. (1976). *Toward a new psychology of women.* Boston: Beacon Press.

Pagels, E. (1979). *The Gnostic gospels.* New York: Random House.

Pittman, F. (1989). *Private lies.* New York: Norton.

Plato. (1948). The symposium. In S. Buchanan (Ed.), *The portable Plato.* New York: The Viking Press.

Rogers, C. R. (1969). Being in relationship. In *Freedom to learn: A view of what education might become.* Charles E. Merrill Publishing Co.

Russell, W. (1989). *Classic myths to read aloud.* New York: Crown Publishers, Inc.

Sanford, J. A. (1980). The Invisible Partners. New York: Paulist Press.

Satir, V. (1988). *The new peoplemaking.* Mountain View, CA: Science and Behavior Books.

Sherman, R., & Fredman, N. (1986). *Handbook of structured technique in marriage and family therapy.* New York: Brunner/Mazel.

Snyder, D. K. (1981). *Marital Satisfaction Inventory.* Los Angeles: Western Psychological Services.

Stone, M. (1976). *When god was a woman.* San Diego: Harcourt, Brace, and Jovanovich.

Swimme, B. (1984). *The universe is a green dragon: A cosmic creation story.* Santa Fe, NM: Bear and Company.

Swimme, B., & Berry, T. (1992). *The universe story.* New York: HarperSanFrancisco.

Tannen, D. (1990). *You just don't understand: Women and men in conversation.* New York: William Morrow, Ballantine.

Williams, S., & Williams, P. (1978). *Riding the nightmare: Women and witchcraft.* New York: Atheneum.

Acknowledgments

The last line of Robert Fulghum's book *All I Really Needed to Know, I Learned in Kindergarten* reads, "And it is still true, no matter how old you are, when you go out into the world, it is best to hold hands and stick together." I have held hands with many people over the past three years who have made this work possible.

The staff of Penn Foundation Employee Assistance Program in Sellersville, Pennsylvania, were the window to the real world and let me know that the ideas in this book actually work in practice. Sharon Mathews, M.Ed., assisted me in training the Penn Foundation staff and encouraged me to pursue the ideas further. And when I did, wasn't I lucky that the first editor to get her red pen on the manuscript was Denise Baron!

Denise spent many hours in my small back office with my slow Mac Plus rearranging words I had written, adding commas, and fixing all of my "theirs and there's." In the end, she made it flow and best of all, let it sound like me. Her first words to me were, "I have to get to know you." I'm glad she did.

And when the manuscript made its way to Brunner/Mazel, my luck continued when Natalie Gilman decided she wanted to take up this project as editor. She has guided me gracefully through the publishing process and helped make the book clear through her editing skills. Thank you, Natalie, for making this work a reality.

If you have to use someone's ideas, I can think of no one better than Harville Hendrix. Harville is more than a brilliant person; he's warm and encouraging too. He has been a part of this book every step of the way and has offered feedback that has polished the shine. Thanks for always believing in this project.

My thanks also to the many Certified Imago Relationship Therapists whose work has crept into this book as they graciously made it available to all of us. They include, but are not limited to, Gary Brainert, Maya Kollman, Bruce Wood, and Bob and Wendy Patterson.

The staff of the Institute for Imago Relationship Therapy—especially Walter Nirenberg, Sanam Hoon, and Mary Lemmon—have been supportive of this work from the beginning, and for that I am grateful.

Thanks to Lisa Kelvin Tuttle for being a great friend and a willing reader and editor of the drafts.

Thanks to the therapists who participated in the research project including Sherry Baker, M.S.W., Anne Carney, M.S.W., Bill Brennan, Ph.D.,

Gerry Brennan, M.S.W., and to Mo Hannah, Ph.D., for her work in the writing of the research appendix.

Thanks also to the Imago Therapists who subjected themselves to the trainings that were based on the early drafts of the book and let me know that the sessions worked in their practices.

But the person I owe the most to is my wife, Marianne, who started it all on a New Jersey beach. She forced me to look at our marriage and myself, and was intuitive enough to find the safest method of all, Imago Relationship Therapy. I am forever grateful to her for my growth, our wonderful children, our relationship that makes us conscious, and her encouragement which produced this book. Thank you my friend. I have enjoyed holding your hand.

HOMEWORK/HANDOUTS

Session One

The Three Parts of the Brain*

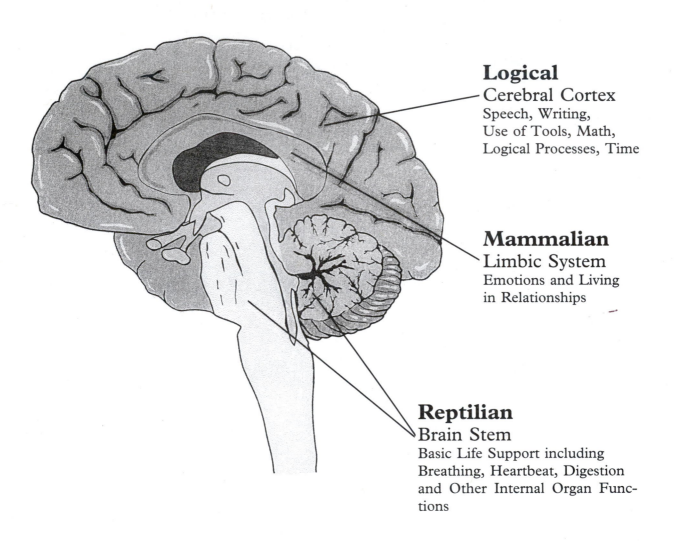

Logical
Cerebral Cortex
Speech, Writing,
Use of Tools, Math,
Logical Processes, Time

Mammalian
Limbic System
Emotions and Living
in Relationships

Reptilian
Brain Stem
Basic Life Support including
Breathing, Heartbeat, Digestion
and Other Internal Organ Func-
tions

Survival: If something is dangerous, we will fight, flee, play dead or freeze, hide or submit.
If it is safe, we will play with it, nurture it, mate with it, work or be creative.

*Based on MacLean (1964).

Couples Dialogue

The following communication tool is the basis for healing in Imago Relationship Therapy. If you and your partner learn and practice this one skill regularly, you will stop the reinjuring process and begin to open the way for conscious healing.

1. MIRRORING

> I heard you say . . . or
>
> If I am hearing you correctly, you said . . .
>
> *Then:*
>
> Did I get that?
>
> Is there more?

Repeat this process in two to three rounds of mirroring and then validate.

2. VALIDATING

Remember, validating is not agreeing. Validating is saying, "I can see how YOU would see it that way. From your perspective, you make sense."

Say something like:

> I can understand that.
>
> That makes sense to me because . . . (*Keep this short.*)

3. EMPATHIZING

That must make you feel . . . (*Pick three feelings from the Feelings List. Feelings are one word, not phrases.*)

Feelings List

Abandoned
Adequate
Adamant
Affectionate
Agony
Almighty
Ambivalent
Angry
Annoyed
Anxious
Apathetic
Astounded
Awed

Bad
Beautiful
Betrayed
Bitter
Blissful
Bold
Bored
Brave
Burdened

Calm
Capable
Captivated
Challenged
Charmed
Cheated
Cheerful
Childish
Clever
Combative
Competitive
Condemned
Confused
Conspicuous
Contented
Contrite
Cruel
Crushed
Culpable

Deceitful
Defeated
Delighted
Desirous

Despair
Destructive
Determined
Different
Diffident
Diminished
Discontented
Distracted
Distraught
Disturbed
Divided
Dominated
Dubious

Eager
Ecstatic
Electrified
Empty
Enchanted
Energetic
Enervated
Envious
Evil
Exasperated
Excited
Exhausted

Fascinated
Fearful
Flustered
Foolish
Frantic
Free
Frightened
Full
Fury

Gay
Glad
Good
Gratified
Greedy
Grief
Groovy
Guilty
Gullible

Happy

Hateful
Heavenly
Helpful
Helpless
High
Homesick
Honored
Horrible
Hurt
Hysterical

Ignored
Immortal
Imposed upon
Impressed
Infatuated
Infuriated
Intimidated
Isolated

Jealous
Joyous
Jumpy

Keen
Kicky
Kind

Laconic
Lazy
Lecherous
Left out
Licentious
Lonely
Longing
Loving(love)
Low
Lustful

Mad
Maudlin
Mean
Melancholy
Miserable
Mystical

Naughty
Needy

Nervous
Nice
Nutty

Obnoxious
Obsessed
Odd
Opposed
Outraged
Overwhelmed

Pained
Panicked
Parsimonious
Peaceful
Persecuted
Petrified
Pity
Pleasant
Pleased
Precarious
Pressured
Pretty
Prim
Prissy
Proud

Quarrelsome
Queer

Rage
Refreshed
Rejected
Relaxed
Relieved
Remorse
Restless
Reverent
Rewarded
Righteous

Sad
Satisfied
Scared
Screwed up
Servile
Settled
Sexy

Shocked
Silly
Skeptical
Sneaky
Sorrowful
Sorry
Spiteful
Startled
Stingy
Strange
Stuffed
Stunned
Stupified
Stupid
Suffering
Sure
Sympathetic

Talkative
Tempted
Tenacious
Tense
Tentative
Tenuous
Terrible
Terrified
Threatened
Thwarted
Tired
Trapped
Troubled

Ugly
Uneasy
Unsettled

Vehement
Violent
Vital
Vulnerable
Vivacious

Wicked
Wonderful
Weepy
Worry(ied)

Zany

HOMEWORK INSTRUCTIONS FOR SESSION ONE

1. When you speak to each other over the next 48 hours, talk using Couples Dialogue only.

    Example:

Partner 1: "Could you pass the salt?"

Partner 2: "I heard you say, 'Could you pass the salt?' I can understand that. That makes sense to me. I imagine that makes you feel dry, anticipating, and wanting."

    The idea of this part of the homework is to learn the process. Have fun with it and learn at the same time. Nothing will get solved at this point—nor is it supposed to. You're learning a skill that at first doesn't seem natural—*but it's the most important skill couples can learn!* After the first two days, return to your normal way of talking, but be sure to use Couples Dialogue for 30 minutes a day on more serious issues. Remember, you are just learning this skill, and you are not expected to be perfect at it yet. Bring back any problems you've experienced with this process to the next session.

2. Three times a day for one minute each (i.e., 3 minutes per day), think a nice thing about your partner. Be sure to sustain that thought for an entire minute.

3. One time per day, say a nice thing to your partner.

HOME EXERCISE SESSION ONE	Day 1	Day 2	Day 3	Day 4	Day 5	Day 6	Day 7
1. Dialogue							
2. Think a Nice Thing (3× per day)							
3. Say a Nice thing (1× per day)							

Thought for the Week:

> When it is dangerous, we will fight, flee, play dead or freeze, hide or submit. When it is safe, we will play, nurture, mate, work, or be creative.

HOMEWORK/HANDOUTS

Session Two

Couples Developmental Scale

Minimizer

	Attachment	Exploration	Identity	Power and Competence	Concern
Minimizer type	Avoider	Isolator	Rigid	Competitive	Loner
Age	0 to 2 years	2 to 3 years	3 to 4 years	4 to 6 years	6 to 9 years
Needs:	Availability and warmth	To be able to explore To be able to come back and tell someone	Mirroring	Praise Affirmation Mirroring	To find friends To find a best friend Third party is a threat
Problems:	Poor holding Not available	Cannot explore Shamed when returned or no one to return to	No mirroring Poor mirroring	Partial mirroring Shaming	Unable to find friend Poor modeling
Maximizer type	Clinger	Fuser	Diffuse	Passive/Manipulator	Caretaker

Normal Development

Maximizer

INSTRUCTIONS TO THE COUPLE FOR FINDING YOUR IMAGO AND CHILDHOOD FRUSTRATIONS/POSITIVE MEMORIES OF CHILDHOOD SHEETS

In the heart figure on the Finding Your Imago sheet, put the positive traits of your male and female caretakers on the top, and put their negative traits on the bottom. Use words such as "kind," "strict," "stern," "hardworking," or phrases such as "always there," "not dependable," or "never there." On the bottom, complete the sentence, "What I wanted and needed most as a child was. . . ." Make this a behavior or attitude such as ". . . to be loved and admired" or ". . . to know that I did things right"—as opposed to a *thing* such as ". . . a bike."

At the top of the sheet that says Childhood Frustrations, list your recurring childhood frustrations, such as "did not get listened to" or "had to stay with my parents constantly." In the second column, list your responses to these frustrations. These should include how you felt and what you did ("screamed and hollered," "went to my room," "went out with my friends"). On the bottom of the page, which is labelled Positive Memories of Childhood, list your positive memories from childhood and, in the column to the right, list how you felt. The instructions are also on the handouts. List as much as you can, and remember to bring these sheets with you to the next session.

Finding Your Imago

In a relaxed and safe state, recall your childhood memories of your caretakers. It is important that you think as a child and recall your caretakers as they were when you were a child and not as they are today. On the top section of the figure below, list the positive characteristics of each caretaker. On the bottom, list all of the negative characteristics of your caretakers. Use adjectives such as "warm," "strong," "cold," "distant," and/or phrases such as "never there," "always there," "not dependable," "not available emotionally."

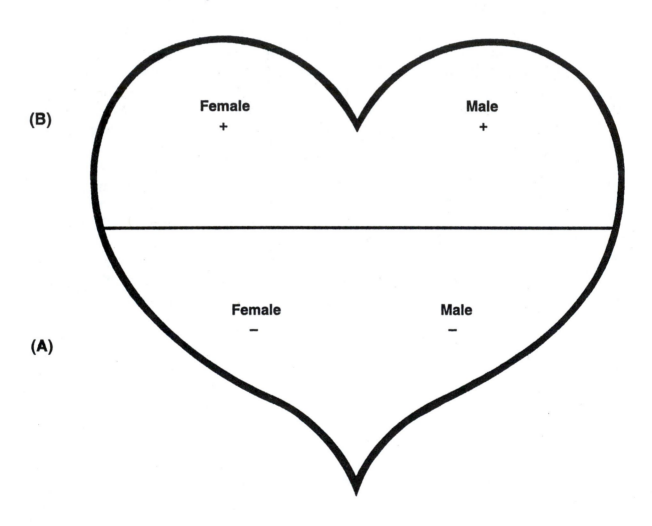

(C) What I wanted and needed most as a child was _____

_____

_____

Childhood Frustrations

In the left column below, list any recurring childhood frustrations such as "did not get listened to," "no one knew I was being hurt," "had to take care of parents or siblings." On the right, list how you responded to these frustrations. This should be how you felt AND your behavioral response (i.e., what you did.).

Frustrations	Response(s)
	(E)

Positive Memories of Childhood

On the left column below, list your positive memories of childhood. This can be specific memories such as "going to the shore in 1960" or "the annual picnic at grandma's house." On the right, list the feelings you associated with each memory.

Memories	Feelings
	(D)

INSTRUCTIONS FOR HOMEWORK SESSION TWO

1. Fill out the two pages given to you with the information you recalled in the guided imagery. Be thorough and complete in filling these out. Remember to bring them back to the next session.

2. Using Couples Dialogue, talk about your childhood memories, both positive and negative, for 30 minutes each, three times this week.

3. Continue thinking a nice thought about each other three times a day for 1 minute and say a nice thing to each other once a day.

HOME EXERCISE SESSION TWO	Day 1	Day 2	Day 3	Day 4	Day 5	Day 6	Day 7
1. Fill Out Memory Forms							
2. Dialogue About Childhood (3× this week)							
3. Think a Nice Thought (3× per day) and Say a Nice Thing (1× per day)							

Thought for the Week:

Emotional safety is the real number one!

HOMEWORK/HANDOUTS

Session Three

My Imago

Using the information from the Finding Your Imago and Childhood Frustrations/Positive Memories of Childhood sheets, complete the sentences below. The letters in parentheses correspond to these sheets and tell you from where to transcribe the information.

I am trying to get a person who is **(A)**_____

_____

_____

To always be **(B)** _____

_____

_____

So that I can get **(C)** _____

_____

_____

And feel **(D)** _____

_____

_____

I stop myself from getting this sometimes by **(E)** _____

_____

_____

Parent–Child Dialogue

Ask your partner the following question and listen with empathy:

"I am your (mother/father/significant caretaker). What was it like to live with me?"

Then ask:

"I am your (mother/father/significant caretaker). What did you need from me that you did not get?"

First one partner talks to one parent, and at another time talks to the other parent. The receiving partner is an empathetic listener. DO NOT ASK QUESTIONS OTHER THAN THOSE ABOVE. Questions pull people out of their feelings and into their thoughts. You want to listen empathetically to your partner's words and feelings.

Then switch roles.

Spend about 20 minutes talking to each parent.

HOMEWORK INSTRUCTIONS FOR SESSION THREE

1. Continue the Parent-Child Dialogue that we started in our session. You should spend 15 minutes on each parent. The listening partner should only ask the questions on the sheet and refrain from making other comments. He or she can invite dialogue, however, by saying "tell me more about that."

2. Do the Holding Exercise started in our session. Each partner should be held for 30 minutes. The holding partner should only mirror back softly the sender's feelings. The idea is to keep your partner in his or her emotions so that you can reimage your partner as wounded and give your partner what he or she did not get as a child. Asking questions pulls people out of their feelings and into their thoughts. Empathy will keep your partner in his or her feelings.

3. In the chart below, write down your partner's wound as you now understand it, and check it out with him or her using Couples Dialogue.

4. In the chart below, write down your wound and talk about it with your partner by using Couples Dialogue.

HOME EXERCISE SESSION THREE	Day 1	Day 2	Day 3	Day 4	Day 5	Day 6	Day 7
1. Parent-Child Dialogue (1× each)							
2. Holding Exercise (30 min. each)							
3. Write/Dialogue Partner's Wound (1× each)							
4. Write/Dialogue Your Wound (1× each)							

Thought for the Week:

Frustrations are a little about now and a lot about the house you grew up in.

HOMEWORK/HANDOUTS

Session Four

Caring Behaviors List

"Hit My Care Button." The things you do now that "hit my care button" and make me feel loved and cared about are . . .

_____

_____

_____

_____

_____

_____

"You Don't Send Me Flowers Anymore." The things you used to do that "hit my care button" and made me feel loved and cared about are . . .

_____

_____

_____

_____

_____

_____

"Go Ahead . . . Make My Day." There are some things that I always wanted to ask you to do that would make me feel cared about and loved, but I have been afraid to ask. (Some typical fears are being needy, outrageous, kinky, extravagant, perverted, disgusting, sentimental, or selfish.)

I am afraid of appearing . . .	But I will manage my fear and ask you to express your care and love by . . .

Mutual Relationship Vision:
My Dream Relationship Worksheet

Working by yourself, write down in the space below all the things you would like in your relationship that would make it a perfect relationship. Start each sentence with the pronoun "We" and write each dream in the present tense as if you already have it.

Mutual Relationship Vision:
John and Jane Doe's Dream Relationship

Working together, using the information from your Dream Relationship Worksheet, design your mutually agreed upon dream relationship. Start each line with "We" and write each dream in the present tense as if you already have it. If you have an item you do not agree upon, skip it. This exercise should be fun and filled with hope. When completed, talk about it using Couples Dialogue, place it in a conspicuous place, and read it together once a month.

Our Dream Relationship

We have fun regularly.

We parent our children well.

We communicate using couples dialogue.

We feel safe with each other.

We support each other's goals.

We work on our relationship each day.

We contain each other's anger.

We have an enjoyable sex life.

We vacation twice a year.

We take care of our bodies.

We are financially secure.

We listen to each other's feelings.

We talk about interesting things.

We eat out once a week.

Mutual Relationship Vision:
Our Dream Relationship Worksheet

Working together, using the information from your Dream Relationship Worksheet, design your mutually agreed upon dream relationship. Start each line with "We" and write each dream in the present tense as if you already have it. If you have an item you do not agree upon, skip it. This exercise should be fun and filled with hope. When completed, talk about it using Couples Dialogue, place it in a conspicuous place, and read it together once a month.

Our Dream Relationship

HOMEWORK INSTRUCTIONS FOR SESSION FOUR

1. Complete the Caring Behaviors List we started in today's session. Make the list exhaustive and review it with your partner using Couples Dialogue.

2. Do at least one of the caring behaviors on your partner's list at least once a day. Remember, pleasure equals safety and you are trying to make the relationship safe. Caring behaviors change the atmosphere of the relationship which, in turn, will promote growth.

3. Have at least three belly laughs or high-energy fun activities this week, even if they are staged.

4. Work on your Mutual Relationship Vision this week. Go over it with your partner before the next session using Couples Dialogue. Post it somewhere visible and review monthly. Believe in it and it can happen.

HOME EXERCISE SESSION FOUR	Day 1	Day 2	Day 3	Day 4	Day 5	Day 6	Day 7
1. Complete and Review Caring List							
2. One Caring Behavior Daily							
3. Belly Laughs/High Energy Fun (3× per week)							
4. Complete Mutual Relationship Vision (Review 1× per month)							

Thought for the Week:

How do you increase Safety?
By Increasing Pleasure!

HOMEWORK/HANDOUTS

Session Five

Socialization and Mate Selection

We express our basic energy, or selves, through four functions:

Thinking • Feeling • Acting • Sensing

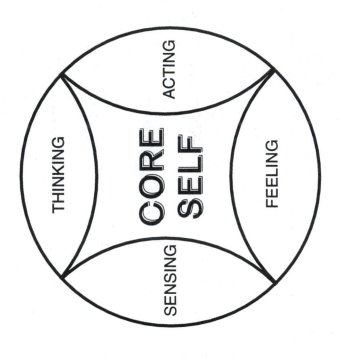

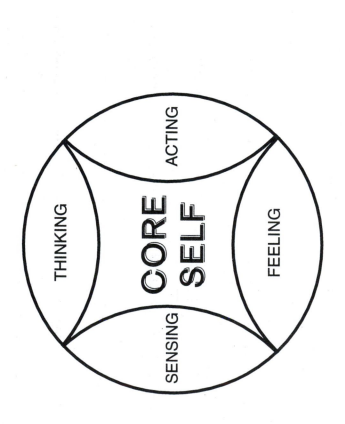

Through the socialization process, we are required to split off parts of ourselves to survive in our environment. We later choose a partner with a complimentary profile.

Frustration Ladder

Rank your frustrations from **1** to **10**, with **1** being the most severe and **10** being the mildest. It is important to tackle the milder ones first. Trying to tackle the most severe ones will only result in failure and more frustration.

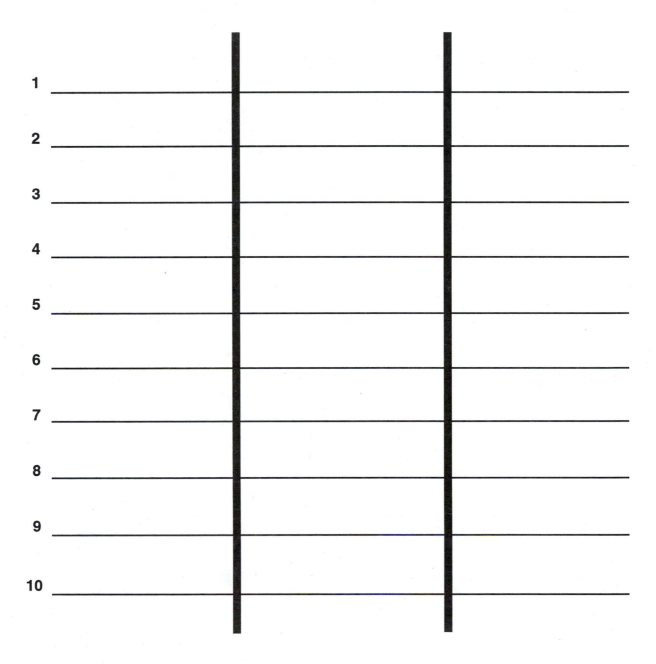

1 _____

2 _____

3 _____

4 _____

5 _____

6 _____

7 _____

8 _____

9 _____

10 _____

As you resolve the milder ones, the ladder will collapse and Number 1 will become much easier to handle.

Sample:
Restructuring Negative Behaviors

A. Desires	B. Behavior Change Requests
I would like you to be on time.	If you are going to be more than 15 mins. late, call me at least ½ hr. before 75% of the time
I would like you to listen to my feelings.	I would like you to listen to me 3 times a week using couples dialogue and mirror back my feelings.
I would like some space.	3 times a week for 1 hr., I would like some time alone without the kids.

Restructuring Negative Behaviors

A. Desires	B. Behavior Change Requests

Sample:
Restructuring Frustrations

1. Write Frustrating Event
What you do that frustrates me is…

> **What Actually Happened**
>
> *you come home late*

2. Write Feeling Response
And I then feel …

> **Emotions—Feelings**
>
> *scared*
> *angry*

4. Write Hidden Fear
to hide my fear of…

> **Fear Your Response Hide**
>
> *That you are dead.*
> *That I will be alone.*

3. Write Behavioral Response
and what I do is…

> **What You Actually Do**
>
> *Pace*
> *scream*
> *Throw things*

5. Hidden Desires
My desires from you are…

> **Desire**
>
> *I would like you to be on time.*

To obtain my desires, I would like to request from you…

> **1. Behavior Change Request**
>
> *If you are going to be more than 15 mins. late, call me ½ hr. before you are due & tell me 75% of the time.*

> **2. Behavior Change Request**
>
> *Surprise me and come home early 10% of the time.*

> **3. Behavior Change Request**
>
> *If you are late and do not call, listen to my feelings using couples dialogue.*

Restructuring Frustrations

1. Write Frustrating Event
What you do that frustrates me is…

> What Actually Happened

2. Write Feeling Response
And I then feel …

> Emotions—Feelings

4. Write Hidden Fear
to hide my fear of…

> Fear Your Response Hide

3. Write Behavioral Response
and what I do is…

> What You Actually Do

5. Hidden Desires
My desires from you are…

> Desire

To obtain my desires, I would like to request from you…

> 1. Behavior Change Request

> 2. Behavior Change Request

> 3. Behavior Change Request

HOMEWORK INSTRUCTIONS FOR SESSION FIVE

1. Complete the Frustration Ladder, placing the mildest frustration at the bottom and the most difficult one at the top. When you begin to work on this, you will start with the mildest frustration first. You do not have to show your partner this form—so be exhaustive and honest.

2. If you've been give the form labelled Restructuring Negative Behaviors, change each frustration into your desire (column A). Then take each desire and change it into a Behavior Change Request (column B). Remember: Be positive, behavioral, and so specific that a stranger could figure out what you want and do it perfectly.

The object of this homework is to begin to EDUCATE your partner about what you need and in the areas in which he or she needs to grow. Do not expect your partner to do these behaviors right away. Doing the behaviors will require your partner to stretch, which will require time. Also, keep in mind that your partner will only change as much as you do.

3. If you have been given the form labeled Restructuring Frustrations, write a frustration in Box 1 and then follow and answer the boxes on feelings, behaviors, fears, and desires as you did in the session with the therapist. This form asks the sending partner to write three Behavior Change Requests for the receiving partner regarding the sender's desire. This gives the receiving partner a choice of behaviors to give to the sending partner that will be accomplished only through growth on both of your parts.

4. Review your Behavior Change Request with your partner using Couples Dialogue. Stay very safe during this exercise because although some of the things on your partner's list may seem impossible, it is more likely that your partner is pushing you on an adaptation that you have developed. Our partner's requests are usually in the areas that we most need to grow into, and growth and change are never easy.

5. Monitor your stretching by observing that each Behavior Change Request will require a stretch into one of the areas you were told to turn off in childhood (Thinking, Acting, Feeling, or Sensing). After reviewing your partner's request using Couples Dialogue, decide which area will require growth in order to accomplish the request and place a check mark next to the appropriate area. You should discover that the request requires a stretch in one or two areas.

Monitoring Stretching—Area of Behavior Change Request			
Thinking ☐	Acting ☐	Feeling ☐	Sensing ☐

HOME EXERCISE SESSION FIVE	Day 1	Day 2	Day 3	Day 4	Day 5	Day 6	Day 7
1. Complete Frustration Ladder							
2. Change these frustrations to Behavior Change Requests							
3. Review Request (Use Couples Dialogue)							
4. Monitor Stretching							

Thought for the Week:

Your partner has the blueprint for your growth.

HOMEWORK/HANDOUTS

Session Six

The Container Process

Before you use this exercise, you should make three protective agreements:

- NO Hitting or Name Calling
- NO Physical or Verbal Attacks
- NO Property Damage
- NO Leaving Until All Seven Steps Are Completed

Partner A = Sender	Partner B = Receiver
1. Ask for an appointment.	1. Agree to a time ASAP.
2. Identify the "trigger" to your frustration; state the frustration in one sentence.	2. Paraphrase your partner's frustration; put on your "psychic armor."
3. Explode feelings.	3. Listen with empathy.
4. Implosion (anger turns to sadness and tears).	4. Provide physical holding, care, and empathy.
5. Separation and rest (optional).	
6. Ask for three behavior changes related to the trigger.	6. Mirror request. Commit to at least one change or offer an alternative.
7. Initiate high-energy play.	7. Participate actively in play.

The Container Record

Date: _____ Sender: _____ Receiver: _____

1. Sender requests an appointment. Receiver agrees ASAP. To begin the Container Process, the receiver prepares his/her armor—gets safe.

2. Sender states the trigger of the frustrating event in one sentence. Receiver mirrors and fine-tunes his or her armor—level of safety.

3. *Explosion Phase.* Senders share anger. Receiver listens and encourages anger. Tell me more about that! Say that louder! Maximum time: 10 minutes.

4. *Implosion.* Anger turns to sadness. Sender shares early wounds. Receiver holds and listens with mirroring and empathy.

5. Separation and rest if necessary.

6. Sender makes three Behavior Change Requests. Receiver writes them down, mirrors, and selects one to which he or she will commit.*

Behavior Change Request	Behavior Change Request	Behavior Change Request
_____	_____	_____
_____	_____	_____
_____	_____	_____
_____	_____	_____
_____	_____	_____

7. Sender initiates high-energy fun or play. Receiver participates with energy.

8. Later, receiver practices at least one Behavior Change Request. The sender recognizes and appreciates when this happens.

---

*The Sender should add all three requests to his or her list of Behavior Change Requests so that he or she can review them regularly to fine-tune them and to be able to recognize them when they occur. The receiver should write all three Behavior Change Requests in his or her list of stretching behaviors. These should be reviewed at least weekly.

Using the Container

There are three ways to use the Container Process and I recommend learning and using all three as a way of developing tools to use in expressing anger.

☐ The Container Process

This is the seven-step process that was taught to you in the session. This process allow safe expression of resentment and rage. It also allows childhood anger or hurt to surface and be heard by your partner. This process replaces all spontaneous fights and is used for intense frustrations. It requires an appointment as well as a commitment to all seven steps, to safety, and to allow adequate time (usually 30 to 45 minutes) with little or no distractions.

☐ The Container Transaction

The Container Transaction is the process used when the anger is mild or for annoyances. For example, leaving a dish out may not require a 45-minute process to express intense anger such as in the Container Process. This can be handled using the Container Transaction, which utilizes the first three steps of the Container Process and a Behavior Change Request. Transactions should last no more than 5 minutes.

Sender	Receiver
1. Make appointment	1. Give appointment.
2. State trigger in one sentence.	2. Get safe and mirror back.
3. Explode anger for 3 minutes.	3. Listen with empathy and mirror back.
4. Behavior Change Request.	4. Mirror request.
5. Optional belly laugh.	5. Participate in belly laugh.

☐ Container Days

As a way of getting started in using Containers, I recommend the following structure: couples should alternate days, each being the Container for a 24-hour period. On the day he is the Container, he will listen to her anger and frustrations all day using only the Container process or the Container Transaction or he can respond with Couples Dialogue. On the following day, you switch and she listens to his anger and frustrations using either the Process or the Transaction. If you get angry or frustrated on the day that is not yours, you must wait until the next day as a promise of safety to the partner whose day it is to express himself or herself. Continue this for three months with both partners being available to each other on Sundays. However, high-energy fun is another option for Sunday.

HOMEWORK INSTRUCTIONS FOR SESSION SIX

1. This is very difficult homework to do. You may want to have some assistance in doing a Container and I, your therapist, will let you know how to get the help you need. I recommend that, for the next three months, you do Container Days, which are described to you in detail on the sheet labeled "Using the Container." Remember, even attempting a Container is probably safer, more structured, and more productive than what you are doing now. Use it as one of the tools in your toolbox that you have learned over the last six sessions.

   Remember to let your partner go through the anger and into the hurt that lies underneath. This is where the real healing takes place. Containers should last no more than 45 minutes and you should do only one per day. The receiving partner must wait until the next day to respond. You want to give your partner the sense that he or she has been heard and understood—even if it means sitting on your own anxiety until the next day.

2. Leaving a dish on the counter or the lid up on the toilet may not need a full Container and probably has no connection to your childhood. For the everyday things, I recommend the Container Transaction, which is also fully described on the sheet labelled "Using the Container." A Container Transaction takes about 5 minutes to complete and gives the sending partner the feeling that he or she has been fully heard. On your day, use the Container Transaction for all the little annoying things.

3. Never forget the high-energy fun at the end of any of the variations of the Container Process. A belly laugh is important to give you back some of the energy you just expended in doing a Container.

HOME EXERCISE SESSION SIX	Day 1	Day 2	Day 3	Day 4	Day 5	Day 6	Day 7
1. Container Days (for the next 3 months)							
2. Container Transaction (use as needed for the next 3 months)							
3. High-Energy Fun (after every Container)							

Thought for the Week:

It is more important to hear than to win!

FOLLOW-UP PLAN

Follow-Up Plan

It is important to know that the work you completed is not the end, but only the beginning. To get the full benefit, you must continue the work you have done on a **daily** basis. In other words, it must become a way of life for you, for your partner, and for your relationship.

This eight-week follow-up program will set you on your way. Try not to think of it in terms of *eight weeks* but as a way to get you started on a lifetime of change and growth. Do not attempt to do any more than is listed in a week, because should you overdo it, you will tire of the work quickly. Remember, your goal is to change a little bit over a long period of time.

Week One

1. Complete any written exercises you started and were unable to finish.
2. Begin a three-month practice of Container Days.
3. Practice Couples Dialogue three times this week for 30 minutes at a planned time.
4. Practice Couples Dialogue in all conflict situations.
5. Reimage your partner as a "wounded child." See yourself healing your partner's wounds. Do this daily.
6. Agree to give each other a gift or appreciation every day.

Week Two

1. Practice Couples Dialogue three times this week for 30 minutes at a planned time.
2. Use Couples Dialogue in all conflict situations.
3. Repeat the Parent-Child Dialogue exercise (I am your mother/father. What was it like to live with me?) Allow yourself to go deeper with this exercise. Use it to continue the process of reimaging your partner as wounded. Each partner should have at least 30 minutes to talk.
4. Review your Relationship Vision.
5. Have a very intellectual 30-minute talk, with both partners participating equally.
6. Remember to give each other a gift every day.

Week Three

1. Ask your partner for his or her Behavior Change Request list:
* Rank the list in order of difficulty for you.

- Memorize this list.
- Starting with the easiest request, gift your partner with a request daily or weekly, as appropriate, until you have completed the list.
- Do it, no matter how you feel.
- When your partner gifts you, acknowledge verbally and also by recording the date on your list so your partner can see it.

2. Say to your partner every day this week, "I understand stretching is difficult, and I will make it safe for you."

3. Review your Relationship Vision and visualize yourself reaching your goals.

4. Use Couples Dialogue to express how you feel about giving and receiving the gifts from your partner this week. Make it safe.

Week Four

1. Use Couples Dialogue in all conflict situations.

2. Have high-energy fun or a belly laugh at least twice this week.

3. Continue gifting your partner with his or her Behavior Change Requests.

4. Do the Holding Exercise about a particularly sad moment in your childhood. Spend 30 minutes each being held. Continue to reimage your partner as wounded.

Week Five

1. Using the Couples Dialogue, share your thoughts about the Container Exercise. Discuss it until you both understand it.
- Share your thoughts about practicing the steps.
- Do a Container Transaction on a minor frustrating behavior your partner does. Make it specific.
- Do a minor Container Process once this week to learn the steps.
- Discuss your experience of doing the Container Process using the Couples Dialogue.

2. Have a 30-minute conversation about something totally silly (for example, the social implications of the Flintstones).

3. Give each other a gift every day.

Week Six

1. Do Caring Behaviors.

2. Do Behavior Change Requests.

3. Do a Container on a more serious subject.

4. Give each other a gift every day.

Week Seven

1. Use Couples Dialogue at least three times this week.

2. Do a Container.

3. Continue doing Behavior Change Requests.

4. Have at least one belly laugh, separate from the Container.

5. Give each other a gift every day.

Week Eight and Every Week Thereafter

These skills must become a part of everyday life. So for *the rest of your life* do the following:

1. Use the Couples Dialogue in all conflict situations.

2. Reimage your partner as wounded, and see yourself as healing those wounds. Do this until your partner tells you his or her wounds are healing or are healed. (This could take years.)

3. Once a month, do a Holding Exercise. Let your partner deal with a deep hurt in a safe environment with you. Visualize yourself healing his or her wounds.

4. Do Caring Behaviors daily. When the Caring Behavior becomes routine, come up with new ones. Keep the relationship safe and fresh. Surprise your partner once a month. Have a belly laugh once a day. Give a gift or appreciation every day.

5. Continue to stretch into the behaviors on your partner's Behavior Change Request list. When you have fully stretched into these behaviors and they are a part of you, ask your partner for a new list. Remember, your part has the blueprint for your growth. See your partner's request as an opportunity to grow in the exact ways that will lead to the recovery of your original wholeness.

6. Do Containers regularly. If these are difficult for you to do alone, commit to each other to find a therapist to help you do a Container.

Every Six Weeks

1. Review your Relationship Vision. Revise it as necessary.

2. Visualize your goals daily and see yourself reaching them.